Watchdogs on the Hill

Watchdogs on the Hill

THE DECLINE OF CONGRESSIONAL OVERSIGHT OF U.S. FOREIGN RELATIONS

Linda L. Fowler

PRINCETON UNIVERSITY PRESS

PRINCETON AND OXFORD

Copyright © 2015 by Princeton University Press
Published by Princeton University Press, 41 William Street,
Princeton, New Jersey 08540
In the United Kingdom: Princeton University Press, 6 Oxford Street,
Woodstock, Oxfordshire OX20 1TW

press.princeton.edu

Cover photograph: Senate Foreign Relations Committee, ca. 1963–1969. From left:
Frank Church, Frank Carlson, George Aiken, Bourke Hickenlooper, J. W. Fulbright
(chair). Courtesy of U.S. Senate Historical Office.

Library of Congress Cataloging-in-Publication Data

Fowler, Linda L., 1945–
  Watchdogs on the hill : the decline of congressional oversight of U.S. foreign
relations / Linda L. Fowler.
      pages cm
  Includes bibliographical references and index.
  ISBN 978-0-691-15161-8 (hardback) — ISBN 978-0-691-15162-5 (paperback)
1. Legislative oversight—United States. 2. International relations. 3. United States—
Foreign relations. 4. United States—Politics and government. I. Title.

  JK585.F69 2015

  328.73'0746—dc23   2014044323

British Library Cataloging-in-Publication Data is available

This book has been composed in Minion Pro
Printed on acid-free paper. ∞

Printed in the United States of America

10 9 8 7 6 5 4 3 2 1

For
_____

Nate, Simon, Welton, Meredith, Tom, John, Brad, Michael, Tom, and Billy—
   fine students and good soldiers all

Contents

Illustrations

Tables

Preface

I BEGAN THIS BOOK IN 2005 moved by concern for the lack of congressional oversight of the wars in Iraq and Afghanistan. As I reviewed the sweep of more than sixty years of legislative involvement in U.S. foreign policy after World War II, I concluded that key Senate committees with responsibility for oversight of the executive showed an unprecedented lack of monitoring *during* a major conflict and a failure to establish accountability *after* hostilities ceased. I wanted to make sense of these patterns, as a scholar, a citizen, and a teacher committed to helping students understand their government. What accounted for the decline of national security oversight, and what can we reasonably expect from Congress in light of past history and current political conditions?

My first encounter with congressional oversight of foreign policy occurred years ago, however, when I served as a young staffer in the House of Representatives at the height of the conflict in Vietnam. By the time I arrived on Capitol Hill in the summer of 1969, U.S. troop levels in Southeast Asia had peaked at over half a million, and total American battle deaths had exceeded forty-five thousand. After assuming office, President Richard Nixon had undertaken a series of initiatives: peace talks in Paris, secret bombings of Cambodia, clandestine meetings in Hanoi between Henry Kissinger and the North Vietnamese, and drawing down troops, eventually leading to the "Vietnamization" of combat operations. Protests consumed college campuses, and stories of atrocities, such as the 1968 massacre at My Lai, had appeared in the press. Increasing numbers of respectable, law-abiding citizens joined student dissidents and more radical critics of the government in the streets. While the country was unraveling, I grappled with a stew of contradictory feelings: anger that my husband had been drafted into the Marine Corps to serve in a war we both opposed; sorrow over the telephone-book-sized list of casualties that arrived on my desk each morning; grudging respect for my boss, who supported the war, but was one of only three members in Congress at the time with a close male relative serving in Vietnam; and disdain for a moribund institution that put the Speaker's gavel and important committee chairs in the hands of octogenarians.

The primary venues for dissent, apart from the streets, were the hearing rooms in Congress. Several passionate war opponents had gained seats in Congress, but they had been unable to bring legislation forcing withdrawal from Vietnam to the floor. Party leaders endeavored to mask the deep fault line in the party's ranks between hawks and doves by preventing amendments and roll call votes to end the war,[1] despite the fact that the Democratic majority no longer worried about protecting the president once Nixon occupied the White House. Eventually, Senator William Fulbright (D-AR), who chaired the Foreign Relations Committee, reactivated critical hearings that he had begun under Lyndon Johnson. At the time of my arrival, however, a period of détente existed between the new administration and Senate committee overseers.[2] The Hill was relatively quiet amid the domestic tumult as lawmakers waited to see whether Nixon really had a peace plan.

The president's approval of incursions into neutral Cambodia in the spring of 1970 catalyzed public outrage, and protesters planned massive rallies for a weekend in early May. Rumors of attacks by the violent Weathermen organization buzzed through the city. Heading to the Rayburn Building garage to get my car that Friday evening, I was dumbfounded at the sight of hundreds of paratroopers and large supplies of military equipment filling the vast underground space. I learned later that other units had been hidden around the city. The troops had arrived by airlift to maintain order in the capital, and the people's House had become a battle station. I picked my way to the car and sat, stunned, amid the noise of walkie-talkies and jeep engines. My strong memory of the U.S. government preparing for war against its own citizens still reminds me why the framers rightly feared concentration of power in the presidency.

Today, some of my students have been in harm's way or have returned from combat in Iraq and Afghanistan to enroll at Dartmouth as veterans. Like those of my generation, they wonder if their government exercised due diligence about the necessity of prolonged war, if their efforts made the nation more secure, and if their fellow citizens truly understood their sacrifices. Surely, the nation's elected representatives owed them a thoughtful review of U.S. involvement in another lengthy land war in Asia.

Instead, a state of confusion prevailed in Washington. Fears of an imperial presidency, which reemerged with the threat of global terrorism, became mired in partisan battles about the policies of individual presidents. Democrats, eager to rein in George W. Bush after the 2006 election, became quiescent during Barack Obama's term. Republicans, ready to concede vast powers to a GOP commander in chief, turned to the much-despised War Powers Resolution in 2011 to challenge a Democrat in the White House over Libya. As the president considered military intervention in Syria in 2013, some members from both parties claimed prerogatives for Congress, but their efforts ended abruptly when

---

[1] The Cooper-Church Amendment, which barred funding for military personnel and air operations in Cambodia, passed the Senate in June 1970, but failed in the House. It was the first time members cast roll call votes on the war in Southeast Asia since the 1964 Gulf of Tonkin Resolution, which Congress repealed in 1971.

[2] Jack Anderson, "Fulbright, Nixon Had Secret Talks," *Washington Post*, May 21, 1972, http://news .google.com/newspapers?nid=1876&dat=19720521&id=qX8sAAAAIBAJ&sjid=DM0EAAAAI BAJ&pg=7191,4185512 (accessed May 17, 2012).

President Obama found a diplomatic means of diffusing the controversy of dealing with the Syrians' use of chemical weapons. Missing from all recent debates about congressional and executive war powers has been serious examination of how the internal workings of the legislature have undermined Congress's capacity to play a responsible role in foreign affairs.

I have undertaken this project because I believe that the threats of global terrorism have exposed *internal* perils to America's democracy. For me, claims about the legislature's constitutional powers in national security depend upon hardheaded analysis of its institutional capabilities. In this respect, I side with Madison, who had limited faith in the "paper barriers" erected by the Constitution and relied on ambition within each branch to preserve its prerogatives. Surveying the record of the past six decades, I see a presidency that has taken on more than it can reasonably handle and a legislature caught up in members' personal and partisan agendas. In effect, there is too much foreign policy ambition in the White House and too little on Capitol Hill.

I harbor no illusions that a legislative branch more engaged in oversight will solve the global challenges confronting the American democracy. Congress is an imperfect institution representing an imperfect people, and it will always be prone to parochialism, shortsightedness, and demagoguery. Nevertheless, Congress can bring the collective wisdom of a diverse nation to bear on difficult problems requiring shared commitment and sacrifice. Through public hearings, its committees can establish an orderly, transparent process that promotes the rule of law and educates the public. Through executive sessions, its designated watchdogs can engage in troubleshooting and negotiation with the executive branch. Sustained evaluation of presidential decisions is especially vital during lengthy conflicts. I hope that shedding light on congressional review of U.S. foreign policy will help citizens and policy makers understand why oversight is vital to ensuring democratic accountability in foreign affairs, why it has become increasingly dysfunctional, and how to think about fixing it.

Acknowledgments

A BOOK ALMOST NINE YEARS in the making imposes on the good will of many different colleagues, students, administrators, friends, and family. Most individuals fit into particular stages of the project, so I acknowledge them sequentially.

First are those who were present at the creation. Richard Fenno, Barbara Sinclair, and Bruce Oppenheimer supported my application to the John Simon Guggenheim Foundation, which funded a year's fellowship to begin the project. Andrew Samwick, director of the Nelson Rockefeller Center at Dartmouth College, provided resources for collecting and coding the hearing data. Dartmouth College granted me sabbatical time at the beginning and end of the process. John Cocklin went well beyond what any scholar can reasonably expect from a reference librarian. Staff members in the Senate historian's office and August Imholtz of the Congressional Information Service educated me about Senate committee hearing records. Rick Barton and Chris Fowler advised me on organizing the initial data sets.

Next were those who provided help as the research began to take shape. Absolutely critical were Brian Law and Seth Hill, both beginning graduate students in political science at UCLA when we connected in 2005. Law collaborated with me in analyzing the decline in prestige and visibility of the Senate Armed Services and Foreign Relations Committees. Hill worked with me in developing the predictors of committee oversight activity. Their intelligence, methodological skill, and wit made the relationships both productive and personally rewarding.

Talented Dartmouth students also played many roles over the years. Research assistants who worked on different pieces of the project include Matthew Slaine, Jared Hyatt, Dan Correa, Alex Kaplan, Mhairi Collins, Gabrielle Ramaiah, Justin Brownstone, Matthew Martin, Sarah Levine, Mark Andriola, Shengzhi Li, and Tatsuro Yamamura.

As I started producing papers, I gained valuable feedback from colleagues at Dartmouth, Emory, Duke, Minnesota, and the Harris School at the University of Chicago and from panels at the Midwest and American Political Science Associations. Will Howell and Doug Kriner aided me at various times with their extensive expertise about the interaction between Congress and the president in foreign affairs, and Eric Schickler and Frances Lee provided valuable comments on individual chapters. Howell, Adam Berinsky, John Carey, and Brent Strathman contributed greatly to clarifying the argument during a review of the manuscript arranged by Ken Yalowitz and Christianne Wohlforth of the Dickey Center for International Understanding at Dartmouth College. James

Wallner helped me understand current Senate practices governing committee assignments, and Tom Long and Welton Chang commented on parts of early drafts. Patrick Lam and Jianjun Hua weighed in with critical advice on methodological issues. Department colleagues Dean Lacy, Michael Herron, Joe Bafumi, Brendan Nyhan, Bridget Coggins, and Yusaku Horiuchi put up with many statistical questions. Elizabeth Adams added sharp editorial skills to improving a final draft. David Mayhew and anonymous reviewers weighed in with insightful suggestions on the penultimate version of the manuscript. Chuck Myers encouraged me to take on the project when he was editor at Princeton University Press, Joseph Dahm provided expert copyediting, and Eric Crahan and his staff were invaluable in seeing it through to completion.

Last come thanks to my friends and family. Never at a loss for words, I now find my ability to express gratitude completely inadequate. If you are reading this, you know who you are. I appreciate your interest in my work, your good nature when I was tedious, and your patience when I was distracted. My husband, Steve Fowler, has weathered many research projects over our long marriage, with this undoubtedly the toughest. If only I could promise him it is the last one.

PART I

INFORMATION, REGULAR ORDER, AND DEMOCRATIC ACCOUNTABILITY IN INTERNATIONAL AFFAIRS

No government is perfect. One of the chief virtues of a democracy, however, is that its defects are always visible and under democratic processes can be pointed out and corrected.

—President Harry S. Truman before a Joint Session of
Congress, March 12, 1947

Oversight Hearings and U.S. Foreign Policy

At the dawn of the Cold War, the United States confronted one of the most consequential foreign policy choices of the post–World War II generation. The Truman Doctrine, which the president announced in a speech to Congress on March 12, 1947, was the signature achievement of his administration and the cornerstone of U.S. strategy for more than four decades. Truman partnered with the Senate Foreign Relations Committee at this unique historical moment to shape the policy and sell it to the nation. The committee conducted public hearings to explain the urgency of restraining Soviet expansion into Greece and Turkey and to garner support from reluctant citizens and advocacy groups. Its members orchestrated secret hearings with administration officials and opposing lawmakers to negotiate compromise language that would give President Truman a convincing legislative victory. The next year, Foreign Relations facilitated the adoption of the ambitious Marshall Plan to reconstruct Europe through a strategic mix of public and executive sessions. Committee oversight hearings in 1947–48 thus proved indispensible for organizing deliberation and ensuring public accountability at a crucial turning point for the United States in international affairs.

Congress has engaged in oversight of the executive branch since the early days of the Republic.[1] The term "oversight" has roots in the verb "to oversee" and implies responsibility for an outcome by making sure that the people and organizations charged with a task complete it satisfactorily.[2] In the federal government, oversight encompasses a wide range of activity: "review of federal departments, agencies and commissions and the programs they administer ... during program and policy implementation as well as afterward."[3] Typically, oversight is retrospective: did the executive carry out the intent of Congress in implementing the law? Yet it also can be prospective: is the president addressing an emerging problem in an appropriate way? By its very nature, then, legislative

---

[1] Inquiries regarding President George Washington's handling of the conflicts with Indian tribes on the western borders were the first congressional probes of foreign policy.

[2] Oversight can also be associated with the verb *to overlook*, which implies a lack of attention to a task, either inadvertently or deliberately.

[3] Aberbach (1990, 2).

scrutiny of agency performance can either exacerbate conflict or bolster cooperation with the White House.

Oversight is built into the U.S. constitutional system to reinforce the rule of law and educate the public. Indeed, noted congressional observer Ralph Huitt asserted a generation ago that "the oversight function is probably the most important task the legislature performs."[4] Contemporary observers continue to assert its importance as the federal government has grown in size and complexity. With respect to foreign policy, oversight entails two vital functions: policing the vast bureaucratic apparatus, which Congress erected after World War II to prosecute the Cold War and later to combat global terrorism; and fostering public deliberation about complex and potentially deadly choices.

Congress has assigned responsibility for oversight to specialized standing committees that conduct formal inquiries, in both open hearings and secret sessions. Although committees are not the sole source of information about the president's conduct of foreign affairs, they enjoy the legal authority and resources to command attention from the White House and focus public awareness that few individual lawmakers can match. They represent the collective interests of the institution and citizens in obtaining reliable, timely information about government policy.

Many committees exert jurisdiction over some aspect of international relations, such as trade, resource management, or drug trafficking, housed in various federal and agencies. However, the biggest administrative players, the Departments of Defense and State, are under the respective supervision of the Armed Services Committees in the House and Senate, and the Foreign Relations Committee in the Senate and the Foreign Affairs Committee in the House.[5] The two Senate committees enjoy greater prestige, higher visibility, and more opportunities for policy entrepreneurship than their counterparts in the House. Such characteristics make them fruitful candidates for in-depth analysis of national security oversight because their actions are more likely to be consequential.

This book examines the formal hearing activity of the Senate's key national security committees, Armed Services and Foreign Relations, from 1947 to 2008, to assess their efficacy in promoting due process and public understanding with respect to international affairs. In particular, I provide extensive anal-

[4] Quoted in Crabb and Holt (1992, 551).

[5] Until the 1970s, national intelligence functions were under the jurisdiction of the Armed Services Committees in the House and Senate and were then transferred to newly created select committees in each chamber. These committees operate under different rules regarding the tenure of their members and have limited capacity for conducting oversight in public or establishing a written record. In addition, observations over time are limited by their shorter history of operation. Comparison with the Senate Armed Services and Foreign Relations Committees thus would be a matter of apples and oranges. In a recent study, Zegart (2011) concluded that intelligence oversight is extremely weak because of the members' limited tenure on the committee and their lack of budgetary power over intelligence operations. Each chamber has a committee charged specifically with oversight, but the focus of these committees generally has been domestic policy.

ysis of how much time the committees spent on public and secret hearings, what factors influenced their decisions to engage in oversight, and how they allocated their efforts to routine program review compared to scrutiny of crises and scandals. The empirical results and case studies suggest that the Senate's national security committees had an uneven record over the sixty-two years of the study that reflected the personal and political agendas of the members rather than the interests of the public. I use the findings, therefore, as a basis for rethinking the nature of national security oversight and proposing several reforms to promote public deliberation and education about U.S. foreign relations.

Overall, I find that the committees' official oversight activity during the sixty-two years of the study was greater than many political observers recognized, but declined markedly since the mid-1990s. Broad institutional changes in the Senate altered the frequency of hearings among all Senate committees, as well as Armed Services and Foreign Relations. The result was less time available for formal oversight, which affect both the amount and type of scrutiny of the executive branch.

Moreover, I uncover various types of bias in how the national security committees reviewed the executive branch. The orientations of the Senate Armed Services and Foreign Relations Committees led to striking differences in the frequency, content, and venues for oversight hearings. Armed Services, for example, tended to shield Republican administrations from public scrutiny of routine program implementation and crisis management, while Foreign Relations heightened broad inquiries into the "state of the world" during periods of divided government. Both committees reacted strategically to changes in federal spending priorities, to the president's use of force, and to major events. Over the period of study, then, oversight activity frequently deviated from orderly processes of review.

Finally, committee concerns about the reputations of the parties inhibited their capacity to generate information regarding the costs of war and incidents of bureaucratic wrongdoing. Both committees were most concerned with inquiries into administrative actions that were of interest to organized constituencies rather than the consequences of foreign policy decisions that citizens cared about. The frequency and content of oversight hearings by Armed Services and Foreign Relations consequently were only weakly connected to public opinion and deliberation about the nation's collective goals in U.S. foreign policy.

On the basis of such wide-ranging results, I conclude that a serious overhaul of these key Senate committees is necessary. I devote the last two chapters of the book, therefore, to proposing changes to the status quo. I outline expectations for national security oversight to restore the balance between the legislative and executive branches consistent with the U.S. constitutional system. I then review current proposals for reform and develop pragmatic incentives for committees to promote the rule of law in international affairs through regular, formal sessions modeled on aspects of a British-style Question Period.

Oversight and Democratic Governance

Oversight is integral to constitutional principles regarding the rule of law and public accountability. Article I, which defines the powers of Congress, contains no mention of the term, but the framers' debate at the Constitutional Convention made it clear that lawmakers would meet frequently to make sure that the president faithfully executed the law as his oath of office required.[6] The separation of powers establishes boundaries between the three branches of government, while the system of checks and balances depends on shared powers that enable one branch to resist encroachments on its prerogatives by another. Formal oversight supports the Constitution's design by monitoring whether the executive follows congressional intent and by bringing the public and the press into the review process. In these ways, oversight facilitates maintenance of the borders between the legislature and executive and offers a potent tool for reining in an incompetent or overly aggressive president.[7]

Although oversight frequently exposes administrative failure or presidential overreaching, it also uncovers the need for a new sequence of policy making, implementation, and evaluation. Consequently, formal congressional review fosters adherence to legitimate procedures for doing the government's business.[8] Such "regular order" serves the rule of law by promoting predictability, continuity, and transparency in governmental decision making.

Oversight is critical, as well, to the framers' idea of representative democracy, which requires extensive deliberation to forge consensus in a diverse nation. Since the nation's founding, the legislative branch has participated in defining the public sphere in both domestic policy and foreign affairs.[9] As Madison affirmed in *Federalist 10*, elected representatives have responsibility to "refine and enlarge the public view" in order to discover common interests.[10] By flagging salient issues and bringing administrators into conversation with members, oversight organizes public discourse about governmental objectives and performance.

---

[6] Madison (1987, 399); Fisher (2003, 1).

[7] The major ones include the power of the purse, confirmation of nominations, ratification of treaties, and override of a presidential veto. Deploying them can be costly in terms of time, potential failure, and escalation of the stakes in a dispute.

[8] Waldron (2013) argues that an orderly sequence in which each branch carries out its defined function of legislation, administration, and adjudication is characteristic of governments that follow the rule of law.

[9] Mayhew (2000).

[10] See also Maass (1983).

Oversight takes many forms in Congress, however. Individual lawmakers issue press releases, give speeches, and appear on television and radio to draw attention to an agency blunder or to challenge a president's decision.[11] They deploy staff members to solve constituent problems with federal programs, and they contact agency officials to ensure that their states or districts obtain governmental resources. They offer advice about policy implementation to department heads through informal channels or communicate privately with the White House. These personal activities constitute an important means of informal negotiation between the branches over policy choices, and they often develop into quasi-permanent issue networks.

To coordinate lawmakers' attention to governmental programs, however, Congress needs institutions, which not only magnify legislative influence over the executive branch but also increase presidential accountability. Organizational support for formal oversight occurs through specialized committees that exercise responsibility over specific policy domains and, since 1946, have been required by law to monitor the executive on behalf of the entire legislature. As agents of the House and Senate, committees represent the collective interests of the institution and consequently enjoy special authority and command formidable resources. Their professional staff members bring expertise and continuity to scrutiny of the executive, and their subpoena power reinforces the ability to call witnesses to testify. Committee-based oversight thus exerts substantial pressure on administration officials to disclose information in ways that most individual lawmakers cannot.

The elevated status of committees inside Congress suits them admirably to educate the public through oversight.[12] They have the means to organize discussion about complex problems and the discretion to examine agency activities in depth. By including members of both parties and allocating staff to the minority, committees bring competing viewpoints into a common space. As authoritative actors who affect government policy, they attract the news media and influence the frame reporters apply to policy deliberations. Generally, the information committees generate has proven to be of higher quality than the views members bring to floor debates.[13] Furthermore, the attributes of committee-led discourse contrast favorably with the disposition of the press toward "soft"

---

[11] Kriner and Shen (2014) demonstrate that lawmakers in districts with relatively high casualties during the war in Iraq increased the number of floor speeches about the conflict.

[12] Krehbiel (1991) analyzes the informational function of committees inside Congress and the rewards committees receive for providing high-quality information. His theory and results focus on the internal uses of information by lawmakers for passing bills rather than the broader public purposes of oversight.

[13] Mucciaroni and Quirk (2006). The authors evaluate the quality of debate on the basis of the accuracy of claims supported by the best available evidence to establish agreement about the facts and "shift disagreement to ... the implications of the facts" (2006, 51).

news and the tendency among individual lawmakers to avoid educating constituents in favor of credit claiming and casework.[14]

Formal committee hearings are the most important form of congressional oversight of the executive branch in terms of both the rule of law and public understanding. Although committees generate many different types of information, such as press releases, reports, and statements by members, hearings have the advantage of following defined processes. The benefits include public announcement in the *Daily Digest*, advance notification to witnesses, norms of discourse to promote civility, rules that compel testimony while protecting against self-incrimination, and written records of testimony and supporting documents. In addition, committee staff members compile the content of open hearings and make the material available in a timely manner, which facilitates public access.

Face-to-face contact between lawmakers and administration officials through formal hearings offers the further advantage of giving a human face to abstract policy debates. In public, personal contact forces the participants to acknowledge their different perspectives and raises the ante for grandstanding or stonewalling. In private, inquiries provide opportunities to build trust and negotiate compromise. The fact that review sessions occur on Capitol Hill, moreover, underscores the constitutional status of Congress as a coequal branch, even if administrators would prefer to keep lawmakers in the dark.

When legislators and executive branch officials clash publicly, their encounters can be riveting, providing the kind of drama and sharply informative exchange that make the Question Period in the British Parliament such popular entertainment. Interbranch confrontation, however, sometimes reveals stupidity, venality, or glaring political opportunism on one or both sides. Nevertheless, at their best, formal hearings enhance the legitimacy of government actions by joining decision makers in serious dialogue and bringing the public into their deliberations.

Oversight Hearings and Foreign Affairs

The need for the rule of law and public education is particularly acute in the realm of foreign affairs. A lawful foreign policy follows regular order and fosters public deliberation. By "regular order," I mean routines that follow a formal, predictable sequence for evaluating alternatives, making decisions, and evaluating their consequences. It is a process that promotes transparency and generates information that citizens can use to evaluate the performance of the president.

---

[14] Baum (2002; 2003); Baum and Groeling (2010). With respect to the behavior of individual lawmakers, see Fenno (1978) and Mayhew (1974).

An imbalance of power between the executive and legislative branches accelerated after World War II, fueled initially by Cold War rivalries and then by the post-9/11 "war on terror." Congress has transferred much of its authority over war to the president and acquiesced to broad uses of executive discretion during states of emergency that have lasted for decades.[15] So much delegation, when combined with the uncertainty of international events and the dire outcomes from presidential miscalculation, has generated a strong need among lawmakers for reliable information, orderly review of past performance, and assessment of likely future outcomes. Although informal contacts have become a common means for reviewing foreign policy, particularly for low-profile issues,[16] oversight hearings introduce procedural regularity into a policy domain that routinely violates criteria of orderly review and accountability.

The responsibility of congressional committees to educate the public in international affairs confronts paradoxical public attitudes, however. The dual functions of the American president as chief minister and head of state combine political and symbolic roles that most democracies keep separate. In addition, Americans have limited interest and knowledge about world events, although they can be acutely sensitive to the costs of war and diplomacy.[17] Consequently, citizens tend to rally around the president in times of crisis, but lose confidence in his handling of events over time.[18] These conflicting patterns produce a high degree of volatility in public opinion polls and pose a dilemma for the committees that oversee an administration's performance with respect to national security.[19] On the one hand, formal hearings cue the public and press to pay attention to an emerging crisis and organize deliberation about the objectives and likely success of the president's policies.[20] On the other hand, information that

[15] The most heated exchanges have arisen over whether the president has unilateral authority to engage U.S. forces in military conflicts and whether legislative resolutions authorizing the president to use force satisfy the spirit (if not the language) of the Constitution. For the "congressionalist" perspective, see Lindsay (1992–93; 1994); Koh (1990); Silverstein (1997); Irons (2005); Fisher (1995; 2000; 2005; 2008); Fatovic (2004); Daalder and Lindsay (2003); Healy (2008); Griffin (2013). For the "presidentialist" perspective, see Crovitz and Rabkin (1989); Cheney (1990); Yoo (2005). Zeisberg (2013) rejects the idea of camps, but does find two different normative traditions in the Constitution.

[16] Hersman (2000).

[17] Holsti (2004); Jentleson (1992); Jentleson and Britton (1998); Burk (1999); Feaver and Gelpi (2004); Gelpi, Feaver, and Reifler (2005; 2007); Karol and Miguel (2007); Aldrich et al. (2006); Eichenberg (2005); Boettcher and Cobb (2006); Berinsky (2007; 2009); Eichenberg, Stoll, and Lebo (2006); Voeten and Brewer (2006); Gartner, Segura, and Wilkening (1997); Gartner and Segura (1998; 2008); Baum and Potter (2008); Hill, Herron, and Lewis (2010); Kriner and Shen (2014).

[18] Mueller (1973; 1994; 2005).

[19] Page and Shapiro (1992); Holsti (2004); Aldrich, Sullivan, and Borgida (1989); Bartels (1991); Aldrich et al. (2006); Page and Bouton (2006).

[20] Zaller (1992; 1994); Zaller and Chiu (1996); Brody (1994); Bennett (1990; 1996); Bennett, Lawrence, and Livingston (2007); Voeten and Brewer (2006); Berinsky (2007; 2009); Howell and Pevehouse (2007, chap. 6); Baum and Groeling (2010).

contradicts the executive's course of action undermines Americans' desire for national unity during times of crisis.

The salience of national security issues for the national reputations of the Republican and Democratic Parties complicates matters, as well. Since the 1980s, polls have documented a substantial Republican advantage among voters for competence in the conduct of foreign policy.[21] As committees weigh the effect of formal hearings on the public's perceptions of executive competence in foreign affairs, therefore, their members' electoral interests often conflict with their institutional responsibilities.

The case of the Truman Doctrine provides a compelling example of how oversight hearings by the Senate Foreign Relations Committee furthered the rule of law and promoted public acceptance of U.S. efforts to contain the expansion of Soviet-sponsored communism. The committee's oversight depended upon the policy entrepreneurship of senior Republican members that was both prospective in setting the foreign policy agenda and retrospective in evaluating whether the early steps toward containment worked. In this respect, the case illustrates the intimate connection between making policy and implementing it. The events of 1947–48 also illustrate the importance of closed sessions in fostering negotiation between the legislative and executive branches and the importance of strategic calculation among committee members in scheduling public hearings. In addition, the informational focus of Foreign Relations Committee hearings varied as senators first prodded the White House to proclaim the growing Soviet threat, modified the president's proposals, vetted opposing arguments in secret, and conducted an exceptionally effective public relations campaign. In other words, formal oversight involved many types of content to balance the executive and educate the public. Finally, the partnership between the president and the committee occurred under divided government. What made the extraordinary alliance work were the political ambitions of key committee members, who provided the institutional prestige, national visibility, and drive to revamp a new Republican majority's approach to foreign policy in the aftermath of World War II.

THE PUBLIC AND PRIVATE MEANING OF S.938

The Cold War was a deadly struggle between two super powers that lasted more than four decades. From the vantage point of the twenty-first century, the logic of the Truman Doctrine appears irrefutable, and the brilliant statesmen who

[21] Petrocik (1996); Petrocik, Benoit, and Hansen (2003–4); Woon and Pope (2008). After 9/11, voters perceived Republicans as superior to Democrats in handling terrorism by more than a two to one margin. Even in 2006, while survey respondents perceived that Democrats would do a better job in Iraq, they still favored Republicans by a margin of 7 to 10 percentage points as better able to handle a crisis. See, for example, http://www.ropercenter.uconn.edu/ (accessed January 2014).

crafted it well deserve their status as heroes of the age. Yet the hearing record for S.938, the bill to provide economic and military aid to Greece and Turkey, indicates how tentative were the first steps on the road to containing Soviet expansion. The ideas came from strategic thinkers in the executive branch, Dean Acheson, George Marshall, and George Kennan, but much of the political deliberation that led to national consensus for restraining Soviet ambitions happened in the chambers of the Senate Foreign Relations Committee.

The aftermath of World War II was chaotic all over Europe, and the terrible conditions suited Joseph Stalin's purposes admirably. One by one, governments in Central Europe fell to communist insurgents, who received abundant help from the Russian Army, but also benefited from the displacement and starvation of local populations and the shaky regimes that attempted to replace Nazi occupiers. Poland, Hungary, Albania, Romania, Bulgaria, and East Germany had all fallen behind what Churchill termed the Iron Curtain by the time Truman appeared before Congress on March 12, 1947, and Czechoslovakia soon followed. Greek and Italian communists were in a particularly advantageous position because of their heroic actions against the Nazis, and in Greece they were getting help from guerillas based in Bulgaria and Albania. Turkey, which had not participated in World War II, nevertheless experienced intense pressure from the Russians along its borders and was struggling with serious financial strains from a constant state of mobilization.

The United States had not responded directly to these events, but the administration was increasingly gripped by a sense of emergency, sparked by George Kennan's famous Long Telegram predicting Soviet expansion and a subsequent secret analysis overseen by the president's trusted advisor, Clark Clifford, in September 1946. Truman's State of the Union message in January 1947, in which he addressed the first Republican majority in Congress since 1932, called for a bipartisan approach to foreign policy, but was short on particulars. In February, Truman met with key lawmakers, including Senator Arthur Vandenberg (R-MI), the new chair of the Foreign Relations Committee, and subsequently dispatched Secretary of State George Marshall to brief other Foreign Relations members privately about the growing Soviet threat in Europe. A report to the Cabinet on March 7 predicted that the Greek government was within a few weeks of complete financial collapse.[22] Subsequently, a leak on March 31 from the British Foreign Office about its decision to withdraw financial and military support from the regime reinforced the president's call to action.

The domestic politics of the looming security crisis were unfavorable to bold action in Europe, however. Truman's party had suffered a dramatic defeat in the 1946 election, and the president himself was subject to ridicule by some in Congress. The newly elected Republicans contained avid anticommunists, such as Senator Joseph McCarthy (R-WI) and Representative Richard Nixon (R-CA),

[22] McCulloch (1992, 545).

who appeared more eager to expose domestic spies than confront the Soviet Union abroad. The old isolationist strains in the GOP lingered, as well, adding to the difficulty of developing an initiative that would commit the country to a larger role in Europe.

The Democrats were a problem, too. Many on the left wanted to continue the wartime alliance with the Russians and had difficulty reconciling differences between an ideology that attracted them intellectually and the alarming behavior of the rulers in the Kremlin. Indeed, Truman's vice president, Henry Wallace, had given a highly controversial speech in 1946 advocating friendlier ties with the Russians. Those liberal internationalists who opposed the Soviet Union, moreover, favored cultivating the United Nations rather than asserting American power directly into Europe. At the very least, they wanted to give the fledgling organization a chance to prove its mettle.

Finally, large swaths of the public simply wanted to be left alone after the intense mobilization of World War II. Millions of veterans were in school under the GI Bill, labor unrest had finally settled down, factories were humming to meet pent-up demand, and Americans were busy producing the Baby Boom generation. Who wanted to think about international crises?

As the administration debated options in February, Senator Vandenberg had advised the president to appear before a joint session of Congress and "scare the hell out of the American people."[23] Several weeks later, Truman followed that advice. His short address exemplified the plain speaking for which he is now admired, as he delivered the essence of the doctrine that bears his name: "It is the policy of the United States to assist free peoples to work out their destinies in their own way."[24] Truman stressed the urgency of the situation in the eastern Mediterranean, the inability of the United Nations to extend help in a timely manner, and the limited nature of the aid, themes that the administration officials later reiterated in public testimony.

While the nation absorbed the president's rhetoric, deliberation between Foreign Relations Committee members and executive officials moved behind closed doors. The first of eight executive sessions began on March 13, 1947, with a small group of senior senators and Under Secretary of State Acheson, Secretary of War Patterson, Secretary of the Navy Forrestal, and several high-ranking military officers. The transcript indicates that neither the administration officials nor the senators believed that the operation would be short-lived or limited in scope.[25] Equally plain, moreover, was the fact that no one in the room had a sense of how far the imaginary line they were drawing in the east-

[23] Quoted in Zelizer (2010, 68).

[24] Address of the President of the United States, House of Representatives, 80th Congress, 1st Session, document 171, http://www.trumanlibrary.org/whistlestop/study_collections/doctrine/large/documents/pdfs/5–9.pdf#zoom=100 (accessed March 2013).

[25] This discussion is based on the transcripts of the hearings published by the Senate Foreign Relations Committee as part of its Historical Series on major U.S. foreign policy decisions.

ern Mediterranean would take them. The meeting's participants were dealing with the practicalities of crafting a policy that could survive criticism from left- and right-wing groups, withstand House and Senate debate, and pass muster with a skeptical public. The absence of grand strategy in the discussion, incidentally, confirms recent scholarship that the policy of containment developed incrementally rather than emerged from the White House as full-blown doctrine.[26]

The senators used these early sessions to assess the extent of the crisis, how much time they had, and the viability of alternative solutions. Once convinced of the need for action, they suggested changes in the bill's language to make it less threatening to the Russians and to disarm domestic critics. They held private sessions, as well, for Senate colleagues to discuss possible amendments with Acheson and other officials and to review strategy for managing the legislation on the Senate floor when debate began on April 7, 1947.

Most striking about the secret hearings before and after the public sessions is the atmosphere of candor and mutual respect that pervades the transcripts as the participants addressed a wide range of issues. Could temporary financing be found while Congress wrestled with the larger concerns? Would the World Bank handle this matter better? Should Turkey, which was in better financial shape than Greece, be included in the package? Would passage of the bill give the president a blank check, when Republican senators had committed to reasserting a role for Congress in foreign policy? Would the United States end up the defender of the British Empire, and should Whitehall be rewarded for having provided so little advance warning of its decision? Would the Russians react aggressively to being designated a threat, albeit not by name? Was the country committing to assist besieged governments around the globe? Could the U.S. government afford to undermine the United Nations with unilateral action before the organization got off the ground? Would the public recognize the limitations on UN action without also losing confidence in the fledgling organization?

Even Senator Tom Connally (D-TX), the ranking minority member, served a useful purpose. His limited understanding of world affairs and penchant for alcohol had prompted Acheson's scornful assessment that he "often doesn't understand what he is told."[27] Yet, his simplistic solutions and constant worries about how ordinary people would view the aid package were a valuable, if irritating, reminder of the formidable challenge of winning over the public.

While quiet deliberation proceeded in the Foreign Relations executive sessions, the committee orchestrated an elaborate public ritual involving five days of open hearings in late March. Acheson led off with remarks that echoed Truman's address, including a stirring quotation from an 1824 speech by Daniel

[26] Johnson (2006).
[27] Johnson (2006, 15).

Webster: "With Greece, now is the crisis of her fate—her great, it may be her last, struggle. Sir, while we sit here deliberating, her destiny may be decided."[28] Remarks followed from the secretary of war, the secretary of the navy, and the ambassadors to Greece and Turkey that stressed the perils these governments confronted and their strategic importance in protecting access to the eastern Mediterranean and Middle East oil. The administration officials elaborated on the need for speed, the magnitude of the destruction in Greece, and the importance of halting communist advances in Europe, although the Soviet Union was never named. Extensive coverage in the *New York Times* during and after the hearings positively reinforced the administration's position.

A large portion of the hearings, however, was given over to thirty-one private citizens and spokespersons for advocacy groups, with heavy representation from peace activists, and several senators, along with the mercurial Claude Pepper (D-FL), who gave an impassioned plea to let the United Nations prove its worth. The committee made a great show of airing alternative viewpoints from groups as diverse as the World Federalists, the Socialist Party, the American Veterans Committee, and the Macedonian American People's League. Publicly, committee members echoed the administration's assurances that aid would be limited, but the executive sessions revealed how little weight the opposing testimony carried and how carefully senators had accommodated potential opponents behind closed doors.

After nine days of floor consideration, the bill passed with amendments on April 22 by a vote of 67–23. The House approved the measure on May 9, voting 287–107, and the two chambers reconciled their differences by mid-May. The president signed the legislation on May 22. Without the adroit use of secret and public hearings in the Foreign Relations Committee, there likely would have been no Truman Doctrine.[29]

When the administration sought authorization of an additional $275 million the following year, the strategic collaboration between the Foreign Relations Committee and the White House continued. Three days of executive sessions brought the secretary of state, the State Department's aid coordinator, and three high-ranking military officers to Capitol Hill. Their assessment of the situation in the two countries was guarded and critical of the corrupt Greek regime, and it fueled members' concern about wasting U.S. funds on a losing cause.

Going public with this information would have not only killed the bill, but also jeopardized the passage of the European Recovery Act, otherwise known as the Marshall Plan. Marshall had proposed the idea of massive economic assistance to rebuild Europe in a speech at Harvard in June 1947, shortly after S.938 became law. His ideas received further elaboration in George Kennan's

---

[28] U.S. Senate Foreign Relations Committee, "Aid to Greece and Turkey," CIS No. 80-S816–10 (March 24, 1947, 4).

[29] Johnson (2006, 20–21).

Foreign Affairs article that summer in which the Truman Doctrine evolved into the broader strategy of containment. Truman endeavored to resurrect the Marshall Plan legislation, which had stalled in the Senate, with a speech in March 1948 in which he famously declared, "We must be prepared to pay the price for peace, or assuredly, we shall pay the price of war."[30] Clearly, the conversations behind closed doors that same month about the lack of progress in Greece would have proved highly damaging to the larger cause of rebuilding Europe. Thanks to the committee's silence, the reauthorization bill eventually passed in April 1948.

The collaboration between the Senate Foreign Relations Committee and the administration during the 80th Congress appears astonishing to contemporary eyes. Truman was unpopular, the Republicans had just taken control of the Congress after a long exile in the minority, and two of the president's most important GOP collaborators, Vandenberg and Lodge, wanted his job. Surely, the conditions were ripe for recrimination, gridlock, and grandstanding rather than cooperation. Instead, Foreign Relations conducted a serious review of a major foreign policy initiative that consumed thirteen days of private and public deliberation, all in the span of ten weeks.

Both sides accomplished important political goals from the collaboration. Truman, who had adopted a tough anticommunist line to protect the domestic legacy of the New Deal from the new Republican majority, achieved a major policy victory.[31] He gained aid from a handful of senior Republicans, who needed to reinvent a foreign policy that would help voters forget how wrong their party had been about World War II and who enjoyed the prestige and visibility to make a deal and garner their colleagues' support. A strong stand in favor of the Truman Doctrine in Europe not only burnished the GOP's anticommunist credentials, but added force to its criticism of the administration's policies in China.[32] The example of S.938 thus drives home how much the cooperation between the two branches depended upon a unique alignment of interests between Democrats and Republicans, remarkable even in an era of relatively low partisan polarization.

The confluence of political ambitions in the White House and the Senate Foreign Relations Committee proved temporary, however. Truman campaigned in 1948 on his approach to contain Soviet expansion in Europe. He dismissed the GOP's embrace of anticommunism as a "smokescreen," contrasted Republican "talk" with his own bold efforts, and pushed the Truman Doctrine and Marshall Plan hard in immigrant communities, which made up 25 percent of the nation's population in 1948 and were concentrated in large northern and

---

[30] McCulloch (1992, 608).
[31] Zelizer (2010, 70–71).
[32] Zelizer (2010, 88).

midwestern cities.[33] His victory and the return of the Democratic majority in the 81st Congress, when combined with Vandenberg's failing health, the weak leadership of Foreign Relations' new chair, Senator Connally, and increasingly aggressive partisanship among Republicans, put an end to the exceptional partnership. Acheson endeavored to collaborate with Lodge, but by 1950 judged the committee to be "unworkable."[34]

Overall, the Senate Foreign Relations Committee's handling of the Truman Doctrine in 1947 and 1948 marked one of the high points of its influence in foreign affairs and conferred an aura of prestige that lasted for more than two decades. Indeed, the committee's prominent position contrasted starkly with the passive role of the Senate Armed Services Committee, which did not seek jurisdiction over the military assistance funds in the plan,[35] and which held no hearings, either public or private, during the initial consideration of the policy or its subsequent review.

Despite the active leadership of Republican senators, the administration was able to claim the lion's share of the political credit because so much legislative effort was out of public view. Nevertheless, the committee's efforts proved indispensible. As Johnson observed, "The conventional image of the congressional role in the early Cold War—somewhat condescending nods to Vandenberg's susceptibility to flattery, or what Acheson dubbed the 'Vandenberg treatment'—seems well off the mark, since the real practitioners of the 'Vandenberg treatment' were [Senators] Smith, Lodge, and Vandenberg himself."[36]

OVERVIEW OF THE BOOK

The Senate Foreign Relations Committee's inquiries with respect to the Truman Doctrine raise compelling questions about the decades of oversight that have transpired since. Did the Senate's national security committees enhance the rule of law in foreign affairs by carrying out orderly processes of review? Did they generate information that citizens could use to hold government officials accountable? In light of this historical experience, what can the public reasonably expect today from the congressional watchdogs that monitor the executive's conduct of international affairs?

In this book, I evaluate the performance of the Senate Armed Services and Foreign Relations Committees in conducting formal oversight of defense and policy from 1947 to 2008. The study begins with the Cold War and ends with the final years of the George W. Bush administration. Between these bookends

---

[33] McCulloch (1992, 679, 683).
[34] Johnson (2006, 42).
[35] Johnson (2006, 13).
[36] Johnson (2006, 21).

are four lengthy, unpopular wars, multiple uses of military force of varying scale, one crisis of nearly apocalyptic proportions over Soviet missiles in Cuba, many diplomatic breakthroughs and failures, numerous scandals, and abundant decisions dealing with treaties, military weapons, and foreign assistance. The sweep of events provides ample fodder for statistical analyses and case studies to illustrate the main arguments about the sources of variation in national security oversight.

The empirical analysis at the center of the project draws on formal hearings by the Senate Armed Services and Foreign Relations Committees in *public* and *executive* sessions. I use the data to first to examine the big picture of the workload of the national security committees, then to narrow the focus to their propensity for oversight, and finally to drill down to the specific content of their hearing agendas. I answer three separate but related questions. Why did the national security committees become less active since the mid-1990s? What motivated variation in the committees' frequency of oversight inquiries and their venues from 1947 to 2008? What influenced committee decisions to favor routine inquiries into the administration of Defense and State Department programs compared to highly salient events of wartime casualties and scandal? I use the results of this analysis to make the case for revitalizing the Senate's national security watchdogs and to develop a set of reforms to accomplish that goal.

Together the Senate Armed Services and Foreign Relations Committees conducted 3,257 public hearings and 2,124 executive sessions for a total of 5,381 observations and 11,276 formal hearing days. Of the total, Armed Services allocated 2,098 days and Foreign Relations devoted 3,423 days to oversight hearings. I coded the content of hearings, as well, to determine if committee activity varied with the types of oversight involved. The breadth and depth of the data set are unique for studying oversight generally and foreign policy specifically.

In addition, I consider a variety of institutional influences on the frequency of committee hearings, ranging from committee prestige, visibility, and assignments per member to party polarization. I also address the effects of external conditions, such as divided government, budgets for defense and diplomacy, use of major force, public opinion, and war casualties, on committee hearing topics. Appendix A describes my methods in coding the committee hearings, and Appendix B summarizes the dependent and explanatory variables.[37]

By limiting the scope of my research to the Senate Armed Services and Foreign Relations Committees, I am able to delve deeply into the processes that influenced the frequency of formal national security oversight for a very long period. With this approach, I connect institutional changes in the Senate directly to committee behavior. I link Senate norms for placing members on

---

[37] Contemporary search engines, as I discuss in Appendix A, have significant limitations in producing consistent results for coding the content of hearings. In addition, they cannot deal with the complicated sleuthing involved in compiling information on executive session hearings.

committees that match their personal political interests to biases in the hearing agendas of Armed Services and Foreign Relations. I assess the disparate effects of external influences on different types of inquiries, including review of budget requests, routine program implementation, crises, or scandal. Thus, I explore aspects of congressional involvement with national security policy that have remained largely out of public view and have been overlooked by other scholars. Along the way, I confirm widespread perceptions among knowledgeable insiders that something is amiss in the Senate and its national security committees.

I recognize that my theoretical and empirical claims may extend no further than the Senate Armed Services and Foreign Relations Committees. Their jurisdictions over defense and diplomacy, after all, pose special challenges in understanding the motives driving their behavior that other committees do not encounter. In foreign affairs, national security oversight has far-reaching strategic, political, and economic consequences, and the president not only enjoys a unique degree of delegated power, but also exercises special prerogatives over statecraft and war. The high-stakes and White House prerogatives, in turn, require an unusual reliance on executive sessions and distinctive approaches to party competition and external conditions. Given the vital national interests associated with war and peace, my findings compel attention in their own right, even if they are not broadly representative of other committees' oversight behavior.

Beyond the substantive importance of national security oversight, the historical trends and statistical relationships that emerge in this study pose challenges for the way that scholars analyze oversight. Since oversight activity depends upon the status of committee work inside the Senate, changes in total hearing activity account for much variation in routine monitoring and investigations that researchers mistakenly attribute to other factors. Moreover, given the considerable diversity in the hearing agendas of the Senate Armed Services and Foreign Relations Committees, scholarly tendencies to treat oversight by committees as an aggregate phenomenon within Congress is quite problematic. Divided government, for example, creates problems for a consensus-minded committee like Armed Service, but generates opportunities for one inclined to debate like Foreign Relations. Its true effects wash out empirically, therefore, unless researchers make appropriate allowances for committee diversity. Finally, high frequencies for oversight, generally, and routine program implementation, particularly, raise questions about the applicability of major theories in the literature regarding congressional control of executive officials. Together, these patterns raise questions, in my mind at least, about issues of research design and efforts to craft an overarching explanation of congressional oversight behavior.

I have written with three audiences in mind: citizens, foreign policy experts, and scholars who focus on American political institutions. Citizens may find the book informative in shaping their expectations about how the president and Congress interact in the realm of national security under the pervasive pull of members' personal political goals and partisan agendas. Foreign policy experts may recognize that I have put meat on the bones of the concept of domestic constraints, if only to challenge their long-held assumptions that the United States is a unitary actor with clearly defined strategic goals. Students of American politics may find that the under-tilled field of oversight yields new insights into ongoing scholarly debates about legislative committees and parties, as well as the nature of Congress's relationship with the president.

James Madison once noted that "war is the true nurse of aggrandizement [of power]."[38] My larger purpose, therefore, is to draw attention to the importance of political institutions and the seemingly arcane process of committee oversight of international affairs in fostering the rule of law in international affairs. Too much legislative deference to the commander in chief can be a slippery slope, a gradual erosion of constitutional responsibility that occurs without fanfare. This study reveals an overall decline in formal processes of review and inadequate efforts to gather information that the public cares about. It is a system in serious need of repair.

The book divides into three sections. Part I explores the big questions regarding oversight and offers a framework for thinking about committee watchdog activity. Having argued that oversight matters to the rule of law in foreign affairs in this chapter, I turn in Chapter 1 to review previous scholarship about congressional scrutiny of the executive branch and about general patterns of legislative influence on foreign policy decisions. I then examine hearing activity of the Senate Armed Services and Foreign Relations Committees from 1947 to 2008 to assess the overall trends in oversight and identify similarities and differences in their behavior. In Chapter 2, I develop theoretical expectations, which address three different committee phenomena relevant to oversight: sources of change in the total frequency of hearings, biases within committees regarding the frequency and venues of oversight hearings as a result of external stimuli, and influences on the content of routine and event-driven review.

Part II examines the extent to which the Senate Armed Services and Foreign Relations Committees contribute to the rule of law and public accountability in the realm of national security. The section is organized to move from broad issues of committee capacity for oversight, to general propensities for conducting review of the executive, to particular types of oversight hearings. Chapter 3 assesses long-term changes in the Senate committee system that devalued committee work and negatively affected the total hearing activity of Armed Services and Foreign Relations. Chapter 4 examines how the distinctive goals of each committee led to strategic choices about how much attention to devote to oversight, particularly in comparison to budget activity. Chapter 5 analyzes partisan

---

[38] Hamilton, Jay, and Madison (1962, *Federalist* 4).

calculations about party reputations as influences on routine and event-driven inquiries, using the classic typology of police patrols and fire alarms. Taken together, these chapters assess the performance of Armed Services and Foreign Relations in promoting regular order and educating the public in foreign affairs.

Part III connects national security oversight to broad constitutional issues of congressional war powers. Chapter 6 takes up normative political issues regarding the importance of legislative oversight in fostering the rule of law and public deliberation about foreign policy. I argue that widespread misconceptions among the public and members of Congress about the constitutional system have impeded the ability of legislators to address the need for change. I also contend that the executive, while enjoying short-term political benefits from congressional impotence in dealing with particular foreign policy issues, pays a high price for the institutional weakness of the legislature. Chapter 7 applies the empirical findings from Part II to the issue of reform and makes practical recommendations for improving the performance of the Senate's national security watchdogs. In addition to challenging the efficacy of proposals currently circulating in Washington, I stress reforms that create greater incentives among members of Armed Services and Foreign Relations to master the complexities of statecraft for the benefit of the institution as a whole and to make foreign policy decisions accessible to the public.

CHAPTER 1

Guarding the Guardians through Oversight

IN THE SPRING OF 2004, the chair of the Senate Foreign Relations Committee proposed public hearings regarding the conduct and objectives of the Iraq War, which was then entering its second year amid rising violence and casualties. The House majority leader attacked his proposal for its disloyalty to the Republican Party and potential harm to President Bush's electoral fortunes.[1] Chairman Richard Lugar (R-IN) went ahead with the inquiry, although the Bush administration dampened publicity for the hearings by sending second-tier officials to testify in place of the secretaries of state and defense. A month later, Senator John Warner (R-VA), chair of the Senate Armed Services Committee, scheduled two days of hearings to investigate abuse of detainees at Baghdad's Abu Ghraib Prison. He, too, drew criticism, this time from his counterpart in the House, for undermining public support for the Iraq War. The tension between the two highly respected committee chairs and their fellow Republicans highlights the fundamental question about the motivations behind congressional oversight: whose interests do congressional oversight hearings promote?

Lugar and Warner, as leaders of the Senate's key national security committees, had institutional responsibilities and personal reputations that required at least some attention to reports of escalating mayhem and appalling photographs coming out of Iraq. Moreover, their committees had reason to engage in oversight in order to pursue members' respective goals of policy debate and support of the military. Nevertheless, the two committees' public review of the Iraq War remained thin.[2] By the 2006 election, Democrats made the lack of congressional attention to the wars in Iraq and Afghanistan a major campaign issue and celebrated their victory with pledges of "oversight, oversight, oversight."[3] Upon attaining the majority, they launched investigations of military contractors, procurement practices, combat equipment, recruitment, and long-

---

[1] David E. Rosenbaum, "In the Fulbright Mold, Without the Power," *New York Times*, May 3, 2004, http://www.nytimes.com/2004/05/03/politics/03TALK.html?th (accessed January 2005).

[2] Ornstein and Mann (2006). Armed Services heard public testimony about Abu Ghraib for another four days in August 2004, although the hearings took place while Washington was preoccupied with the presidential nominating conventions.

[3] Anna Mulrine, "Armed with History," *U.S. News & World Report*, February 4, 2007, http://www.usnews.com/usnews/news/articles/070204/12skelton.htm (accessed July 2008).

term strategies. As two seasoned political observers noted approvingly, "The Hill is alive with the sound of hearings."[4]

At first glance, the shift in oversight activity by the Senate Armed Services and Foreign Relations Committees appeared to be a straightforward story of party competition in which unified control of the executive and legislative branches initially depressed the frequency of formal oversight hearings, while divided government later stimulated it. Closer examination of the hearing record reveals a more complicated set of motives; for the condition of split party control did not explain the variation in national security hearings on Iraq in the Senate as well as one might one have expected. Armed Services, for example, conducted many of its inquiries behind closed doors to contain the threat to its internal consensus about supporting the military. Foreign Affairs scheduled public oversight hearings about various international hot spots, but devoted relatively few of them to Iraq. Despite news accounts of heightened review of the Bush administration, as we shall see, the frequency of oversight hearings did not increase appreciably after Democrats took control of Congress in 2007, although each committee launched critical investigations. Overall, the weak scrutiny of the Iraq and Afghan Wars was not conducive to orderly processes of review and readjustment as the conflicts dragged on, nor did it foster public understanding of the stakes involved.

Complex motivations for oversight pervaded the entire sixty-two years of the Senate Armed Services and Foreign Relations Committees activity in international affairs. Each committee varied its formal inquiries substantially over time, and the two differed in the frequency of their hearings, often strikingly during the same year. Armed Services showed a decided bias toward budget hearings and routine program administration; Foreign Relations tended to focus on informational hearings about the "state of the world." Divided government produced differences between the two committees. Yet Presidents Truman, Eisenhower, Johnson, Carter, and Reagan experienced high levels of public scrutiny at the hands of their fellow partisans on both committees. In short, committee orientations and external contexts appear to have been major factors in the number and content of oversight hearings of executive branch performance in international affairs.

Viewed more broadly, the frequency and the distribution of formal committee hearings in both public and executive session expose gaps and contradictions in the way that scholars have understood oversight. First, the inclusion of executive sessions inflates the hearing tally, revealing both committees to have been more engaged in national security oversight than many critics have recognized. Second, several patterns in the hearings of the Senate Armed Services and Foreign Relations Committees raise issues about the way that scholars generally approached the topic of foreign policy oversight. The recent reduction in

[4] Ornstein and Mann (2006).

the total number of public hearings by the Armed Services and Foreign Relations Committees, for example, appears to have arisen from institutional changes affecting the entire Senate committee system, a trend researchers have omitted from their analyses of oversight activity in general. Third, the distribution of hearing content for each committee suggests that multiple goals motivated oversight rather than the single objective of agency control, which researchers have assumed to be the driving force behind oversight. Fourth, routine program review, or what scholars term "police patrol" oversight, received considerably more space on the hearing agendas for both committees than theorists would have predicted. Finally, examination of crises and scandals, what scholars term "fire alarm" oversight, varied within a relatively narrow range over time, even as the committees' total hearing agendas shrank.

Perhaps national security represents a special case for congressional watchdogs. Nevertheless, the patterns I discuss in this chapter are integral to inferences about the political processes that generate oversight hearings of defense and foreign policy. In the next section, I discuss what scholars know about congressional involvement in U.S. foreign policy, what they have concluded about oversight more generally, and why these perspectives do not appear to fit together. I then present data on the formal hearings of the Senate Armed Services and Foreign Relations Committees to illustrate the puzzles that drive my analysis. In working through various historical trends, the reader will become familiar with the complexities of national security oversight and gain understanding of the characteristics of the Senate hearing data that support the statistical analyses in subsequent chapters.

SEPARATE WORLDS? PERSPECTIVES ON NATIONAL SECURITY AND CONGRESSIONAL OVERSIGHT

Congressional oversight of national security arises from a perennial question in democratic societies, which dates back to Plato. "Who will guard the guardians?" is the simple, but damning, charge against the philosopher king. The dilemma of unaccountable discretion strikes with particular force in the United States over the president's conduct of international affairs. The public has limited capacity to monitor the domain of statecraft, and its disadvantages have grown with the global scale of foreign relations and America's superpower status. The people's representatives in the legislative branch take up the slack in ensuring the legitimacy of U.S. foreign policy, although congressional inadequacies have sparked concern for years.[5] Knowledgeable observers consequently

---

[5] Koh (1990); Silverstein (1997); Fisher (1995; 2000); Irons (2005); Rudalevige (2006); Griffin (2013). Lindsay (1994) argued, however, for a middle ground between those who thought that Congress was too passive in foreign affairs and those who considered it meddled too aggressively.

have raised alarms about a dangerous atrophy of congressional war powers in the last decade.[6]

In some respects, scholars have documented a great deal about what Congress does or does not do in the realm of foreign affairs. Extensive literatures addressed the constitutional responsibilities of the legislative branch and critiqued the expansion of presidential power.[7] Recent historical accounts challenged conventional wisdom that members of Congress were bit players in the dramas of the Cold War and its aftermath.[8] Numerous case studies examined interactions between lawmakers and individual presidents and demonstrated congressional influence over specific foreign policy events.[9] Several inquiries highlighted the importance of legislators in shaping elite discourse and popular understanding about foreign affairs.[10] Formal theories regarding the role of domestic politics as a constraint in international relations emerged to complement the field's conventional focus on state actors.[11] Finally, statistical analyses identified the size of a president's congressional majority as a limit on his ability to initiate or sustain military action.[12]

These disparate studies have indicated that congressional involvement in defense and foreign policy mattered over the post–World War II period, despite the dominance of the executive branch. The various books and articles lacked explanations, however, for the triggers that motivated lawmakers responsible for defense and foreign policy to engage the president. Why did the designated committees move aggressively in some international situations and turn a blind

---

[6] Fisher (2000; 2005; 2006; 2008; 2013); Ackerman (2010); Auerswald and Campbell (2012); Griffin (2013). Wolfensberger argued, however, lawmakers denied President Bush a "blank check" by imposing procedural controls in the PATRIOT Act that the president resisted, but eventually accepted (2005, 349).

[7] See, for example, Koh (1990); Silverstein (1997); Fisher (1995; 2000; 2006; 2008); Irons (2005); Fatovic (2004); Yoo (2005); Cheney (1990); Crovitz and Rabkin (1989); Rudalevige (2006); Healy (2008); Griffin (2013).

[8] Zelizer (2010); Johnson (2006).

[9] Destler (1985); Burgin (1991); Ripley and Lindsay (1993); Lindsay (1992–93); Hinckley (1994); Henderson (1998); Prins and Marshall (2001); Mayhew (2000; 2005); McCormick and Wittkopf (1990); Hersman (2000); Vanderbush and Haney (2002); Scott and Carter (2002); Wolfensberger (2005); Zegart (2011); Zeisberg (2013). Chapters in Auerswald and Campbell (2012) by Towell, Balunis and Hemphill, Johnson, and Epstein contain case studies of the congressional oversight of defense authorizations, homeland security, intelligence, and foreign aid since 9/11. A pattern of periodic activism emerges in this research, although Hinckley noted that conflict did not necessarily produce better foreign policy decisions or greater accountability during the Reagan years.

[10] Fite (1991); Mayhew (2000); Schickler (2007); Howell and Pevehouse (2007); Carter and Scott (2009); Groeling and Baum (2008); Kriner (2009); Berinsky (2007; 2009).

[11] Bueno de Mesquita and Lalman (1992); Fearon (1994); Clark (2000); Bueno de Mesquita et al. (2003); Schultz (1998; 2001; 2003); Huth and Allee (2002); Clark and Nordstrom (2005); Slantchev (2006); Carson (2011).

[12] Howell and Pevehouse (2005; 2007); Kriner (2009; 2010).

eye in others? The literatures on Congress and foreign affairs offered partial answers to these questions through qualitative observation of specific cases or cross-sectional statistical studies of public opinion during wartime. Yet researchers interested in foreign affairs have not engaged in systematic study of the oversight process in Congress, the site of the majority of formal interaction between the legislative and executive branches.

Oversight is a perennially under-tilled field in American politics, which has hindered the development of theory and evidence. As one scholar recently summarized the topic, there is extensive variation in oversight activity, but "relatively is known about what drives it."[13] Academic studies devoted to congressional oversight in the broadest sense have appeared episodically over the past six decades but focused primarily on domestic policies.

One wave of research appeared in the mid-1970s and drew uniformly critical conclusions about the failure of congressional committees to undertake sufficient oversight of the executive.[14] The inadequate performance, they argued, occurred because lawmakers saw few electoral payoffs in pursuing activities that were good for the institution but undervalued by the voters. Other scholars, however, demonstrated that committees launched inquiries that appeared to be at odds with their incentives to cater to constituent interests and instead provided a means to pursue policy advocacy and institutional power.[15] In addition, oversight emerged as part of larger battle over prerogatives between the legislature and the administrative state.[16]

A second, more extensive body of work on oversight addressed the problem of political control over regulatory agencies when legislative principals attempted to monitor their bureaucratic agents, despite severe disadvantages in information about agency programs.[17] Since oversight activities are costly, theorists hypothesized, lawmakers would write statutes to restrain agencies' abuse of their discretion, effectively handing oversight to third parties, such as judges, interest groups, journalists, or constituents. The result would be relatively few formal inquiries but a higher level of control than met the eye. Most of this research examined the effects of different types of statutes to compel bureaucrats to follow the preferences of the legislative branch so that formal hearings would

---

[13] McGrath (2013, 354).

[14] See Ogul (1976); Ogul and Rockman (1990); Ripley and Franklin (1990); and Aberbach (1990) for critiques of the inadequacy of congressional oversight more generally.

[15] Diana Evans (1994).

[16] Dodd and Schott (1979); Sundquist (1981).

[17] The idea is to ensure that bureaucratic agents will carry out the wishes of their legislative principals, a classic problem of accountability in economics made particularly acute by asymmetries in information that favor agency officials. See, for example, Weingast and Moran (1983); McCubbins and Schwartz (1984); Shepsle and Weingast (1987); Weingast and Marshall (1988); Epstein and O'Halloran (1999); Cameron and Rosendorff (1993); Diermeier and Fedderson (2000); Balla and Wright (2001); Bendor, Glazer, and Hammond (2001); Volden (2002); Shipan (2004). See Wood (2011) for an overview of the literature on congressional delegation to the executive.

not be necessary. Supporting evidence regarding congressional control drew largely from examination of regulatory agencies.

A third approach to oversight focused on investigations of executive wrong-doing.[18] Probes of scandal and mismanagement have provided the most visible form of congressional monitoring, often generating front-page headlines and dramatic testimony before television cameras. Relatively few in number per legislative session, investigations nevertheless occupied a disproportionate amount of attention from the press and the public. Scholars focused on divided government as the prime motivation behind this type of oversight, but obtained conflicting results using different data and methods. Nyhan argues, moreover, that scandal arises from political calculation by the president's opponents and in many instances connects only weakly to the facts about agency performance. Some major missteps avoid scrutiny, for example, while other, relatively minor infractions generate lengthy inquiries.[19]

Generally, the expectation in the scholarly literature has been that formal oversight hearings would be relatively uncommon. Yet, committees increased their oversight activities rapidly throughout the 1970s and 1980s and retained a comparatively high level of hearings into the 1990s, before reducing their activity to the level of the 1950s.[20] Moreover, influential policy entrepreneurs engaged in oversight to provide a counterweight to presidential dominance of the federal government.[21] Variation in the frequency of formal oversight hearings indicated that Congress was not relying on statutory restraints alone and that other motivations were at work in the politics of oversight.[22]

An unexamined problem with the literature on congressional oversight surfaced when Aberbach updated his classic study and noted an overall decline in congressional hearings.[23] His observation posed difficulties for the way scholars evaluated evidence about oversight, although no one followed up. Empirical

---

[18] Mayhew (1991); Kriner and Schwartz (2008); Parker and Dull (2009; 2012); Kriner and Schickler (2012); Balla and Deering (2013); Kriner and Schickler (2014). Deering (2001; 2005) provides discussion of oversight in foreign policy generally; Marshall (2003) examines it for the House; Schickler (2007) looks at the period from 1937 to 1946; and Zeisberg (2013) provides a case study of the Munitions Inquiries in the 1930s and the Iran-Contra investigation in the 1980s. Kriner's (2009) and Kriner and Shen's (2014) examinations of the different tools Congress used to raise questions about the Iraq War are the most comprehensive efforts to analyze formal and informal oversight, but they address a single conflict.

[19] Nyhan (2014).

[20] Aberbach (1990; 2002); McGrath (2013). Aberbach's earlier study examines the years from 1961 to 1983, and his later analysis runs through 1997. McGrath's study runs from 1947 to 2006. The former coded oversight hearings from the *Daily Digest*, while the latter used search parameters of the Policy Agendas data set on congressional hearings to select those that involve terms, such as "review, investigate, budget, etc." The two accounts present similar patterns for the 1960s and 1970s, but diverge somewhat for the 1990s.

[21] Carter and Scott (2009); Schickler (2007).

[22] McGrath (2013); Balla and Deering (2013).

[23] Aberbach (2002).

researchers on congressional inquiries continued to count the frequency of oversight hearings, whether routine program oversight or investigations, without taking account of changes in the underlying pattern of committee activity in Congress. In other words, they looked at movement in the numerator without considering changes in the denominator.[24] When scholars failed to control for the overall trends in committee hearings as a whole, they risked making incorrect inferences about the influences on watchdog activity.

A further issue overlooked by scholars who have done empirical work on oversight is the distinction between domestic and foreign affairs. Generally, researchers count all oversight days together regardless of the policy domain, but several factors suggest that committee review of defense and foreign policy involved different calculations than, say, the Food and Drug Administration. In war and diplomacy, Congress and the president claim shared and separated powers, which frequently blur the lines of accountability. Since the Pentagon and State Departments are agents of both the legislature and the president, ambiguity arose when legislative intent and presidential prerogatives conflicted. In addition, the use of statutory provisions to restrain administrators *ex ante* has limited applicability in foreign affairs. Congress often uses vague language to give the president leeway for managing foreign policy crises: for example, the resolutions to authorize action against the North Vietnamese in 1964 after the incident in the Gulf of Tonkin or in 2002 to approve the possible use of force against Saddam Hussein in Iraq in 2003 were purposefully ambiguous. Moreover, the courts very seldom intervene in disputes between the legislative and executive branches over foreign policy, and when they do hear cases, they typically defer to the president.

Further differences arise in foreign relations oversight from public constraints on committee watchdogs who launch inquiries about the president's conduct of international relations, particularly when pressures to present a united front to an external enemy are present. Finally, the U.S. national security apparatus since 1947 has attained unparalleled size and scope,[25] and major wars have reconfigured politics throughout American history in ways that few domestic crises have matched.[26] Given the extensive disparities between domestic and international policy implementation, oversight of international affairs

[24] For purposes of illustration, suppose that a researcher observed that committees, on average, conducted 100 oversight hearing days per year in 1990 and 70 per year in 2000. If committees also had reduced their total annual hearing agenda from an average of 200 days to 140 days per year over the decade, the relative valuation of oversight remained the same even though the raw frequency was lower. The potential error for researchers is attributing the change in frequency to a particular set of covariates, when the actual source of variation was change at the institutional level generated by a different set of variables.

[25] Whittington and Carpenter (2003) strongly argue that the scale and secrecy of the national security bureaucracy mean that conventional principal-agent mechanisms do not operate effectively in foreign affairs.

[26] Mayhew (2005); Howell, Jackman, and Rogowski (2013).

seems likely to have followed a distinctive path that scholars need to take into account.

An Overview of National Security Committee Hearings

The hearing record of the Senate Armed Services and Foreign Relations Committees demonstrates the complexities underlying the politics of national security oversight. Observed trends from 1947 to 2008 indicate the importance of institutional change, committee differences, and types of hearing content to explain variation in the oversight of defense and foreign policy over time. One set of patterns raises questions about how much Armed Services and Foreign Relations foster the rule of law in international affairs by engaging in orderly processes of review. These include (1) noticeable declines in public hearings after the mid-1990s for the two national security committees, a trend that also applied to *all* Senate committees; and (2) biases in Armed Services and Foreign Relations toward the frequency of oversight hearings compared to budget hearings. Another set of trends speaks to the role of formal committee hearings in educating the public about national security. Most important is the relatively large number of secret sessions, as well as the disproportionate emphasis on program implementation, compared to topics the public cares about, such as conflicts that produce high casualties or scandals. Each trend frames the analysis for subsequent chapters.

I obtained data about the frequency and content of committee hearings from several sources. Information about public committee hearings is available through the Congressional Information Service, or CIS, which provides summary information and an abstract for each inquiry, along with a list of witnesses and their testimony. I coded the date and number of days for each hearing topic and classified the content according to its type, such as budget, oversight, statute, treaty, or nomination. I then examined all oversight hearings to determine whether they involved general policy review, program administration, treaty progress or implementation, international crisis, scandal, and mismanagement. I gathered information for executive session hearings from the *Daily Digest*, which publishes the daily calendar for each committee. The typical entry listed the date, purpose of the session, and witnesses. I also examined the various Historical Series published by the Senate Foreign Relations Committee that compiled public and secret testimony on major foreign policy events. Finally, I collected data on the frequency of all Senate committee hearings from the website of the Policy Agendas Project, which derives its information from the CIS abstracts and does not include executive sessions. The Policy Agendas Project codes for many types of hearing content, but does not identify oversight hearings. I developed my own scheme, therefore, and in Appendix A, I discuss the procedures I used to ensure the reliability of the coding and the differences in my approach from other scholars who study oversight.

Hearing Frequencies and the Rule of Law

Committee oversight hearings, I have argued, foster the rule of law when they promote "regular order" in the policy process. They need to occur routinely, adhere to consistent procedures, and operate transparently. Such review is integral to the constitutional system and essential for Congress to ensure faithful execution of its will and identify needs for new or revised policies. Trends in the hearing data over sixty-plus years indicate lapses by both committees in meeting basic expectations for effective oversight.

Figure 1.1 presents the frequency of total public hearing days for the Senate Armed Services and Foreign Relations Committees from 1947 to 2008. Generally, the two committees exercised wide latitude in how much public attention they devoted to defense and foreign policy, respectively. Both committees were active until the mid-1980s, averaging fifty to sixty public hearing days per year

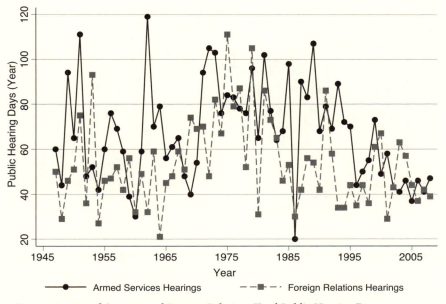

Figure 1.1. Armed Services and Foreign Relations Total Public Hearing Days, 1947–2008.

with periodic peaks and valleys. Notably, Foreign Relations conducted relatively few hearings in the election years of 1948, 1954, and 1964, and Armed Services hit a record low in 1986, the year of the Iran-Contra Scandal. Then, a downward shift began in the 1990s, and it accelerated for Foreign Relations over the next two decades, while Armed Services maintained a more ambitious public hearing calendar at least until 2001. The years of extensive military engagement in Iraq and Afghanistan consequently stand out as being well below the intensity of public hearing activity during the height of the conflicts in Korea or Vietnam, as well as the brief war in the Persian Gulf in 1991.

The Senate Armed Services and Foreign Relations Committees were not alone, however, in their propensity for holding fewer public hearings in the last two decades. Figure 1.2 tracks the frequency of public hearing days for all Senate committees from 1947 to 2008.[27] As was the case with the national security committees, the years of the Nixon administration and the post-Watergate pe-

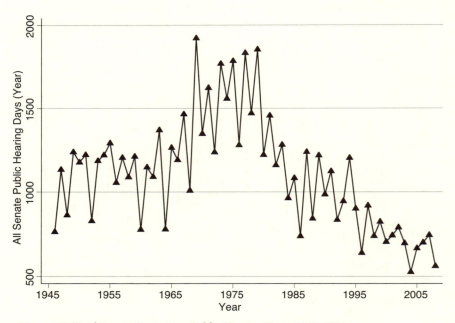

Figure 1.2. Total Senate Committee Public Hearing Days, 1947–2008.
Source: Baumgartner and Jones, Policy Agendas Project, http://www.policyagendas
.org/page/datasets-codebooks (accessed January 2014).

[27] Data and codebooks for the Policy Agendas Project are available at http://www.policyagendas
.org/page/datasets-codebooks (accessed January 2014).

riod marked the peak of committee hearing activity for the Senate as a whole, with two notable differences. First, Senate committees *in toto* were not as busy relatively speaking as the Armed Services and Foreign Relations Committees, especially during the first two decades of the Cold War. Second, the rate of decline in public hearing activity that began in the mid-1990s was comparatively steeper for Senate committees in the aggregate than for the national security committees.

Over the study period, the national security committees, as well as Senate committees overall, did not follow consistent routines. Armed Services and Foreign Relations varied their hearings from year to year and differed substantially from each other in the frequency of hearing days, with 1962 a particularly striking example. Moreover, the pattern of public hearing days for the two committees reveals period effects in the data, roughly from 1947 to 1969, from 1970 to 1995, and from 1996 to 2008. The grouping of hearing frequencies into distinctive eras shows up even more strongly in the aggregate trends for all Senate committees.

The wide variation in total public hearing activity is relevant to the question of regular order with respect to oversight on two counts. First, the national security committees could not conduct a systematic process of public review if they did not schedule hearings. In this respect, the early Cold War period and the post-9/11 period stand out as eras when the use of oversight to promote the rule of law in foreign affairs was potentially less robust than the interim period. Second, the disparate public hearing counts for Armed Services and Foreign Relations suggest that each national security committee operated with different motivations and approached its watchdog responsibilities with expectations that other Senate committees did not share. The systematic trends in the data thus indicate that the interaction between Senate committees and their executive counterparts depended upon institutional parameters that extended beyond individual committee efforts to exercise statutory control over bureaucratic discretion.

Transparency is another facet of a regularized committee review process of executive action. Figure 1.3 breaks down the total number of hearing days for each national security committee to highlight the frequency of executive sessions. Again, distinctive patterns for Armed Services and Foreign Relations are evident. Whether other Senate committees showed similar types of differences is unknown, because comparable data do not exist and would be extraordinarily difficult to compile. The highly sensitive nature of diplomacy, military strategy, and weapons technology suggests, however, that Armed Services and Foreign Relations likely were unusual in their heavy reliance on secret meetings.

Armed Services conducted executive sessions extensively throughout the sixty-two years of the study, carrying out its business behind closed doors in some years more than half its scheduled hearing days, for example, in 1959 and

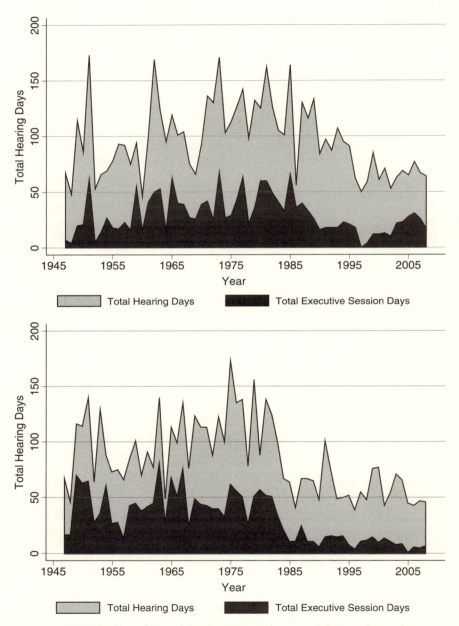

Figure 1.3. Comparison of Armed Services (top) and Foreign Relations (bottom) Executive Sessions with Total Hearing Days, 1947–2008.

1986. As a result of its large number of secret hearings, Armed Services ended up with a higher total of hearing days than Foreign Relations in many Congresses. We see modest period effects in the pattern of secret hearing days for Armed Services in the early years and again in the late 1980s, although executive sessions remained relatively high in the post-9/11 period in contrast to Armed Services' drop in public hearings. Foreign Relations, in comparison, relied disproportionately on closed-door meetings throughout the Cold War, but it shifted to consistently low levels of secret meetings in the mid-1980s and stayed there.

It is hard to know what to make of the high incidence of executive sessions on the national security committee dockets with respect to the rule of law. Clearly, transparency was not a major goal of either committee for much of the post–World War II period. The so-called Cold War Consensus that followed adoption of the Truman Doctrine reflected a level of trust between lawmakers and administration officials for much of the period, which later created issues of legitimacy for the committees as President Johnson escalated U.S. involvement in Vietnam. Nevertheless, Armed Services and Foreign Relations became relatively more transparent as tensions with the Soviet Union eased in the late 1980s with fewer hearings held behind closed doors. As with public hearings, the primary message from Figure 1.3 is that the national security committees varied from each other in their use of executive sessions, as well as across time.

Hearing Content and Public Education

Americans' episodic attention to international affairs places a heavy responsibility on the Senate's national security watchdogs to generate information that citizens care about and can access in a timely manner. Figures 1.4 and 1.5 address the issue of hearing content for the Senate Armed Services and Foreign Relations Committees, respectively. Again, similar data are not available for other committees, although the differences in content between the two national security committees reinforce the idea that total committee activity is relevant to thinking about oversight.

For Armed Services, budget hearing days (depicted in medium gray) consumed a disproportionate amount of the committee's agenda from the mid-1960s on. The committee relied on annual authorization of expenditures to assert control over the Pentagon,[28] but its overall policy priorities had less to do with the public interest in how tax dollars kept the nation safe and more to do with responding to the demands of organized constituencies in the defense establishment.[29] Budgets consumed the majority of Armed Services' executive session days, too.

---

[28] Deering (2001; 2005); Hersman (2000).
[29] Rundquist and Carsey (2002); Thorpe (2014).

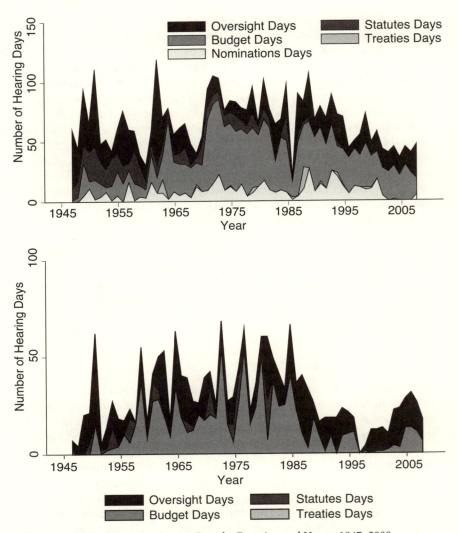

Figure 1.4. Armed Services Hearing Days by Function and Venue, 1947–2008.
Top: Armed Services Public Hearing Days; bottom: Armed Services Executive Hearing Days.

A strong signal of Armed Services' orientation is the heightened attention it gave to public budget hearings between the aftermath of the Vietnam War and President Reagan's first term. This was a period of intense dispute, first, over how to allocate the peace dividend resulting from the wind down of the war; then, how to sell Reagan's promised buildup of American military might; and, finally, how to defend Pentagon programs during the ensuing battles between Republicans and Democrats over spending priorities as deficits became a political issue. Some scholars consider budget review to be a form of oversight,[30] but, as Aberbach noted, advocacy rather than program review is a major purpose of such hearings.[31] Moreover, the purpose of budget hearings is less about ensuring accountability of Department of Defense expenditures and more about senators making sure that money flows to their home states and favored military contractors.

Nevertheless, oversight was the second most important subject of public committee hearings for Armed Services. Such hearings focused heavily on personnel policies, training and benefits to members of the armed forces around the country, as well as on the performance of weapons systems. In this respect, Armed Services appears to have found electoral advantage from oversight in engaging organized constituencies; the puzzle is why so much of it occurred behind closed doors. Whether all this activity about budgets and program review contributed to the education of the general public is debatable, however.

The rest of the Armed Services hearing agenda involved approval of the large number of presidential appointments to run the national security bureaucracy and to award commissions to high-ranking officers. Statutes dealing primarily with personnel and real estate issues consumed a modest number of public hearing days and almost no executive session days after 1980.

The Senate Foreign Relations Committee presents a contrasting profile in Figure 1.5. It devoted considerable public attention to oversight beginning in 1947, but its frequency of oversight hearing days ballooned after 1965 compared to other types of hearing content. Statutes and budgets were modest items on the committee's docket until the mid-1990s, when they declined to minimal levels. Various observers have remarked on the conflicts engendered by expenditures for foreign aid and international organizations and pointed out the repeated failures of the committee to develop authorizing legislation since 1985.[32] Treaties, which consumed variable amounts of time across the decades, all but disappeared as a topic by 2000. Similarly, the committee routinely considered nominations through public hearings, particularly between 1970 and 1985, but conducted only cursory review of appointments since.

The tilt toward oversight on Foreign Relations is even more pronounced in examining the frequency of hearing days in executive session. Since 1995, virtually the only content of secret hearings was oversight. Although former senator Joseph Biden viewed the committee's mission as education when he served as chair in 2001–2 and 2007–8, the high frequency of secret oversight hearings challenges the idea of public information as its primary mission.

---

[30] McGrath's (2013) definition of oversight includes budget hearings.
[31] Aberbach (1990).
[32] Deering (2001; 2005); Hersman (2000).

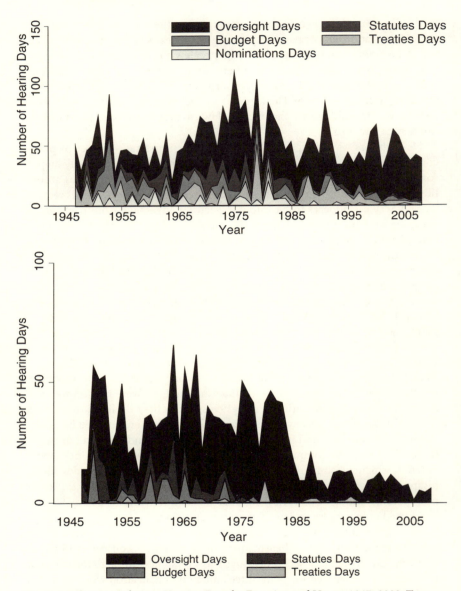

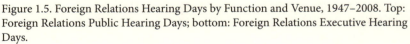

Figure 1.5. Foreign Relations Hearing Days by Function and Venue, 1947–2008. Top: Foreign Relations Public Hearing Days; bottom: Foreign Relations Executive Hearing Days.

The question remains whether Armed Services and Foreign Relations examined topics that the public cared enough about to pay attention to the committees' activity. Figure 1.6 looks at the distribution of all oversight hearing days by *type of oversight* for each committee, as well as the public or closed nature of the session. The upper-right-hand segment of the pie chart starts with the lightest colors (very pale gray) for treaty oversight, with public hearings in a darker shade than executive session hearings. This category includes progress on negotiating a treaty and issues implementing a ratified treaty, but not the hearings pertaining to actual ratification. Neither Armed Services nor Foreign Relations spent much time on presidents' diplomatic strategies or the subsequent impact of treaties.[33]

Moving clockwise, the next slices are what I term general oversight (light gray), which includes hearings on the state of the world, a region or a country. These hearings are purely informational and represent committee efforts to highlight an issue or to provide an opportunity for a new administration, a new Congress, or a newly confirmed appointee to consider an overview of foreign policy challenges. The general briefings had broad titles, such as "Democratic Developments in Sub-Saharan Africa: Moving Forwards or Moving Backwards?" The Armed Services Committee engaged in less of this type of oversight, only about an eighth of its hearings over sixty-two years. Foreign Relations, however, conducted many such hearings, almost a third of its total oversight days, primarily in public.

Continuing around the circle, program oversight (in medium gray) included review of the implementation of specific statutes and policies. This domain is where Armed Services directed a disproportionate amount of its hearing days, slightly more than a third of its overall oversight effort, with a heavy emphasis on public review. The pattern is not surprising, given the enormous size of the Defense Department. A typical hearing, for example, covered the technological, defense, and foreign policy issues associated with the National Missile Defense System, popularly known as Star Wars. Foreign Relations devoted almost a quarter of its hearing days to this type of oversight, with a slight preference for public scrutiny of issues, such as interpretation of the Pressler Amendment as it applied to commercial military sales to Pakistan in 1992.

Continuing clockwise, crises (shades of dark gray) emerge as a major preoccupation for both committees, with roughly a quarter of all oversight hearing days for each. Within this category, I included hearings regarding full-scale war, engagement by U.S. armed forces in lesser conflicts, and the imminent or probable use of force. Examples include the wars in Korea, Vietnam, the Persian Gulf, Iraq, and Afghanistan; naval blockades or strategic positioning of ships,

---

[33] Auerswald and Maltzman (2003) demonstrate that although most treaties receive Senate approval, those with high stakes often include reservations that are added after it has been signed to ease passage through the ratification process.

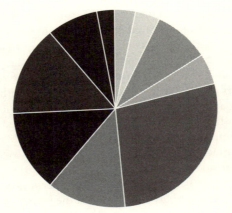

 Public Treaty Oversight   Exec Treaty Oversight

Public General Oversight   Exec General Oversight

Public Program Oversight   Exec Program Oversight

Public Crisis Oversight   Exec Crisis Oversight

Public Scandal Oversight   Exec Scandal Oversight

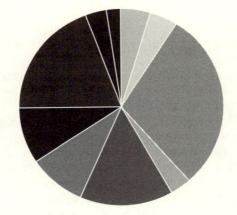

 Public Treaty Oversight   Exec Treaty Oversight

Public General Oversight   Exec General Oversight

Public Program Oversight   Exec Program Oversight

Public Crisis Oversight   Exec Crisis Oversight

Public Scandal Oversight   Exec Scandal Oversight

Figure 1.6. Distribution of Armed Services and Foreign Relations Public and Executive Session Oversight. Top: Total Armed Services Hearing Days (%); bottom: Total Foreign Relations Hearing Days (%).

such as the Strait of Hormuz; bombing campaigns in countries with which the United States was not at war, such as Serbia and Libya; commitment of ground troops for limited objectives, as in Panama, Somalia, and Grenada; conflicts involving close U.S. allies that might require intervention, such as the Yom Kippur War; and hostile interactions with rival states with the potential for escalation into full-blown conflicts, such as the blockade of Berlin. The chief difference between the two committees was the tendency to use open and closed sessions in roughly equal numbers by Armed Services and the preference for closed meetings about crises by Foreign Relations.

Completing the circle, we find the percentage of all oversight hearing days (black and near black) allocated to allegations of mismanagement and scandal. Given the scope of Defense Department activities, it is not surprising to observe that Armed Services devoted a larger proportion of its inquiries to investigations, about an eighth, than did Foreign Relations, although one might wonder why the share was not even larger. Interestingly, the great majority of the Armed Services probes occurred in public settings. Typically, they involved inquiries regarding the well-being and performance of American service personnel, such as rates of drug use and desertion during Vietnam; faulty equipment that resulted in noncombat deaths; problems with military contractors; or operational issues in a combat area, such as Iraq. Foreign Relations showed much less interest in carrying out this type of inquiry, although charges of mismanagement at the United Nations attracted its scrutiny during the mid-1990s.

Scholars typically distinguish types of oversight with the typology of "police patrols" and "fire alarms."[34] The former entail routinized, active surveillance of programs, including reports, inspections, and hearings, to discourage agency officials from deviating from congressional intent. The latter involve informal methods that enable third parties to trigger interventions or investigations by responsible officials, who may or may not include members of Congress. To establish how frequently the national security committees engaged in patrol oversight compared to alarm oversight, I collapsed the various types of oversight into two categories and used budget hearings as a comparison. The police patrol category includes general oversight, program oversight, and treaty oversight, while the fire alarm category includes crisis and scandal.[35] In foreign affairs, the actors that set off alarms were not only citizens and groups in the United States, but also other nations, subnational groups, and international organizations. Scandals went hand in hand with crises, since warfare tended to create opportunities for mismanagement that heightened scrutiny of executive performance.

[34] McCubbins and Schwartz (1984).

[35] Recall that hearings regarding the ratification of treaties are not included because they represent a special case that is closer to statutory hearings, but is a unique type of activity.

Figure 1.7 presents the frequency of *total* hearing days devoted to budgets, police patrols, and fire alarms for each committee. Given the near constant state of emergency that prevailed in the United States from 1947 on, the committees' preferences for patrols and budget hearings over fire alarm oversight confirm the views of critics that congressional watchdogs were lax in monitoring the executive branch.

The trend lines for Armed Services reinforce the message of previous figures about the committee's preoccupation with the authorization of military spending. They also confirm qualitative evidence that budget review was the primary means of supervision of the Pentagon, especially between 1970 and 1980.[36] The dramatic exception was 1951, the eventful year following North Korea's crossing of the thirty-eighth parallel, the landing of U.S. troops at Inchon, and China's entry into the conflict. Yet interesting deviations emerge in the figure, as well. The frequencies of police patrol and budget hearing days, for example, were not that far apart in the early decades of the Cold War and during Reagan's presidency. By the 1990s, however, police patrols often consumed fewer days than fire alarms. Nevertheless, the committee typically undertook very few fire alarm hearings; the total number exceeded twenty days in only ten of the sixty-two years (1949, 1963, 1966–67, 1973, 1993, 2002–3, and 2007–8) and approached zero in several years.

For Foreign Relations, budget authorization received short shrift throughout the time series compared to police patrols and fire alarms, with the exception of 1949 and 1953. The high incidence of patrols contrasts with the pattern for Armed Services, especially during the post–Vietnam War era. This category remained large after the collapse of the Soviet Union, due largely to the committee's propensity for state of the world hearings. The Foreign Relations Committee ranged widely around the globe, highlighting existing trouble spots and attempting to engage various presidents in issues it considered important. The committee's attention to crises and scandals was low until the mid-1960s and the escalation of the U.S. intervention in Vietnam. It remained comparatively high before receding after 1985, but, on average, the total number of crisis and scandal hearings was below twenty per year. Unlike Armed Services, however, the committee never passed a year without at least one fire alarm, although it came close to zero in 1956, 1988, and 1996.

The distribution of hearing content suggests an uneven performance by the two committees in educating the public. Armed Services' emphasis on the budget and Foreign Relations' interest in the state of the world reveal the committees' orientations toward organized policy elites rather than ordinary citizens. People are most likely to care about events that directly threaten American security, that put U.S. military personnel in danger, or that reveal waste of taxpayer dollars. If public relevance matters, then fire alarm oversight is the

[36] Deering (2001; 2005).

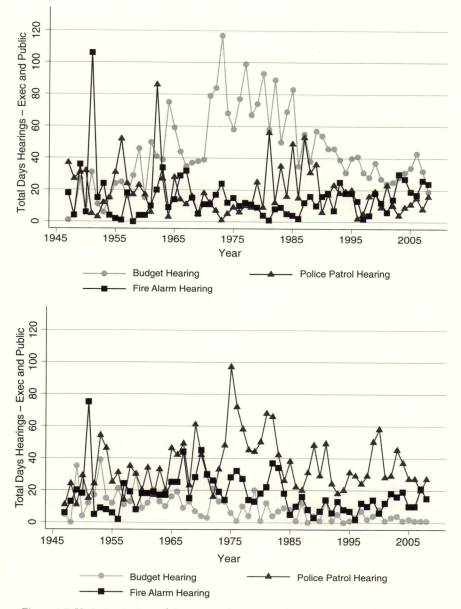

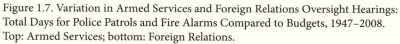

Figure 1.7. Variation in Armed Services and Foreign Relations Oversight Hearings: Total Days for Police Patrols and Fire Alarms Compared to Budgets, 1947–2008. Top: Armed Services; bottom: Foreign Relations.

appropriate benchmark for measuring the educational value of defense and foreign policy oversight.

By this standard, we see a lot of variation. The bombing of the barracks housing U.S. Marines sent to Lebanon for peacekeeping duty occurred in 1983, for example, and sparked some inquiry by Foreign Relations, but elicited little reaction from Armed Services. The invasion of Panama in December 1989 to seize its former president, Manuel Noriega, on drug charges did not motivate a serious probe by either committee. Public opinion polls reveal that the Lebanon incident generated considerable public concern, while the use of troops in Panama was initially very popular. Thus, the public's interest and the information generated by the committees did not necessarily coincide.

A more serious limitation apparent in Figure 1.7, however, is the seeming absence of sustained attention to foreign policy crises and scandals in years when the United States was engaged in major conflicts. A public that is not typically engaged in foreign affairs requires two things of congressional watchdogs: (1) multiple days of open hearings about one topic to cue citizens to pay attention and (2) repeated closed-door sessions with executive officials to delve deeply into a crisis or scandal when it is too complicated or sensitive for the public. Looking at the frequency of total hearings in Figure 1.7, the Korean War stands out for the relatively intense scrutiny it received from Armed Services in 1950 and 1951 and from Foreign Relations in 1951. The years in which the conflict in Vietnam escalated represent another seemingly serious attempt by the two committees to probe the goals and execution of the Johnson administration's policy, although they disagreed vehemently about the proper course of action. In contrast, the total hearing days during the years when the United States waged war in Iraq and Afghanistan represented a middling level of inquiry by Armed Services in 2003–4 and somewhat less by Foreign Relations. The period after Vietnam and before the war on terror saw the country involved in numerous international crises and scandals to which the national security committees paid only modest attention.

Overall, the record of the Armed Services and Foreign Relations Committees in educating the public and probing performance of the Departments of Defense and State appears uneven. More oversight occurred than many scholars would predict, but it did not necessarily lead to the procedural regularity and public education that hold the executive accountable for foreign policy decisions.

IRAQ: OVERSIGHT AND PUBLIC LEGITIMACY OF A DISCRETIONARY WAR

Oversight of the Iraq War illustrates the complex factors driving the performance of the Senate national security committees. As Armed Services and Foreign Relations reduced the frequency of formal hearings after the mid-1990s, the committees generated fewer opportunities for probing the strategy and operations of the U.S. invasion and its aftermath. Critics consequently charged that the Republican-led Congress had turned a blind eye to the Bush administration's conduct of the war. The Armed Services Committee appeared inactive partly because a large number of its inquiries occurred in executive sessions. The Foreign Relations Committee seemed inattentive because it pursued other foreign policy concerns, such as Iran. The chairs of both committees were quoted regularly in the major news media, and several prominent lawmakers not on either committee, such as Senator Ted Kennedy (D-MA), repeatedly raised questions about the objectives and strategy of American troops. The formal, sustained, and open inquiries so necessary for the rule of law in a discretionary war did not take place, however, leaving the public confused and skeptical about its necessity and outcome.

The Senate Armed Services Committee met as early as September 2002 to discuss Iraq and held at least ten secret hearings in 2003. In the spring of 2004 alone, while Senator Warner was under attack from his fellow Republicans in the House for public hearings about the Abu Ghraib scandal, his committee heard secret testimony about Iraq: three times in March, three in April, and two in May. In addition, multiple secret sessions regarding authorization of the Pentagon budget provided opportunities for senators to ask questions about the war. Indeed, as the situation in Iraq deteriorated over the next several years, the committee met regularly in private with Defense Department officials, contradicting at least in part the charge of critics that Congress had "checked out."[37] The heavy use of executive sessions, as we saw in Figure 1.3, reflected a long-standing pattern for Armed Services.

The lack of visible oversight by Congress during the Bush years had serious public consequences, affecting both press coverage and popular understanding of the war. The press provided numerous reports on the debate regarding authorization to use force against Iraq in the fall of 2002, but greatly reduced attention to the conflict once the resolution passed in October.[38] Prominent newspapers, such as the *New York Times* and *Washington Post*, later apologized to their readers for neglecting to probe the rationale leading up to the war and its subsequent prosecution. The papers' failure to a large extent reflected the lack of authoritative sources on Capitol Hill that publicly reviewed the war and offered alternative views to the Bush administration's version of events.[39]

Citizens depend upon a variety of political elites to organize national discourse about a particular crisis or war.[40] Lawmakers who go public with criticism

[37] Ornstein and Mann (2006).

[38] Howell and Pevehouse (2007, chap. 6).

[39] See Cook (1998) for the reasons why the media rely on sources in official positions, as well as Bennett (1996) and Bennett, Lawrence, and Livingston (2007).

[40] The term "political elite" encompasses a wide array of actors, including lawmakers, journalists, party activists, and interest group advocates. Brody (1994), Zaller (1994); Zaller and Chiu

of the executive stimulate press coverage of alternative views, especially if the doubters are from the president's own party or occupy authoritative committee positions.[41] Sustained oversight hearings in Congress generate press coverage, which in turn cues citizens to scrutinize foreign policy. When citizens receive sufficient information, they tend to develop coherent views that are grounded in real-world events.[42]

In the absence of serious, open review of the prosecution of the Iraq War, widespread public ignorance about the rationale for the invasion persisted long after the facts came to light. Large percentages of citizens continued to believe (incorrectly) that weapons of mass destruction had been found in Iraq, that Saddam Hussein had allied with al-Qaeda, and that most U.S. allies backed the military operations in Iraq.[43] In addition, citizens' party identification defined their perceptions of the war, leading to an intensely polarized view of its rationale and likely success.[44]

Despite the lack of oversight in Congress, the public turned against the war in the 2006 elections.[45] Americans have a history of ambivalence toward casualties. Sometimes they have tolerated very large losses, as in World War II; at other times, they have supported a conflict initially and then withdrawn support as battle deaths mounted; and at still other times, they have reacted severely to modest losses, as in Somalia in 1993.[46] Iraq appears to be an example of a war in which initial public skepticism before the invasion gave way to enthusiasm over the rapid fall of Baghdad and then generated widespread dismay. By April 2006, 64 percent of respondents to a Gallup/*USA Today* poll rated the job the Republican Party was doing in Iraq as poor or very poor,[47] and public support continued to erode thereafter.[48] Popular perceptions of GOP compe-

---

(1996); Bennett and Paletz (1994); Bennett (1996); Bennett, Lawrence, and Livingston (2007); Aldrich et al. (2005); Baum and Groeling (2010).

[41] Berinsky (2007; 2009); Groeling and Baum (2008); Howell and Pevehouse (2007); Kriner (2009).

[42] Aldrich, Sullivan, and Borgida (1989); Page and Shapiro (1992); Baum (2002; 2003); Holsti (2004); Aldrich et al. (2006); Baum and Potter (2008).

[43] Kull, Ramsey, and Lewis (2003–4).

[44] Jacobson (2006).

[45] See Grose and Oppenheimer (2007); Gartner and Segura (2008); Gelpi, Feaver, and Reifler (2005; 2007).

[46] Mueller (1973); Page and Shapiro (1992); Holsti (2004); Gartner and Segura (1998; 2008); Gartner, Segura, and Wilkening (1997); Jentleson (1992); Jentleson and Britton (1998); Karol and Miguel (2007); Grose and Oppenheimer (2007); Gartner (2008); Gelpi, Feaver, and Reifler (2005; 2007); Boettcher and Cobb (2006); Eichenberg (2005); Eichenberg, Stoll, and Lebo (2006); Kriner and Shen (2014).

[47] iPOLL Databank, Roper Center for Public Opinion Research, University of Connecticut, http://ropercenter.ucon.edu/ipoll.html (accessed January 2009). See also Berinsky (2009); Eichenberg, Stoll, and Lebo (2006).

[48] Kriner (2009); Kriner and Shen (2014).

tence in Iraq had declined significantly by 2006, although the party's long-standing reputational advantage among voters continued.[49]

In the absence of serious deliberation on Capitol Hill, the popular repudiation of the Iraq War was visceral and uninformed about alternative strategies. Hearings could have brought proponents and critics together to air their differences and might have forced Democrats to take responsibility for doing more than urge the president to set a timetable for withdrawal, which was the option they pursued once they were in the majority. Voters lacked any sense of how the nation should go forward, therefore, once they had decided the Iraq invasion had been a mistake.

Although the absence of oversight did not protect the Republican majorities in the House and Senate in 2006, it fostered a perception of unconstrained presidential power. Numerous journalistic and insider accounts emerged that analyzed the lead-up to and prosecution of the war in Iraq. With few exceptions, these narratives focused on President Bush and the small group of decision makers around him.[50] Whether praising or condemning his leadership, the authors agreed on one thing: Iraq was "Bush's war." Their narrative reinforced perceptions of an imperial presidency on the rise and also let Democrats off the hook for supporting the authorization in 2002.

Congress has rarely stopped presidents from deploying military force or compelled them to remove troops from the battlefield once fighting began.[51] Given the climate of fear in the nation after 9/11, it seems unlikely that legislators would have overcome President Bush's determination to invade Iraq. Nevertheless, oversight might have made a difference as the war dragged on. Members of the Foreign Relations Committee, for example, raised the issues of postinvasion reconstruction in the spring of 2003, but they expressed their worries in a single executive session and did not revisit the issue. Had the same questions come out in public hearings, the hawks in the White House might have had less success silencing skeptics, such as General John Shalikashvili and Secretary of State Colin Powell. At the very least, the administration might have abandoned the belief that it created the "reality" to which the rest of the world adapted.[52]

By avoiding hearings or moving them into executive session, the Senate national security committees allowed the president to frame events according to his own lights. The actions of the Armed Services and Foreign Relations Committees, therefore, neither fostered the rule of law nor met the public's need for reliable information in foreign affairs.

---

[49] Petrocik (1996); Petrocik, Benoit, and Hansen (2003–4).

[50] Woodward (2002; 2004; 2006); Daalder and Lindsay (2003); Suskind (2004); Packer (2005); Mayer (2008).

[51] Kriner (2010) argues that the unwillingness of Congress to challenge the president directly should not blind us to the many ways in which it influences foreign affairs indirectly.

[52] Suskind (2004).

Conclusion

The nation's guardians wield vast discretion over international security that increasingly is beyond the control of citizens. Congress has the constitutional power and its committees have the legal authority to act as agents of the people in promoting a democratically accountable foreign policy. The Senate Armed Services and Foreign Relations Committees appear to have been remiss, however, in carrying out an orderly process of review of the Iraq War and educating the public about its prospects. Viewed in historical context, their behavior is something of an anomaly, or at least part of a downward trend in formal hearings that began in the 1990s and affected the entire Senate. The result was a process that appeared on the surface to be deeply partisan, though it entailed a more complex set of motives.

Despite the importance of legislative watchdogs in promoting the rule of law and public understanding, oversight remains an underdeveloped field of study in the domains of U.S. foreign policy and American politics. The historical trends described in this chapter indicate large swings in oversight activity by both Armed Services and Foreign Relations and major differences between them in terms of hearing content and venues. The resulting patterns may result from the unique circumstances of defense and foreign policy in the United States, but they also suggest gaps in scholars' understanding of how congressional committees approach international affairs. In addition, many of the findings presented in this chapter appear to be at odds with established theories and diverse empirical studies of oversight. Having provided an overview of the Senate Armed Services and Foreign Relations Committees' hearings for more than six decades, I turn next to the conditions that motivate legislators to ask questions regarding the nation's foreign policy.

CHAPTER 2

Committee Motivations for Oversight

THE VIETNAM WAR REPRESENTS the nadir of congressional influence over foreign policy in the eyes of many political observers. Legislators had given President Lyndon B. Johnson a blank check in the 1964 Gulf of Tonkin Resolution and then struggled for over a decade to define their role before defunding military engagement in Southeast Asia under President Ford in 1975. Congress came off badly, whether considering the enormous casualties from the conflict or the chaotic airlift from the U.S. embassy in Saigon. The Senate's national security committees had quietly reviewed the use of military advisors and aid in Vietnam, and their activity intensified as LBJ escalated U.S. involvement in Southeast Asia. The Senate Foreign Relations Committee soon became the locus of congressional pressure for winding down the war, while the Armed Services Committee provided a platform for hawks seeking to ramp up the use of force. In hindsight, the Vietnam era represented a turning point in oversight of national security: Senate committee hearing days exploded in its aftermath, differences between Armed Services and Foreign Relations that had always been present stood out more clearly, and bipartisan agreement between Democrats and Republicans on foreign policy eroded. These diverse trends reflected the three major factors responsible for variation in national security oversight: changes in the value of committee activity, systematic differences in the goals and behavior of individual committees, and strategic calculations about party reputations for competence in international affairs.

The performance of Armed Services and Foreign Relations during the Vietnam era was notable because it marked the beginning of long-term shifts in senators' orientations toward committee work. The Senate evolved from an intimate club dominated by committee barons to a more decentralized institution that fostered policy entrepreneurship broadly among members and that, since the 1990s, polarized along ideological lines. As successive cohorts arrived in Washington, they brought new political agendas and norms of behavior, which altered the institutional context in which the Armed Services and Foreign Relations Committees conducted their business. In the decade following Vietnam, formal hearings rose dramatically for all Senate committees, not just those dealing with defense and foreign policy, and then gradually returned to pre-Vietnam levels after the mid-1990s. As overall committee activity expanded and then contracted, the opportunities for oversight rose and fell, as well.

In addition, the distinctive goals of senators on each committee came into clear focus during the Vietnam era. Biases in the frequency, content, and venues of Armed Services and Foreign Relations hearings had been present throughout the Cold War era, but they became more visible during the contentious Vietnam period and pervaded the committees' post-Vietnam patterns of oversight. These disparate approaches to oversight promoted members' personal political agendas over the informational needs of the public. Armed Services adopted a protective stance toward the military, while Foreign Relations pursued wide-ranging discussions about the state of the world. The committees, therefore, differed in their tolerance for internal conflict, which affected their propensity for oversight, their attention to budgetary matters, their reactions to the president's use of force, and their use of secrecy. Both committees were more attuned to the interests of organized constituencies and policy elites than the public at large.

Finally, the contrasting approaches of Armed Services and Foreign Relations during Vietnam signaled the collapse of the so-called Cold War Consensus, with its bipartisan agreement on containment of the Soviet Union and its deference to presidential authority. Party rivalries did not immediately affect the proceedings of the national security committees, since senators conducted aggressive interrogations of officials in the Departments of Defense and State into the 1990s, irrespective of their ties to the occupant of the White House.

Eventually, both committees had to deal with the gradual realignment within their party cohorts, as well as a deepening split between the parties. Senate Republicans, for example, embraced neoconservative ideas about deploying America's military might around the globe and shed their liberal internationalist colleagues during the Reagan years. Senate Democrats, in contrast, stressed diplomacy and international alliances as a means of promoting U.S. interests abroad, although they divided along state lines over defense spending and military bases. Once the reputations of the two parties became closely tied to international relations, the Armed Services and Foreign Relations Committees confronted a problem of managing the political fallout from international events, particularly rising casualties, public opinion, and the party of the president.

How does one account for such a complex mix of institutional dynamics, committee biases and partisan motivations? Congressional scholars disagree about which theories best explain committee and party behavior,[1] prompting

---

[1] Three rival theories to explain committee behavior include *distributional* theories in which "high demanders" self-select onto committees to create coalitions for channeling particularized benefits to states and districts (Shepsle 1978; Shepsle and Weingast 1987); *informational* theories that postulate assignment of representative lawmakers who were induced by procedural controls over getting bills to the floor to report legislation that satisfied the chamber's median member (Krehbiel 1991); and *partisan* theories in which members reflected majority party views and de-

one astute observer to conclude, "Rather than seek a single, universal account of congressional politics—whether distributional, informational, partisan, or anything else—we should recognize that all of these considerations operate in varying degrees and that the variation is systematic and predictable. Different member motivations will interact with different issues to create a variety of contexts."[2]

Scholars do concur, however, that members support rules and structures inside the Congress that facilitate whatever activities they perceive as most valuable and that they adopt new ways of doing business when the old ones no longer serve their interests.[3] Sometimes scholars can point to specific procedural changes or new organizations and say, "yes, things were different after that moment in time."[4] Yet institutions have "sticky" qualities that make them resistant to internal reform efforts and external pressures,[5] especially in the Senate where minority factions enjoy veto power. Over time, lawmakers modify some aspects of the legislative process while continuing the status quo with respect to others. Moreover, lawmakers' behavior can evolve gradually as electoral forces send new cohorts to Washington with different political goals.[6] Noted political scientist Eric Schickler summarized the complex forces at work in Congress this way: "institutional change is consistently characterized by the interplay of competing coalitions promoting multiple, potentially conflicting interests."[7]

Although an overarching theory of oversight appears beyond reach, considerable qualitative and quantitative research documents continuity and change in Congress that are relevant to committee oversight. I draw on this scholarship to develop expectations for how the Senate Armed Services and Foreign Relations Committees engaged with the executive branch in international affairs.[8] First, I focus on longitudinal shifts in the value of committee work that appear

---

ployed the committee's gatekeeping prerogatives as agents of the party leadership. Each approach captures an important aspect of committee operations in the House and, to a lesser extent, the Senate, yet no one theory has prevailed.

Theories of party influence also are mixed. Krehbiel asks "where's the party?" and instead offers a theory of pivotal politics (1993; 1998). Kiewiet and McCubbins (1991) and Cox and McCubbins (2005) see party power as being exercised indirectly through agenda control of the floor to promote the interests of the majority party. Aldrich (1995b) and Aldrich and Rohde (2001) postulate that lawmakers embrace stronger party discipline when they are internally cohesive and ideologically distant from the opposition.

[2] Rohde (1995, 134).

[3] Aldrich (1995b).

[4] See Wawro and Katznelson (2014) for an outstanding assessment of how congressional scholars approach institutional change.

[5] Adler (2002).

[6] Rohde (1991).

[7] Schickler (2001, 26).

[8] Adler and Lapinski (2006) use the term "macropolitics" to describe the emerging literature on congressional performance, which looks beyond the internal operations of the Senate and House to outcomes and interactions with other branches of the federal government.

to have affected the frequency of public hearings from 1947 to 2008 throughout the Senate. Second, I consider the stability in committee goals that promoted systematic differences in the frequency and venues of oversight between Armed Forces and Foreign Relations, as well as their response to fiscal priorities and the president's use of force. Third, I show how concerns for party reputations drove the two committees' choices of oversight content in order to manage the effects of external events on public perceptions of the parties. I develop three different sets of expectations that address specific aspects of oversight: the total number of hearings committees undertake, the differences in committee goals and strategic calculations, and the short-term shocks introduced by war casualties and scandal that affect the national brands of the Republican and Democratic Parties.

Institutional Change and Senate Committees

Historically, committees have been the locus of institutional and personal power in Congress. Woodrow Wilson observed more than a century ago that "Congress in committee is Congress at work"; Richard Fenno affirmed in his classic work that "committees matter."[9] Of less importance in the Senate than in the House, committees nevertheless were the defining feature of most senators' careers for more than a century. Given their centrality to the legislative process, committees frequently became the target of reformers. Change in the formal rules governing committee activity was not the only source of adaptation, however. Members altered the way they used committees to accomplish their political goals, and if enough lawmakers developed a similar set of expectations, new patterns of activity evolved. The question is what political stimuli induced the distinctive patterns of total public committee hearings that we saw in Chapter 1 from 1947 to 2008.

The motivations behind the dramatic rise in Senate hearings in the 1970s and 1980s are well documented. Barbara Sinclair's striking account of the transformation of the Senate, for example, demonstrated that newer cohorts arrived on Capitol Hill in that period with the common objective of policy entrepreneurship and political independence, even though they differed in terms of their party, constituency, and ideology.[10] Although they rejected norms of apprenticeship and specialization, the junior senators directed their energies at

---

[9] Wilson (1885); Fenno (1973, xiii).

[10] Sinclair (1989). Dodd and Oppenheimer's outstanding series *Congress Reconsidered*, which includes ten editions from 1981 to 2012, has documented the institutional changes within the House and Senate: from the decentralizing reforms that produced subcommittee government in the 1970s, to the reassertion of the Speaker's power in the 1980s and 1990s, to the Republican-led revolution in the House that tightened party discipline in the era of polarization. Rather than cite individual chapters, I have summarized the gist of the trends documented in each volume.

committees to enhance their personal influence and expand their reach into multiple issue domains.[11] The number of subcommittees rose dramatically, as did the opportunity for chairmanships and the number of professional staff, enabling lawmakers to pursue their individual agendas.[12]

With the explosion of interest groups and their related PACs that began in the 1970s, committees increased in value as a resource for attracting support from contributors and activists. Senators found it particularly advantageous to spread their attention across multiple committees instead of concentrating their energies on a few.[13] In 1947, senators averaged 2.1 committee assignments per member; by 2008, they averaged 4.1 assignments per member. In addition, they reduced their time in Washington, with the notable exception of 2005, in order to devote attention to constituencies at home.[14] Figure 2.1 depicts these shifts in emphasis over the sixty-two years of the study. The idea that senators would gain power in the chamber through policy specialization, mastery of procedure, and behind-the-scenes negotiation lost currency in the chamber.

While senators were busy modifying the old committee system in favor of a decentralized model that would generate more information, the press lost interest in covering Congress. The decline in stories about the legislative branch was part of a larger trend of reduced newspaper presence in the nation's capital, but it also reflected a shift in focus to the presidency and executive agencies.[15] Congress, as many observers have noted, is difficult to cover because of its multiple personalities and fragmented structures of authority. The right-hand axis in Figure 2.2 indicates that articles in the *New York Times* mentioned Congress frequently until the 1990s.[16] Committees attracted attention if they offered drama and conflict, something Foreign Relations provided regularly until the

[11] Sinclair (1989).

[12] Aberbach cites increased numbers of staff as a factor in the rise in oversight hearings from 1961 to 1983. In recent years, both Armed Services and Foreign Relations have retained large staffs, even though their agendas of formal hearings shrank.

[13] Fowler and Law (2008a; 2008b).

[14] Mann and Ornstein (2006). The number of session days emerged as an important explanation in Aberbach's (1990) analysis of oversight in the middle of the time series, and critics of the most recent Congresses have faulted lawmakers for short work weeks (Ornstein and Mann 2009).

[15] Graber (1989); Hess (1994); Lichter and Amundson (1994); Rozell (1994); Cook (1998); Farnsworth and Lichter (2006); Kingdon (1995); Bennett (1990; 1996); Bennett, Lawrence, and Livingston (2007).

[16] The measures were created using a variety of search parameters in the ProQuest Historical and LexisNexis databases. The data were corrected for irrelevant mentions, such as social notes, and adjusted for errors (Congress of Industrial Organizations) through a statistical procedure developed by Brian Law. The data include nearly 825,000 raw observations, which makes this measure the most comprehensive longitudinal indicator of media coverage of Congress ever compiled. The committee-specific measures do not include local stories or campaign coverage unless they involved committee business. Most scholars who compile data on newspaper coverage typically use the front page rather than the whole newspaper. Further details about these data are in Fowler and Law (2008b) and are described in Appendix C, as well.

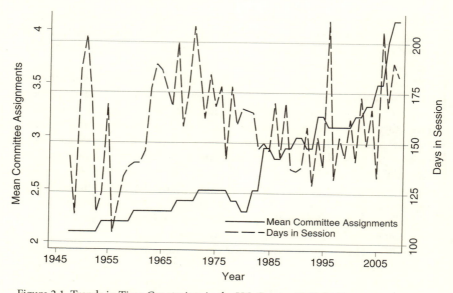

Figure 2.1. Trends in Time Constraints in the U.S. Senate, 1947–2008.
Source: The Mean Committee Assignment measure on the left was calculated by the author from the *Congressional Directories*, 1947–2008. It shows a dramatic rise in the committee portfolios for senators beginning in 1983. The number of days per session on the right was derived from the calendar of Senate sessions for each year published in the *Congressional Directory*. It shows downturns in the second session of a Congress and periodic peaks and valleys.

1990s. In 1951, according to the left-hand axis, the *Times* contained almost six hundred mentions of the committee, a figure that plummeted to roughly sixty in 2008. Armed Services adopted a relatively low profile by the late 1950s, a pattern it pursued throughout the study period with the exception of the Gulf War in 1991. Eventually, journalists gravitated toward the beats that fed them news on a regular and easily accessible basis—the White House and the executive agencies.

Finally, the ideological polarization that began to take root in the House and Senate in the 1970s accelerated in subsequent decades.[17] Scholars debate the causes of polarization and differ about its consequences,[18] but one undeniable result was the elevated status and visibility of political parties. Senators resisted the impulse to give up their personal autonomy and did not embrace the rules and procedural controls that produced high levels of party discipline in the

[17] Poole and Rosenthal (1997); McCarty, Poole, and Rosenthal (2008); Theriault (2008).
[18] Poole and Rosenthal (1997); McCarty, Poole, and Rosenthal (2008); Roberts and Smith (2003); Theriault (2008); Lee (2009); Sinclair (2006; 2012a).

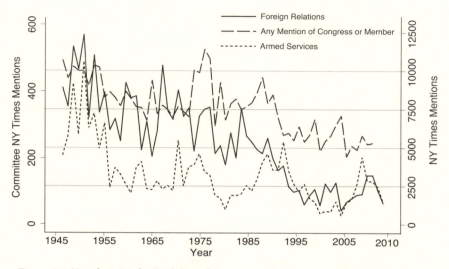

Figure 2.2. Trends in Media Visibility of Congress and Senate Armed Services and Foreign Relations Committees, 1947–2008.
Source: Fowler and Law (2008a; 2008b) and updated by Fowler in 2010. The yearly figures represent the number of mentions in the entire *New York Times* identified using the ProQuest Historical Newspapers database and corrected for errors.

House.[19] Nevertheless, ideological polarization within committees undoubtedly made it more difficult for committees to agree on an agenda of public hearings.

No single, observable cause drove these phenomena, but each had the potential to affect the orientation of senators toward their committee work. Initially, the ambitious new senators grabbed influence for themselves by democratizing the committee system and creating news events that resulted in an explosion of hearings. As external actors gained importance in funding campaigns, senators increasingly relied on committees to shape their identities for donors and consequently expanded their committee portfolios. Eventually, polarization of the Senate chamber penetrated committees and made cross-party bargaining more difficult. Paradoxically, senators increased their committee assignments, even as they were less likely to define their political careers in terms of the specialized knowledge and insider influence that committees fostered.

Lacking individual-level data, such as longitudinal surveys or interviews, I cannot test these expectations directly. But I can use aggregate trends to offer partial confirmation that broad institutional changes explained the dra-

---

[19] Sinclair (2006; 2012a; 2012b); Smith (2007); Den Hartog and Monroe (2011).

matic changes in the frequency of public hearing days. I tackle this problem in Chapter 3.

Member Goals and Committee Differences

Richard Fenno's classic study of congressional committees began with the assertion that "committees differ from one another . . . and they differ systematically."[20] Fenno identified three factors to explain why committees diverged and produced disparate types of policy outcomes. First, personal *goals*, which included constituency benefits, policy preferences, or institutional power, motivated legislators to seek membership on specific committees. When combined with strong norms inside the Senate to grant individual member requests, member preferences led committees to develop distinct identities. Second, *environmental influences*, such as pressure from organized groups or the executive's political clout, constrained what lawmakers could accomplish on their chosen committee. Third, *strategic premises* mediated between members' individual priorities and the milieu in which the committee operated, resulting in generally agreed upon rules of thumb that guided committee decision making. Together, these aspects of committees, Fenno argued, produced consistent patterns of activity over time.

Fenno's observations of committee behavior spanned a decade from the mid-1960s to the early 1970s, a period that in hindsight appears to have enjoyed remarkable institutional stability. The basic ideas behind Fenno's depiction of committee differences proved robust, however.[21] Throughout the post–World War II period, senators brought distinctive expectations to the Senate Armed Services or Foreign Relations Committees that had a profound impact on their hearing agendas and their approaches to oversight. The earlier patterns persisted because both parties continued to honor member requests, although after 1995, Republicans imposed a limit of three terms on committee chairs.

Armed Services' members sought seats on the committee to create close ties to the Department of Defense. Most members focused on the economic benefits of military spending in their home states. In addition, many held hawkish

---

[20] Fenno (1973, xiv).

[21] Christopher Deering and Steven Smith (1984; 1997) mapped the committee landscape in both chambers in the 1980s and mid-1990s, and Larry Evans (1991) conducted in-depth analysis of six Senate committee chairs in 1985–86. Deering and Smith compared committees across several dimensions, including recruitment and internal operations, such as chairs, subcommittees, and staff. These authors provided invaluable comparisons of the House and Senate, as well as changes in committee practices resulting from the Republican revolution after the 1994 election. Unfortunately, the last version of their study appeared in 1997. Evans demonstrated how Senate committee chairs varied their strategies for passing bills depending upon the level of consensus on the committee, the salience of the issue, and their personal goals. Neither Armed Services nor Foreign Relations was on the list of committees Evans examined.

views regarding security policy or had prior experience in uniform. In addition to the Pentagon, the committee's environment included military contractors, service personnel stationed at bases in their home states, and defense policy think tanks and experts. Over time, the committee proved remarkably consistent in targeting economic resources to local economies and supporting U.S. military actions around the globe.[22] Scholars classified the committee, therefore, as having mixed goals of serving the constituency and policy interests of its members.[23]

Armed Services encountered two challenges that shaped its strategy for accomplishing committee goals. First, the committee was sometimes in intense competition with the White House for control over priorities in defense spending and the deployment of U.S. forces. Second, it periodically encountered resistance from legislators and citizens, who sought cuts in the defense budget to pay for domestic priorities. The committee adopted operating premises, therefore, of containing internal conflict over defense policy that might otherwise undermine the flow of defense dollars and promoting a positive image of Pentagon performance. These two rules of thumb lead to several predictions about Armed Services' behavior:

1 Avoid controversy, especially during periods of divided government
2 Concentrate on budget authorization and focus oversight on program implementation to ensure that defense expenditures flow to their intended beneficiaries
3 Pay attention to the needs of military personnel by monitoring the use of force

Senators joined Foreign Relations, in contrast, to pursue the "high politics" of statecraft and historically to nurture ambitions for presidential office.[24] Moreover, the committee's responsibility for treaties, diplomacy, and the perennially controversial foreign aid program attracted some of the most liberal and most conservative senators within each party over the years. It acquired the label of a pure policy committee,[25] whose members sought the national spotlight and lacked the glue of common constituency interests to dampen party rivalries. The committee's goal of stimulating policy debate, present even during the heyday of the Cold War Consensus, encouraged it to engage in partisan politics and cultivate media visibility.

The political environment in which Foreign Relations operated posed several challenges for achieving the committee's dominant goals. The president commanded powerful constitutional prerogatives over diplomacy that put senators

---

[22] Rundquist and Carsey (2002); Thorpe (2014).
[23] Deering and Smith (1984; 1997, 80).
[24] McCormick (1993).
[25] Deering and Smith (1997, 80).

in a secondary role of "advice and consent." In addition, the public viewed the foreign aid budget with suspicion, if not outright hostility. Finally, the political parties, especially the GOP, began to draw their presidential nominees from the ranks of governors rather than the Senate which decreased the value of membership. Having enjoyed the reputation for being the most prestigious in Congress for more than a century, the committee declined dramatically in status after the mid-1970s.[26] It also faded in terms of national media visibility, as noted above.

The Foreign Relations' objective to engage in policy debate thus encountered obstacles. On the one hand, its members sought to foster elite discourse and frame competition between the parties about foreign affairs. In effect, the members agreed to disagree. At the same time, senators on the committee were hindered in satisfying this goal by the public's dislike of foreign aid, its suspicions of international organizations, and its expectations that the country unite behind the president during times of crisis. Several patterns of committee behavior arose from the committee's efforts to address its paradoxical situation of promoting public deliberation about foreign policy for a citizenry frequently disinclined to listen. The strategic premises that emerged as the committee pursued its goal of policy debate included the following:

1   Deemphasize budget authorization for foreign aid and the State Department to focus on broad foreign policy themes
2   Use public hearings to bolster the reputation of the Senate majority and individuals with presidential ambitions for promoting the nation's security interests
3   Exercise caution in challenging the president during times of international tension, unless the tide of public opinion has shifted

Taken together, the operating rules of the Senate Armed Services and Foreign Relations Committees served the interests of their members, but did not necessarily further their broader responsibilities to promote regular order and public understanding of international affairs. It is common for congressional committees to generate information that yields private utility for their members, while slighting collective benefits for lawmakers and the public as a whole.[27] Congress consequently has developed many devices to encourage committee members to promote the interests of the chamber and the polity, even as they pursue their own ends.[28] The problem, however, is that none of the mechanism

---

[26] Stewart and Groseclose (1999); Canon and Stewart (2002); Fowler and Law (2008a; 2008b).

[27] Moe (1985); Moe and Howell (1999); Huntington (1973).

[28] In effect, legislatures seek to generate positive externalities from individual behavior. Alternatively, we might say that they create conditions in which a small number of people with a high value for a particular collective good of information will provide it for the entire group. Such behavior, which is common in politics, is often described as the exploitation of the few by the many.

that scholars have identified as constraints on committees' information generation applies to oversight.[29] Despite the statutory responsibilities placed on committees, expectations in the 1946 law were vague and have not been codified in any systematic way. Committees that were seriously deficient eventually could be penalized through a reduction in professional staff, but as a practical matter, they operated relatively freely in deciding the frequency, venues, and topics of oversight.

One consequence of the disparate goals and premises for the two committees was the inconsistent relationship between divided government and frequency or content of national security oversight. In addition, the committees' performance in satisfying the criteria for the rule of law in international affairs was uneven. Armed Services, for example, faced strong incentives to monitor the Pentagon, but it was equally motivated to put a positive face on military performance. It carefully followed routines consistent with the rule of law, but suffered from problems of bias and lack of transparency in the way it generated information. Foreign Relations satisfied the internationalist proclivities of its members, but often at the expense of adherence to procedural regularity with respect to diplomacy and expenditures for aid. The committee generated much accessible material for the public, but it struggled to find a balance when the president's policies, senators' partisan interests, and public demands for unity were at odds. I explore the consequences of this mismatch between the committees' goal-driven behavior and their institutional responsibilities with respect to oversight in Chapter 4.

PARTY REPUTATIONS AND EXTERNAL SHOCKS

The Senate as an institution presents a puzzling orientation toward political parties. On the one hand, it lacks many of the features that promote party discipline and loyalty; on the other hand, it presents clear signs of party impact on decision making. Senators' staggered, six-year terms insulate them to some extent from national political tides, and norms of seniority allocate committee leadership roles to members with the safest seats, rather than to those with the most loyal voting records. Furthermore, permissive chamber rules enable individual members to offer amendments and engage in unlimited debate without fear of reprisal from party leaders. Despite the apparent absence of tools to induce senators to follow the party line, partisan influences over legislative outcomes

---

[29] Krehbiel (1991). In the House, the gatekeeping powers of the Rules Committee and the influence of party leaders over the calendar provide mechanisms for sanctioning self-interested committees. In the Senate, the absence of restrictions on amendments and debate partially insulate committees from reprisal, although their bills could be subject to a filibuster or modification during debate if they get too far out of line.

are apparent in Senate roll call voting.[30] Whether oversight in the Senate is susceptible to party effects is an open question, however.

In general, the relative autonomy of committees is closely linked to the power of parties.[31] Historically, committees have been strongest, when parties have been weakest; and vice versa. Most of what scholars know about the relationship between congressional parties and committees pertains to the House, however, which exercises much stronger procedural constraints over committees' access to the floor than in the Senate. Polarization has expressed itself in the Senate through higher rates of party cohesion on roll call votes, but analysts have not looked beyond the Senate floor to examine its impact on committee behavior,[32] although a few researchers have studied the effect of divided government on the frequency of investigations with mixed results.[33] Moreover, evidence has emerged of greater party influence in Congress over international affairs after 9/11 as a result of polarization.[34]

Committee members' concerns over parties' national reputations seem a likely motivation for oversight of defense and foreign policy for several reasons. First, Senate seats became more competitive in the 1980s, because senatorial elections were more likely than House races to attract strong challengers. Second, the emergence of senatorial campaign committees in both parties and the efforts of interests to nationalize congressional races made it more difficult for senators to separate themselves from national tides. Most important, the Republican Party placed heavy emphasis on its reputation for competence in national security beginning with Ronald Reagan's exploitation of perceived Democratic weakness in confronting the Soviet incursion into Afghanistan and the Iranian hostage crisis in the 1980 election.

Public opinion often coalesces around perceptions of each party's strength resulting in ownership of a particular issue.[35] For decades, Democrats had the advantage among voters of caring more about working people and the middle class and defending programs for seniors. To counteract this view, Republicans portrayed themselves as being strong on defense and vigorous defenders of U.S. interests abroad.

---

[30] Sinclair (2006; 2012a; 2012b); Smith (2005; 2007); Gailmard and Jenkins (2007); Monroe, Roberts, and Rohde (2008); Den Hartog and Monroe (2011).

[31] Aldrich (1995a); Rohde (1995).

[32] David Rohde and various coauthors have examined the appropriations process in order to evaluate the influence of parties on key committees in the House. Kriner and Schwartz (2008) include a measure of ideological distance between Congress and the president in their study of investigations.

[33] See Aberbach (1990; 2002) and McGrath (2013) regarding broad oversight. And see Kriner and Schwartz (2008); Parker and Dull (2009; 2012); and Balla and Deering (2013) on investigations.

[34] Oleszek and Oleszek (2012).

[35] Petrocik (1996); Petrocik, Benoit, and Hansen (2003–4); Woon and Pope (2008).

Generally, congressional parties have used floor action and the passage of legislation to promote a party brand.[36] Although no studies have examined the reputational effects of congressional oversight, it seems plausible that lawmakers and voters would make that connection. Certainly, the pressures discussed in Chapter 1 on Senators Warner and Luger to avoid damaging President Bush's reelection chances with inquiries about the Iraq War confirm this view.

Several factors thus appear likely to have influenced the frequency and type of oversight activity by the Senate Armed Services and Foreign Relations Committees. First, the parties began to differentiate themselves with respect to defense and foreign policy after World War II, despite the Cold War Consensus. Second, the public varied in its concern about national security issues in response to major wars and events. Third, the GOP brand stressed competence in foreign affairs, so a Republican president had the most to gain or lose from congressional scrutiny of his performance. Together, these trends lead to a set of expectations that are pertinent to the committees' allocation of oversight between routine monitoring, what scholars term "police patrols," and review of the president's handling of crises and scandals, which scholars label "fire alarms."

For Armed Services, the choice of oversight content reflected the need to diffuse the salience of costly conflicts and scandals, while speaking to organized constituencies with stakes in defense. The committee, therefore, pursued the following rules of thumb:

1 Avoid public fire alarm oversight of presidents of the opposition party, especially Republican presidents who generally would have been predisposed to support the Pentagon
2 Use police patrols to bolster public support of the military and be openly attentive to the needs of military personnel during wartime
3 Employ executive sessions to interrogate defense officials about the costs of war

For Foreign Relations, strategies with respect to oversight content represented an attempt to balance challenges to the president with public expectations for national unity:

1 Embrace public fire alarm oversight of Republican presidents if a Democratic majority controls the committee
2 Schedule patrol hearings rather than alarm hearings to avoid the appearance of undermining national unity when the public is aroused about international issues
3 Attend publicly to the rising costs of war

---

[36] Cox and McCubbins (2005).

These hypotheses complement expectations about member goals in explaining why divided government is not necessarily a consistent predictor of national security oversight. In addition, they lead to more nuanced explanations of the variation in content of Armed Services and Foreign Relations oversight behavior. At the beginning of the Cold War, public anxiety ran high, and both national security committees engaged in oversight without paying much attention to the party of the president while favoring secret hearings. When party reputations diverged on foreign policy after Nixon, the national security committees had to deal directly with short-term partisan calculations. Republican majorities in the Senate expected their national security committees to manage public anxiety regarding the use of force abroad. In addition, the hawkish tendencies of many Republican presidents after Eisenhower made them potential allies to the Armed Services Committee. Democratic majorities, conversely, had greater incentives to focus on a Republican president's performance in domestic policy, unless international events aroused the public sufficiently to pay attention to foreign policy. The asymmetries of party reputation and ideology, the public salience of foreign policy, and the party in control of the Senate were all likely influences on the content of oversight involving routine program implementation, crises, and scandal. I develop these propositions in Chapter 5.

Oversight of the Vietnam War demonstrates how member goals shaped the inquiries of the Senate Armed Services and Foreign Relations Committees. In addition, the hearings of this highly contentious period set the stage for the transformation of Senate committees into the entrepreneurial organizations that increased formal hearings and oversight into the 1990s. Finally, the patterns of hearing activity presaged the growing sensitivity to party reputations among the Senate's national security watchdogs.

A TALE OF TWO COMMITTEES

As U.S. troop commitments to the South Vietnamese government escalated in 1965, two critical moments occurred in the Senate that illustrated the importance of committee differences in oversight of international affairs. The first event took place on February 1966 in the Senate Foreign Relations Committee under the chairmanship of J. William Fulbright (D-AR); the second occurred sixteen months later in the Senate Armed Services Committee under the aegis of Senator John Stennis (D-MS).[37] Initially, the two committees approached the early stage of the conflict from relatively similar vantage points; both adopted a strong stance against the spread of communism in Southeast Asia. Chairman Fulbright, however, gained a reputation as an ardent foe of the war, while his Senate colleague, John Stennis, a stalwart friend of the military who eventually

[37] Fry (2006).

became chair of Armed Services, attacked the constraints imposed on the generals by civilian leaders in the Pentagon and White House. Together, Fulbright and Stennis framed the narrative of America's bitterly divisive war: the former as a tragic error best ended quickly, the latter as an unnecessary defeat imposed by clueless civilian leaders. Their different approaches were not simply a matter of personal preferences, but also reflected the general dispositions of their respective committees. In the hearings of the Vietnam period, stark contrasts emerged between the Senate's national security watchdogs and signs of future trends emerged.

The United States had sent military advisors to South Vietnam since the early 1950s, first to assist the French and then to provide direct aid to the Diem regime in Saigon after the signing of the Geneva Accords ending French rule in 1954. By 1961, American troops numbered more than three thousand, and financial assistance had risen dramatically to over a hundred million dollars. The hearing records of the Armed Services and Foreign Relations indicate some intermittent oversight of the growing American involvement with the ARVN (Army of the Republic of Vietnam) forces of South Vietnam, but both committees at the time were deeply engaged in the decade after Geneva with events in Europe, Korea, China, and Latin America.

The committees' initial reactions to the increasing U.S. commitment were relatively muted and conducted out of public view, as shown in Figure 2.3.[38] Armed Services held just one public hearing to discuss S. J. 189, the resolution "To Promote the Maintenance of International Peace and Security in Southeast Asia," which was the Johnson administration's 1964 request for authorization to respond with military force to the alleged firing on U.S. patrol boats in the Gulf of Tonkin by the North Vietnamese. The committee also held two days of executive session hearings to discuss the resolution and privately considered the situation in Southeast Asia for another two days during the year. Foreign Relations held three days of public hearings on the president's Gulf of Tonkin request and devoted eleven sessions behind closed doors to events in Southeast Asia.

Although the two committees shifted their attention to Southeast Asia after the Gulf of Tonkin incident in August 1964, they continued to handle the situation in Vietnam privately throughout 1965. Neither held a public hearing on the topic, despite the commencement of the campaign to bomb the North, Operation Rolling Thunder. Each held fourteen days of secret sessions, however.

---

[38] To compile the list of hearings, I identified all hearings that were coded as crises, scandals, authorizations of military force, or resolutions between 1964 and 1975. I then deleted any that were not connected to Vietnam. Armed Services had eighteen executive sessions listed simply as "Briefing" during 1967 and 1968. These typically followed a closed-door session specifically designated as a Vietnam hearing and involved the same witnesses, so that one could infer that the hearing was a continuation of the same topic. I deleted five such briefings, which probably were about Vietnam, but could not be confirmed.

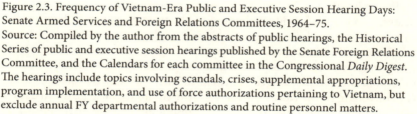

Figure 2.3. Frequency of Vietnam-Era Public and Executive Session Hearing Days: Senate Armed Services and Foreign Relations Committees, 1964–75.
Source: Compiled by the author from the abstracts of public hearings, the Historical Series of public and executive session hearings published by the Senate Foreign Relations Committee, and the Calendars for each committee in the Congressional *Daily Digest*. The hearings include topics involving scandals, crises, supplemental appropriations, program implementation, and use of force authorizations pertaining to Vietnam, but exclude annual FY departmental authorizations and routine personnel matters.

The divergence in the national security committees' approach to Vietnam emerged in 1966. An initial supporter of U.S. engagement in Vietnam, Fulbright became convinced that the conflict was not sustainable, that its costs far exceeded its security benefits, and that administration officials could not be trusted to tell the truth. Indeed, Fulbright coined a memorable phrase, "the credibility gap," to challenge the testimony of executive branch witnesses before his committee. What changed Fulbright's mind was a lengthy letter from a reporter who had traveled widely in Southeast Asia and conducted extensive interviews with military personnel and intelligence officers that conveyed a bleak picture of U.S. efforts.[39]

Called to testify in January that year regarding a supplemental bill authorizing additional aid to South Vietnam, Secretary of State Dean Rusk reported sub-

[39] http://www.senate.gov/artandhistory/history/minute/Vietnam_Hearings.htm (accessed May 2013).

stantial progress in executing the U.S. strategy. Rusk asserted that if the United States stood firm, the communists eventually would give up and leave South Vietnam. Angered by the Johnson administration's apparent lack of candor, Fulbright decided to launch a series of public "educational" hearings that took place over five days in February. The hearings were televised and included as star witnesses James Gavin, a retired general, and George Kennan, an architect of America's policy of containment of communism. These highly respected experts warned against further buildup of military forces and urged a course of prudent withdrawal. When Secretary Rusk, General Maxwell Taylor, the commander of operations in Vietnam, and David Bell, the administrator for AID, took their turn to testify, Fulbright immediately put them on the defensive.

For many citizens, Vietnam was the first "living room war." The nightly newscasts brought battle scenes directly into people's homes and covered dramatic testimony in congressional committee rooms about the strategic goals of military action and the combat performance of U.S. troops. The hearings were good television with human drama and plenty of sharp exchanges, and the press covered them extensively. They had the effect of legitimizing public criticism of the war and undermining support for the president's conduct of operations in Vietnam. Johnson's approval ratings regarding handling of the war slipped from 63 percent to 49 percent by the spring of 1966.[40] The bulk of Foreign Relations' oversight throughout that momentous year occurred behind closed doors, however, with eighteen days of hearings overall.

Figure 2.3 indicates that the Senate Armed Services Committee held twice as many public hearings as Foreign Relations in 1966, but the committee's agenda was geared to sessions about military hardware, readiness of the troops, POWs, and long-term operational capabilities. The senators invited Defense Department officials to tell the Congress what they needed to make war in Southeast Asia. Given the absence of confrontation, the media response was predictably understated. In addition to these efforts to build support for the Pentagon's agenda, the committee also conducted eighteen executive sessions.

By 1967, however, Senator Stennis had become outraged by the restraints imposed by the White House on the bombing over North Vietnam and the president's micromanagement of target selection. The full committee met in secret on twenty different occasions that year to discuss Vietnam. In August, the chair appointed Stennis to head a special investigatory subcommittee that conducted five days of public hearings on the air war over North Vietnam in which Secretary of Defense Robert McNamara was the target of particularly aggressive questioning. The subcommittee published a scathing summary of its findings, moreover, that took direct aim at the civilian leadership of the DOD for preventing the Air Force from doing its job. Rather than attack the military's

---

[40] http://www.senate.gov/artandhistory/history/minute/Vietnam_Hearings.htm (accessed May 2013.

strategy and tactics, Stennis established a recurrent theme in later debates about Vietnam that America would have defeated the Vietcong and its allies in the North had the generals been given a free hand to exercise their professional judgment.

Figure 2.3 indicates that for the next two years both national security committees emphasized executive sessions over public scrutiny of the war. Armed Services, still chaired by Senator Richard Russell (D-GA), held only four days of open hearings in 1968 to discuss problems of desertion in the ranks and malfunctioning M-16 rifles, and it did not engage at all in public oversight throughout 1969. Foreign Relations maintained a discreet silence in 1968, as well, with only two days of public testimony regarding U.S. involvement in Southeast Asia. As bad as things were between Fulbright and Johnson, the committee's Democratic majority refrained from further attacks. Privately, however, the committee met frequently in 1968 to evaluate the events leading up to the Gulf of Tonkin Resolution and concluded that President Johnson had misled Congress about the nature of the attack and his intentions in seeking authorization for the use of force.

After an initial period of détente between Fulbright and the newly elected President Nixon in 1969, the chairman resumed his public pressure on the White House with eleven days of inquiries into military operations in Laos and Cambodia as the war widened. Nixon pursued an increasingly unpopular course of action in 1970 and 1971, but Armed Services, then chaired by Stennis, remained relatively quiescent. When the committee engaged in oversight, however, it dealt with scandal publicly and privately, including problems of drug abuse, weak security for servicemen in Thailand, and fraud and mismanagement of defense contracts. Indeed, scandal dominated its oversight agenda for the remainder of the war, especially security leaks, drug problems, illegal intelligence gathering by the CIA, and the bombing of Cambodia.

The most vigorous efforts to challenge the president occurred in Foreign Relations beginning in 1970, as Fulbright intensified his public criticism of Nixon's actions. By 1971, the struggle between Foreign Relations and the president peaked. Congress had rescinded the Gulf of Tonkin Resolution that January, and Foreign Relations followed up with the dramatic hearings that included testimony on April 22, 1971, from Lt. John Kerry, later a Democratic senator from Massachusetts and eventually his party's nominee for president in 2004. Before the cameras, Kerry, a highly decorated Navy lieutenant, posed a question on behalf of the Vietnam Veterans Against the War to the senators and the American public: "How do you ask a man to be the last man to die in Vietnam? How do you ask a man to be the last man to die for a mistake?"[41]

---

[41] John Kerry, Testimony Before the Senate Foreign Relations Committee (1971), 7, http://www.lib.berkeley.edu/videodir/pacificaviet/kerry.pdf (accessed May 2013).

By 1972, both committees had reduced their oversight of the war as the national debate between hawks and doves played out in the presidential election between President Nixon and the liberal, antiwar senator, George McGovern (D-SD), who was a member of Foreign Relations. Armed Services spent five of six public hearings on drug abuse among military personnel in Vietnam and two executive sessions on authorizing a supplemental spending bill for DOD. Foreign Relations held no public hearings about the conflict, although it scheduled four closed-door sessions to consider reports from senators and staffers on trips they had taken to Southeast Asia. A sign of the poisonous atmosphere between Fulbright and the White House, however, was the comment of an aide who dismissed the role of the Senate in foreign policy: "Today, if you go to Congress and consult with them ... I am not saying it's like consulting Hanoi, but it's almost."[42]

With Nixon's reelection, Armed Services continued its focus on problems with military personnel and examined the bombing of Cambodia. Foreign Relations turned its attention to scandal, as well, especially illegal surveillance of U.S. citizens by the CIA and the role of Henry Kissinger in authorizing wiretaps to deal with leaks. Generally, the Watergate scandal and Nixon's eventual resignation in 1974 eclipsed other types of national security investigatory activity.

The imminent collapse of the Saigon government in 1975, however, prompted a flurry of activity by both Senate committees. Armed Services heard three days of secret testimony about the dire situation in South Vietnam, while publicly continuing to address scandals in the Pentagon regarding procurement costs and contracting. Foreign Relations was silent under its new chair, John Sparkman (D-AL), who headed the committee after Fulbright's defeat in the 1974 election, although the committee conducted a lengthy review of conditions in Vietnam, Cambodia, and Laos.

Over the twelve-year period from 1964 to 1975, when the last American personnel were airlifted out of Saigon, Armed Services and Foreign Relations conducted a total of 345 days of hearings about national security. Of the total, 137 days were public and 208 days were behind closed doors. Armed Services was responsible for 147 of these open and closed days of inquiry, 90 percent of which dealt with crises and scandals associated with Southeast Asia. Foreign Relations met for a combined 198 days, 63 percent of which dealt with crises and scandals related to Vietnam and its neighbors. The high level of attention by committee members to oversight of a major conflict and the extensive secret contacts that went on between the executive and legislative branches contrasted sharply with the behavior of the Senate national security committees during the wars in Afghanistan and Iraq.

---

[42] Jack Anderson, "Fulbright, Nixon Had Secret Talks," *Washington Post*, May 21, 1972, http://news.google.com/newspapers?nid=1876&dat=19720521&id=qX8sAAAAIBAJ&sjid=DM0E AAAAIBAJ&pg=7191,4185512 (accessed May 17, 2012).

Distinctive patterns emerged in the venues and content of the two national security committees, highlighted by the frequencies in Figure 2.3 regarding Vietnam. Armed Services conducted comparatively fewer open hearings and focused its efforts on the needs of the military at a time of rising pressures on resources and operational capabilities. Given growing national controversy over the draft and the personnel problems in the military, the committee's reticence reflected its strategic premises. In public at least, the committee refrained from questioning the rationale for the war, although it did raise issues about strategy and tactics. It is noteworthy, for example, that it never scheduled an open hearing on the My Lai scandal, in which Vietnamese civilians were massacred, or the perceived failure of the military during the Tet Offensive. When the committee could no longer ignore the widespread disaffection with the war, Armed Services turned its attention to problems within the ranks and scandals involving contracts and procurement, but continued to avoid larger issues that targeted the Pentagon directly or divided the committee internally.

Foreign Relations, in contrast, put major emphasis on debate and education, and it responded swiftly and very publicly to growing public concern over casualties and the draft. In addition, the committee structured its public hearings to make them newsworthy. The witnesses before the committee generated conflict between senators and administration officials and provided a human face to abstract arguments about diplomacy and war. Most important, the hearings involved authoritative actors challenging the president from within his own party. Unable to galvanize lawmakers or public opinion to put an end to the war, however, Fulbright became an isolated figure in the Senate before losing his 1974 bid for reelection.

In hindsight, congressional committee oversight was not sufficient to change the course of determined presidents with respect to Vietnam. LBJ had groused about the temerity of committee chairmen who, he noted sarcastically, thought that "they should run the strategy of the war rather than the President."[43] According to one biographer, Johnson's escalation of U.S. involvement grew partly from a fear that Democratic and Republican hawks in Congress would blame him for losing the battle against communism in Southeast Asia.[44] Nixon rejected the very idea that Congress had authority over the war as he pursued a multipronged strategy of escalating military pressure on the North, pursuing secret negotiations with Hanoi, and gradually drawing down American troops. With such strong divisions between the Senate's key national security committees, oversight hearings conveyed mixed messages that made it easier for each president to chart his own course.

The intense scrutiny of Vietnam set the stage for the increased Senate hearing activity that followed over the next two decades. Fulbright became the highly

---

[43] Fry (2006, vii).
[44] Goodwin (1976).

visible champion of the antiwar movement in the Senate and demonstrated the power of dramatic hearings to attract the attention of the press and build a national reputation. In doing so, he created space for other, more junior senators on his committee, such as McGovern and Frank Church (D-ID), to launch subsequent presidential bids. Indeed, Church conducted a series of high-profile investigations of domestic spying and unlawful assassination and money laundering in the CIA that shocked the public and produced major reforms of intelligence gathering.

Finally, the Vietnam case contains intimations of the struggles between Democrats and Republicans over foreign policy that escalated during the Carter and Reagan years. Concerns about party reputation initially were not evident. Both Democratic chairmen deferred to President Johnson in the early stages of the war because they shared his anticommunist stance. After breaking ranks with him, however, they went public with their criticism, despite their shared partisanship. Both committees fell silent during the 1968 and 1972 presidential elections, however, as the committees let the party nominees lay out their respective approaches to Southeast Asia. The newly elected President Nixon enjoyed a year's honeymoon in 1969 while Armed Services and Foreign Relations gave him the opportunity to implement his campaign peace plan.

Once Nixon's intentions to continue the war became apparent, the two committees turned their attention to scandal. Partly, this response reflected war fatigue on the part of the public; and partly, it was a way of rebalancing power between the executive and legislative branches after a period of deference. Nevertheless, Nixon was engaged in a high-stakes game to remake the Republican Party's image in foreign affairs and had ably depicted his 1972 opponent, Senator McGovern, as naive and dangerously weak in halting the spread of communism. Investigations by Armed Services and Foreign Relations offered a different narrative,[45] which directly undercut Nixon's claims of superior leadership by exposing severe problems of command and operations as the war dragged on. Their focus on the troops, particularly the widespread problems of morale and drug abuse, contrasted starkly with Nixon's pursuit of grand strategy at the Paris peace talks.

Conclusion

The historical trends outlined in Chapter 1 point to a complex pattern of motivations at work in the Senate's national security committee hearings. Although

---

[45] The coincidence of war and scandal appears throughout the data set and poses issues for coding hearing content. Hearings about drug abuse among soldiers and faulty weapons, for example, could be read either as inquiries into policy implementation or as probes into mismanagement. When the hearing title and tone indicated bureaucratic wrongdoing, such inquiries warranted the code of scandal.

institutional change resulted in similar trajectories in formal public and executive hearings for Armed Services and Foreign Relations, selection effects in membership produced distinctive patterns in their propensity for oversight, use of executive sessions, attention to budgets, responses to presidents' initiation of force, and depth of individual inquiries. Party conflict, so important to most aspects of congressional behavior, contradicted conventional explanations about unified and divided control of the Senate and White House, but was a factor in the differences between the two Senate committees. Understanding oversight of defense and foreign policy thus requires systematic thinking about the variation in all three patterns.

The theoretical perspectives in this chapter lead to several conclusions. First, the optimum behavior for each senator is not necessarily the most beneficial outcome for the public or Congress as a whole. Second, the biases built into the assignment of senators to specific committees affect the way individual committees carry out their responsibilities for promoting the rule of law and educating the public with respect to international affairs. One consequence of the disparate strategies committees employ is public confusion when authoritative actors, such as Fulbright and Stennis, provide conflicting signals about the president's conduct of defense and foreign policy. Third, committees' diverse motives and behaviors imply that no single reform will induce members to do a better job under the incentives currently in place. Overall, a system of national security oversight that depends upon private motives to accomplish collective objectives is likely to fall short of public expectations.

PART II

OVERSIGHT HEARINGS AND REGULAR ORDER IN U.S. FOREIGN RELATIONS

The question of war and peace, in a country like this, is not to be compressed into the compass that would befit a small litigation. It is not to be made to turn upon a pin ... [but] should be regarded as a great question, not only of right, but also of prudence and expediency.

—Daniel Webster, addressing the House of
Representatives, 1814

CHAPTER 3

Institutional Change and Senate Committee Hearings

WHEN RONALD REAGAN DEBATED President Gerald Ford during the 1976 primary, he adopted a tough stance toward the Panama Canal, declaring, "We bought it. We paid for it. It is ours."[1] Reagan's words crystallized the internal splits within Republican and Democratic ranks about the role of the United States in the world after Vietnam, and he heralded a divide that eventually pushed the two parties far apart on foreign policy. These developments occurred within a broader set of institutional trends that affected the frequency of hearings by Senate committees in the aggregate and by the Armed Services and Foreign Relations Committees individually. Although Senate committees expanded formal inquiries of all types in the decade following the collapse of the Cold War Consensus, they eventually reduced their hearing workloads to historic lows. Such long-term shifts in the operation of the Senate committee system deserve a closer look because they limited opportunities for oversight.[2] With fewer hearings, senators were less likely to conduct regular reviews of executive branch performance. In this chapter, I demonstrate that long-term, institutional changes, especially the decision by senators to diversify their policy portfolios through increased committee assignments, influenced the frequency of all types of committee hearings for the entire Senate, as well as for Armed Services and Foreign Relations.

After the long nightmare of Vietnam, Congress reasserted its institutional prerogatives in international affairs. Lawmakers passed the War Powers Act in 1973, publicized a long list of CIA abuses, terminated funding for military operations in Southeast Asia, formed intelligence committees in both chambers to oversee clandestine activities, asserted greater control over the president's distribution of military aid, and trimmed defense spending. The Senate Foreign Relations Committee was in the vanguard of the resurgence of Congress in

---

[1] My collaboration with Brian Law was critical to developing the variables for this chapter. For the Reagan quote, see http://news.google.com/newspapers?nid=1314&dat=19770809&id=TDxOA AAAIBAJ&sjid=1O0DAAAAIBAJ&pg=3104,3165779 (accessed May 2013).

[2] Binder (2011) demonstrated that the denominator matters when evaluating the performance of Congress in her study of legislative gridlock.

international affairs through a special investigative subcommittee with a broad mandate to probe covert executive branch activities. The exposure of substantial wrongdoing gave congressional doves powerful evidence to bring the defense establishment to heel.

Eventually, the hawks pushed back, demanding a more confrontational relationship with the Soviet Union, aggressive anticommunism in the Third World, and increased investment in military equipment and personnel. The transfer of sovereignty over the Panama Canal in 1979 became a potent symbol of this larger debate between liberal internationalists and neoconservatives regarding détente with the Soviets and U.S. relations with developing nations. Reagan used Panama to realign the GOP toward a harder line on foreign policy,[3] and though he lost the 1976 primary, he and his supporters turned repeatedly to the canal issue to mobilize conservatives in subsequent elections. The Senate battle over the treaty and its aftermath fueled perceptions among the public that Democrats were less effective on international affairs than Republicans.[4] Indeed, Zelizer described the dispute over Panama as key to a larger failure "to revitalize the Democratic national security agenda."[5] Coincidentally, the Panama case represented a challenge for the Foreign Relations Committee from which it never recovered.

In hindsight, the battle over the Panama Canal coincided with gradual changes in the Senate committee system outlined in Chapter 2. Because time has always been a scarce resource in Congress, senators typically reveal their priorities through the activities they choose to emphasize.[6] With respect to committees, new cohorts of senators initially perceived committee work as a means of pursuing personal power and policy interests, but eventually they appeared to regard membership on specific committees as a tool for courting political activists and donors. Paradoxically, larger committee portfolios among senators meant fewer days of hearings. The increase in the mean number of committee assignments documented in Chapter 2, as we shall see, had the most powerful effect on the frequency of public hearings for *all* committees, as well as for Armed Services and Foreign Relations.

Similarly, the end of the Cold War Consensus over national security corresponded to a period of defense and foreign policy activism, along with a surge in social regulation and other domestic initiatives. As we saw in Chapter 1, however, committee appetites for conducting hearings had dissipated by the 1990s. In addition, all committees dealt with heightened ideological polarization and shortened legislative sessions, although the effects of these trends turned out to be relatively weak. The loss of press coverage dealt Foreign Relations an espe-

[3] Farnsworth and McKenney (1983, 153).
[4] Zelizer (2010, 286).
[5] Zelizer (2010, 298).
[6] Hall (1996).

cially powerful blow, but had relatively little effect on aggregate Senate hearings or Armed Services inquiries. The reluctance of senior senators, especially Republicans, to build careers on Foreign Relations adversely affected the committee's frequency of executive sessions, as well.

This chapter begins with a review of expectations and measures regarding the influence of the shifting institutional context on Senate committee hearings generally and on Armed Services and Foreign Relations sessions particularly. The discussion then shifts to statistical analysis of the effects of various long-term changes on the frequency of public hearings first by Senate committees in the aggregate and then by Armed Services and Foreign Relations. Next, the empirical analysis focuses on influences on the frequency of executive hearing days by the two national security committees. Finally, the discussion turns to the Panama Canal to illustrate the confluence of trends that created a watershed moment for the Senate Foreign Relations Committee. Together, long-term institutional changes, some affecting the entire Senate and others limited to Armed Services and Foreign Relations, provide the backdrop for assessing the national security committees' approach to oversight in later chapters. The career motives and contextual factors responsible for declining hearing activity matter because they undermined the capacity of the national security committees to foster regular order and public education in international affairs through oversight.

SOURCES OF LONG-TERM CHANGE IN SENATE COMMITTEE HEARINGS

Many political observers have remarked on the dramatic changes in the Senate since the end of World War II. Two trends outlined in Chapter 2, a rise in the mean number of committee assignments and a modest drop in the length of legislative sessions, represented a choice among lawmakers about how they wanted to spend their time. In addition, external conditions altered the context in which Senate committees operated, including the end of the Cold War Consensus, the diminished media coverage of Congress, and the increased ideological polarization between Democrats and Republicans. Having outlined general expectations about the link between committees' adherence to regular order and historical change in Chapter 2, I turn here to specific hypotheses about the effect of such changes on committees' total hearing activity.

The Effects of Senators' Allocation of Time

The steady climb in mean committee assignments represented a dramatic change in the Senate in which senators nearly doubled their policy portfolios from an average of 2.1 to 4.1 committee assignments per senator. The widespread move to diversify rather than specialize represented a different attitude toward committee work.[7] Indeed, it likely captured some underlying dimension about senators' perception of their careers. As senators increased their assignments, the value of any one committee diminished along with the priority senators attached to its total hearing effort. Thus, the growth in the number of positions per senator paradoxically appears to have reduced the frequency of formal inquiries by individual committees throughout the Senate, as well as in the Armed Services and Foreign Relations Committees. The rise in mean committee assignments also seemed to have had a negative impact on the frequency of executive sessions.

Senators found it beneficial to spend more time away from the Capitol cultivating constituency groups as Senate campaigns became more costly and more races became competitive. The length of legislative sessions varied substantially between 1947 and 2008, as noted in Chapter 2, but a slight downward trend emerged after the 1980s, punctuated with several sharp peaks. Shorter sessions likely resulted in fewer public hearings, all else equal, and should have had a particularly strong, negative effect on executive sessions, which tended to be discretionary in nature.

The Effects of Context

The years of Cold War Consensus from 1947 to 1968 represented an anomaly in U.S. politics in many respects. Although overall conditions were not as harmonious as the name implied, it was a remarkable time, notable for the nation's emergence as a nuclear superpower, extraordinary economic growth, increased income equality, and general mood of optimism and trust in government. Lawmakers had a full plate dealing with the aftermath of World War II and constructing the national security apparatus that supported the policy of containment. They also addressed a backlog of policy problems and demonstrated a willingness to expand the power of the federal government into traditional areas of state and local control, such as creation of the national highway system and funding for education.[8]

With such a political climate, we might expect all Senate committees to have been unusually busy throughout the 1950s and 1960s. Their activity was constrained, however, by the hierarchical structure of the Senate committee system

---

[7] The rise in the numbers of congressional staff members coincided with the expansion of committee portfolios and grew from fourteen in the 80th Congress to well over forty in the 110th Congress. Committee staff is positively related to the frequency of oversight hearings. As I note in Appendix C, the counts of staff were so highly correlated with the mean committee assignments variable that I dropped them from the analysis.

[8] War typically affects domestic politics in the United States, frequently stimulating policy innovation (Mayhew 2000). Howell, Jackman, and Rogowski (2103) contend that the power of the presidency to nationalize policy issues during periods of conflict enables the White House to exert greater influence on Congress over domestic issues.

during the early Cold War era. Senior committee chairs, disproportionately from the Democratic South, tightly controlled their committees' agendas and frequently allied with conservative Republicans to block legislation that would expand the size and influence of the federal government. A dummy variable for the period from 1947 to 1968 thus captures the control imposed by committee barons on their members. Generally, the consensus period appears to have discouraged public hearing activity throughout the Senate's committees, as well as the Armed Services and Foreign Relations Committees. Nevertheless, the intensity of the Cold War required a great deal of secret negotiation with administration officials, so the national security committees had incentives to expand the frequency of executive sessions during these years.

Again, recalling Chapter 2, press coverage of Congress and its members experienced a downward drift, particularly after the mid-1980s. Higher visibility in the press had the potential to encourage lawmakers to actively engage the executive branch, all else equal. The aggregate measure of congressional coverage is not specific to individual Senate committees, but rather captures all types of legislative actors in terms of their visibility. For total Senate committee hearings days, then, the effect was likely to have been be positive, but weak.

The two national security committees showed marked differences in media visibility over time. Foreign Relations, we saw in Chapter 2, commanded fully 4 percent of all *New York Times* mentions about Congress and its members at the beginning of the Cold War, but slipped dramatically in press coverage, especially after the mid-1980s. Members of Foreign Relations traditionally had viewed the committee as a means of developing national reputations, so the relationship between the frequency of Foreign Relations hearings and its press mentions was likely to be strongly positive. Given Armed Services' historically lower profile, the relationship between its hearings and media attention should have been modestly positive. Press coverage likely had no effect on the frequency of executive sessions because of their secrecy.

Party polarization, which has attracted so much attention from scholars and pundits, requires additional discussion to assess its likely relationship to committee hearings.[9] As I noted in Chapter 2, polarization appears to have begun in the 1970s, picked up speed in the 1980s, and blossomed by the mid-1990s.[10] The question is whether ideological divisions in Congress affected the frequency of committee hearings.[11] A number of congressional scholars contend

---

[9] See Sinclair (2006; 2012a; 2012b) for a discussion of the pervasive effects of polarization in the Senate.

[10] Polarization has occurred because of partisan realignment among voters, largely in the South but also in the Northeast and West, with the result that the parties have become more homogeneous internally and moved further apart along a conservative-liberal dimension (Rohde 1991). See also Theriault (2008); McCarty, Poole, and Rosenthal (2008).

[11] Polarization has been most visible on the floor of the House and Senate, partly because it is easy to measure roll call votes and partly because conflicts about procedures that govern debate and

that polarization strengthened the hands of party leaders, not only over rank-and-file members on the floor, but also over committees.[12] Not all congressional experts agree that parties exercised more clout over lawmakers, however, and some contend that party effects in the Senate operated on members indirectly.[13]

The key issue with respect to oversight is whether individual committees experienced polarization at different rates and to different degrees and how that affected their hearing dockets. Less desirable committees with high turnover, for example, would have polarized more rapidly than committees with stable memberships. Nevertheless, selection biases that motivated senators to seek out specific committees would likely have produced distinctive ideological orientations, despite chamber-wide trends. For both reasons, the effects of polarization on the frequency of hearings likely varied considerably over time and by committee. Figure 3.1, which depicts the changes in ideological differences for the full Senate and for the Armed Services and Foreign Relations Committees, confirms that polarization was highly variable for the national security committees and differed from the Senate in the aggregate.[14]

Expectations regarding the impact of polarization on total hearing activity are unclear because theories of parties and committees conflict. Under the models of party cartel behavior or conditional party government, polarized committees would be expected to use hearings to further the interests of the Senate majority. In contrast, informational theory regarding committees predicts that polarized committees would generate information that is suspect in the eyes of the median senator on the floor. It is unclear how the majority or the median lawmaker would articulate demand for more or fewer total hearings and whether either had the means to impose its will on the hearing count.

---

amendments have produced the clearest splits along party lines (Lee 2009). Scholars have not examined its effects on committee oversight, however.

[12] Sinclair (2006); Aldrich and Rohde (2001); Cox and McCubbins (2005).

[13] Scholars, such as Krehbiel (1998) and Poole and Rosenthal (1997), are deeply skeptical that parties induce lawmakers to deviate from their overall ideological orientations. Aldrich and Rohde (2001) and Cox and McCubbins (2005; 2007) adopted a different view, contending that party influence is "conditional" on ideological agreement within the party and is maintained through negative agenda control. The problem with their argument is that party influence emerges as strongest for bills when internal consensus is high and do not need constraints to pass. Smith (2007) contends that party influence occurs in many less visible arenas off the floor. Den Hartog and Monroe (2011) uncover party influence in making minority obstruction in the Senate more costly. Notably, the debate about the effects of polarization has focused on floor procedures and bill passage rather than oversight.

[14] The measures are based on a scaling procedure that ranks individual members on a single liberal-conservative dimension from most liberal to most conservative developed by Poole and Rosenthal (1997) and available at VoteView.org. The index is the difference between the median Republican and Democratic senators in the chamber as a whole and in the two national security committees. The result was multiplied by –1 to produce an index that varies from 0 (*no polarization*) to 1 (*full polarization*).

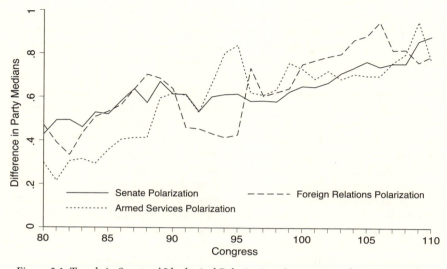

Figure 3.1. Trends in Senators' Ideological Polarization: Senate, Armed Services, and Foreign Relations, 80th–110th Congress.
Source: Voteview, http://voteview.com/dwnominate.asp (accessed June 2009).
Polarization is measured as the difference in first-dimension DW-Nominate scores between the median Republican and median Democratic senators in the chamber as a whole and in the Armed Services and Foreign Relations Committees. The values have been multiplied by–1 so that 0 represents no polarization and 1 represents complete polarization.

If we assume that committees operated relatively autonomously in scheduling hearings, the incentives remain murky. On the one hand, committees might have scheduled more public hearings to air their differences, especially if they experienced gridlock over legislation; or, they might not have been able to agree on an agenda of hearings and consequently scheduled fewer inquiries. On the other hand, senators might have pursued more consensual strategies within their respective committees and generated lots of hearings, despite their records of polarized roll call votes on the Senate floor.[15]

Whatever the underlying logic for each committee, the measure of polarization for the full Senate probably would not produce statistically significant coefficients for committee hearings in the aggregate. The statistical impact likely would wash out given the variation in the rate and extent of the polarization for individual committees.

The two national security committees, however, might have experienced polarization in distinctive ways. Armed Services, according to Figure 3.1, was

[15] I am grateful to Wendy Schiller for this observation.

consistently less polarized than either the Senate as a whole or Foreign Relations for most of its history because of the heavy concentration of conservative, southern Democrats among its members. The exceptions were the 93rd to 95th Congresses (1973–77) after Vietnam and the 109th Congress (2005–6) at the height of the violence in Iraq. Airing policy differences for Armed Services would have been counterproductive for a committee eager to build popular support for the Pentagon. Consequently, I expect polarization to have had little effect on the frequency of Armed Services public hearings. On the other hand, it seems likely that the committee would have moved more of its business behind closed doors at high levels of polarization, all else equal.

Foreign Relations, in contrast, tended toward greater polarization than Armed Services or the Senate as a whole throughout the sixty-two years of the study. Although the committee displayed a remarkable degree of consensus between the 90th and 95th Congresses (1967–77), it then experienced a big spike in ideological conflict in 1979 as divisive issues, such as the Panama Canal, began to realign the parties on foreign affairs. Ideological divisions within Foreign Relations continued to rise sharply for more than a decade with the defeat of liberal Republicans and their replacement with conservative GOP newcomers. The effects on public hearing days from polarization, therefore, were likely to have been positive in keeping with the members' penchant for policy debate. Nevertheless, at some point, internal differences within the committee might have made it difficult to agree on a public hearing agenda. The opposite would have been true for executive session hearings.

Overall, change in senators' expectations about how to use their time, combined with contextual factors, shaped Senate committees' penchant for public and executive committee hearings. Taken together, these trends suggest that the forces affecting committee activity have been extremely complex. Table 3.1 presents a brief summary of the predicted relationship between the various types of institutional change and the total workload of Senate committees.

ESTIMATING THE FREQUENCY OF SENATE PUBLIC COMMITTEE HEARINGS

Public hearings promote regular order and citizen education in congressional committees. In addition, they are the only type of committee hearing for which data on the full Senate are available. I begin, therefore, with analysis of the aggregate number of public hearings for all Senate committees, depicted previously as Figure 1.2, and the total number of public hearings for the Senate Armed Services and Foreign Relations Committees, as portrayed earlier in Figure 1.1. The independent variables include the mean number of committee assignments per senator; the length of the legislative session; a dummy variable for the Cold War Consensus from 1947 to 1968; the number of *New York Times*

Table 3.1. Expected Relationships between Senate Committee Hearing Days and Institutional Change

Type of Influence	Change in Committee Hearing Activity		
	All Senate	Armed Services	Foreign Relations
Public Hearing Days			
Effects of Senators' Allocation of Time			
Mean # Committees	Reduce	Reduce	Reduce
Days in Session	Increase	Increase	Increase
Effects of Context			
Cold War Consensus	Reduce	Reduce	Reduce
Media Visibility	No effect	Slight increase	Increase
Polarization	No effect	No effect	Increase
Executive Session Hearing Days			
Effects of Senators' Allocation of Time			
Mean # Committees	NA	Reduce	Reduce
Days in Session	NA	Increase	Increase
Effects of Context			
Cold War Consensus	NA	Increase	Increase
Media Visibility	NA	No effect	No effect
Polarization	NA	Increase	Reduce

mentions of Congress and its members and the specific number of *New York Times* mentions for the Armed Services and Foreign Relations Committees and their members; and the level of partisan polarization in the chamber and within each national security committee. Appendix B contains the descriptive statistics.

The analysis employs a Poisson regression model, which is a standard technique for examining count data and is explained in Appendix C.[16] The statistical results appear in Appendix C as Tables C.1 through C.3, along with discussion of a variety of methodological issues related to the robustness of the findings.

Beginning with the aggregate public hearings for all Senate committees, Figure 3.2 depicts the effects of variables relevant to senators' allocation of time and external contexts on total public hearing activity from 1947 to 2008. The graph contains predictions for the mean impact of each variable on total hearing days as it takes estimated values at the 10th through the 90th percentile with all other variables held constant at their mean and Cold War Consensus fixed at zero (post–Cold War Consensus).[17] The dummy variable for the era of Cold

[16] Count data violate the basic assumptions of ordinary least squares. Poisson regression is used when the mean and variance are equal; in this case, the distribution of the dependent variables came very close to meeting the requirement. I discuss a variety of estimation models and tests in Appendix C.

[17] The values were calculated using Clarify software (Tomz, Wittenberg, and King 2001).

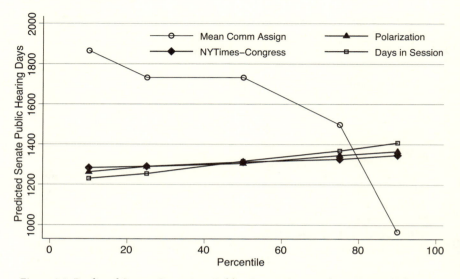

Figure 3.2. Predicted Senate Committee Public Hearing Days and Institutional Change Variables, 1947–2008.
Note: Points are predicted values for the mean number of hearings per year as each independent variable increases from the 10th percentile to the 90th percentile holding other variables at their mean and Cold War at zero. Estimates were obtained using the Clarify procedure (Tomz, Wittenberg, and King 2003). The significant coefficients (p values = .05 or better) have hollow symbols and include Mean Committee Assignment and Days in Session. Cold War is significant and has a negative sign. Consequently, the predicted lines for each variable if Cold War = 1 (for 1947–68) have the same slopes, but are lower, by roughly 400 predicted days for polarization, 425 for *New York Times*, 600 for Mean Committee Assignments, and 400 for Days in Session.

War Consensus is significant, with a negative sign, so if it were set at 1, the predicted values would appear lower, but have the same slopes. The effect of the mean number of committee assignments, which is highly significant, appears as a strongly negative influence on the total number of public hearing days, all else equal. This variable, on average, produces a change in predicted mean committee public hearing days of all Senate committees from 1,866 days at the 10th percentile to 966 days at the 90th percentile.

Recalling from Chapter 2 that senators held the fewest committee slots in the 80th Congress and the greatest number in the 110th, the magnitude of the shift in senators' orientations away from committee specialization becomes even more striking. To get a more concrete sense of what happened, I plugged the actual values of the independent variables into the model for 1947, 1981, and 2007. The predicted mean public hearing days were 2,103, 1,492, and 530 days, respectively. I then estimated what the number of Senate committee hearings would have been in the 110th Congress if senators had operated with the same number of committee assignments as those at the beginning of the time series and without the constraints of the Cold War Consensus. The predicted mean number of public hearing days would have been 2,585, or more than five times greater. Clearly, the shift in the way senators allocated their time has been costly to the operation of regular order and public education by all Senate committees.

The length of the legislative session is also a significant variable, and its positive slope indicates that, all else equal, Senate committees averaged more hearings in the aggregate during longer sessions. In some early years of the Cold War Consensus, when the Senate held relatively short sessions at the 10th percentile, the predicted mean number of public hearings days was 1,230; when session length was extended and took the value at the 90th percentile, the estimated number rose to 1,408 days, all other variables held constant. Recall from Figure 2.1 that the high and low values for days in session occurred at various points in the time series and fluctuated quite dramatically, even over the last two decades.

As expected, the effects of external changes in the political context washed out when examined in the aggregate for Senate committees. Neither party polarization nor mentions of Congress and its members in the *New York Times* was statistically significant. In addition, the figure reveals that their substantive effects while positive, were negligible as expected.

Overall, Senate committees held more public hearings when their members were policy specialists with relatively small committee portfolios. Nevertheless, it is important to recognize how the period of Cold War Consensus with its hierarchical committee structure mediated the relationship between mean committee assignments and public hearing days for Senate committees as a whole. Figure 3.3 plots predicted hearing days for the full Senate on the y-axis against the standardized values of the committee assignment variable, controlling for this distinctive era. A grouping of black circles, representing the years from 1947 to 1968, clusters at the left-hand end of the scale, as they should, given the high correlation of mean assignments and time. The interesting feature of the graph is the cluster of gray triangles in the upper-left corner, which indicates a very high level of predicted total Senate hearing days even though the values for committee assignments were very close to those prevailing in the Cold War era. In effect, senators remained relatively specialized and grounded in a few committees in the decade after 1969. It is the expansion beyond the mean portfolio of 2.7 committees that triggered the rapid decline in the Senate's public hearing days for the more recent Congresses.

Turning to the Armed Services Committee in Figure 3.4, we see a pattern of public hearing days that has some marked similarities to Senate committees as a whole. The dummy variable controlling for the Cold War Consensus is highly significant and negative, as it was for aggregate Senate committee hearings. The same dramatic, negative effect emerges for mean committee assignments holding

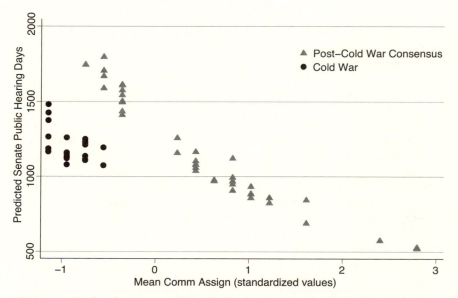

Figure 3.3. Predicted Senate Committee Public Hearing Days by Cold War Consensus and Mean Committee Assignments, 1947–2008.

all variables at their means and the Cold War Consensus dummy at zero. Again, given its negative slope, Cold War Consensus would produce lower predicted values, but lines with the same slopes if the variable were set at 1. At the 10th percentile for mean committee assignments, the predicted mean number of public hearing days is eighty-nine, which falls to sixty-three days at the 90th percentile. Similarly, there is a positive impact for the number of days in a legislative session, seventy-two predicted mean number of public days at the 10th percentile, rising to eighty-three predicted days at the 90th, although the variable is not statistically significant.

The major differences between Senate committees in the aggregate and Armed Services appear in the slopes for the contextual variables. First, the sign for ideological polarization within the committee is negative and the slope is fairly steep, although the variable is not significant, largely because it is highly correlated with the mean committee assignment variable. The predicted drop in mean public hearing is eleven days, moving from the 10th to the 90th percentile. This is a larger substantive effect than expected. The media visibility variable has a modest, positive effect of roughly the same magnitude, although the variable is not statistically significant.

The trends in the graph provide powerful evidence that Armed Services reacted to the changing norms in the Senate regarding committee work and adapted to the changing political context. Plugging in the actual values for the

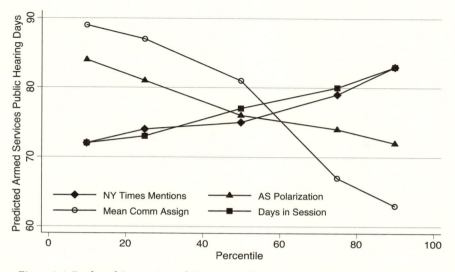

Figure 3.4. Predicted Senate Armed Services Public Hearing Days and Institutional Change, 1947–2008.

Note: Points are predicted values for the mean number of hearings per year as each independent variable increases from the 10th percentile to the 90th percentile and holding Cold War constant at zero. Estimates were obtained using the Clarify procedure (Tomz, Wittenberg, and King 2003). The significant coefficients (p value = .05 or better) include Mean Committee Assignments, which appears as a hollow symbol, and Cold War, which has a negative sign. The predicted lines for each variable if Cold War = 1 (1947–68) have the same slopes, but are lower because of the coefficient's negative sign, by roughly 25–30 predicted days for polarization, for *New York Times*, for Mean Committee Assignments, and for Days in Session.

years 1947, 1981, and 2007, the predicted mean public hearing days range from sixty-seven, to sixty-five, to forty-nine days, respectively. Again, had Armed Services members operated in the 110th Congress with the same number of committee assignments as in the 80th Congress (and Cold War set at 0), the predicted mean public hearing days would have been seventy days, an increase of roughly 40 percent.

The experience of Foreign Relations in Figure 3.5 appears to have been very different. As for other Senate committees, the Cold War Consensus variable is highly significant for Foreign Relations and has a negative sign. The mean committee assignment variable is not significant, however, although it has a moderate substantive effect on the predicted mean number of public hearing days. Holding Cold War Consensus constant at zero and the rest of the values at their means, the change from the 10th percentile to the 90th percentile for mean assignments works out to a decline from seventy-one predicted mean hearing

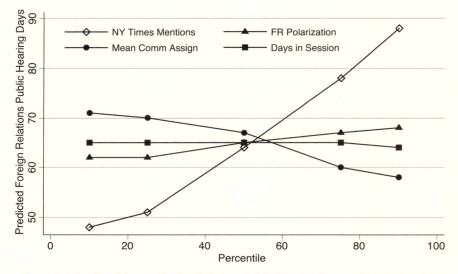

Figure 3.5. Predicted Senate Foreign Relations Public Hearing Days and Institutional Change, 1947–2008.

Note: Points are predicted values for the mean number of hearings per year as each independent variable increases from the 10th percentile to the 90th percentile holding other variables at their mean and Cold War constant at zero. Estimates were obtained using the Clarify procedure (Tomz, Wittenberg, and King 2003). The significant coefficients (p value = .05 or better) include *New York Times* Mentions, which appears as a hollow symbol, and Cold War, which has a negative sign. The predicted lines for each variable if Cold War = 1 (1947–68) have the same slopes, but are lower because of the coefficient's negative sign, by between 22 and 32 predicted days for polarization, for *New York Times*, for Mean Committee Assignments, and for Days in Session.

days to fifty-eight predicted days. Contrary to expectations, neither the length of the legislative session nor the polarization of the committee yields significant coefficients or much in the way of substantive impact on the predicted mean number of public hearing days.

The big driver of Foreign Relations' behavior was the change in its media visibility, which exerts a powerful statistical effect. The coefficient is highly significant and has a positive sign, and its substantive effects are dramatic. Holding all variables constant at their means and Cold War Consensus constant at zero yields predicted values of forty-eight public hearing days at the 10th percentile and eighty-eight public days at the 90th, a difference of more than 90 percent. In interpreting the magnitude of the change, it is important to remember that Foreign Relations was at its maximum visibility (the 90th percentile) in three different eras: (1) at the very beginning of the Cold War; (2) during the mid-1960s, as the United States escalated its involvement in Vietnam; and

(3) in 1981, the first year of the Reagan presidency. Plugging in the actual values for 1947, 1981, and 2007, produces predictions of mean number of hearings of eighty-eight days, seventy-six days, and thirty-seven days, respectively. To put these numbers in context, the predicted number of public hearing days would be fifty-four days for 2007 if the mean committee assignment variable took on its 1947 value. The predicted number would have been one hundred public hearing days, however, if Foreign Relations had commanded the visibility it enjoyed in 1951.

As with the full Senate, we see in Figure 3.6 the mediating effects of the Cold War era with its tightly controlled committee system on both national security committees with respect to mean committee assignments. For Armed Services (top panel), predicted public hearing days were quite variable during the early days of the Cold War period, ranging from over eighty days to just over fifty. Yet the cluster of gray triangles indicates that Armed Services appears to have enjoyed a "sweet spot" similar to that operating for Senate committees in the aggregate. It held numerous public hearings in the aftermath of the post-consensus era when its membership remained relatively specialized in defense policy. Foreign Relations (bottom panel), too, enjoyed a surge similar to other committees before its members became spread too thinly, although it conducted comparatively fewer public hearings compared to Armed Services during the period leading up to 1968.

Generally speaking, the dearth of public Senate hearings that contemporary critics of Congress have deplored is not an accident. Senators have allocated their time and attention to committees in a way that diminishes their capacity to generate public information. The limitation was largely self-imposed as members pursued their political interests in an institution lacking incentives for them to do otherwise. Moreover, the result was a level of national security activity well below the performance of Armed Services and Foreign Relations when they had been dominated by a handful of powerful chairmen in the early Cold War era or by policy specialists in the following decade. Foreign Relations, moreover, operated with the further disadvantage of increasing indifference on the part of the press. Taken together, these statistical results suggest that returning the Senate Armed Services and Foreign Relations Committees to a level of public activity that would support an orderly process of oversight would be a formidable challenge.

ESTIMATING THE FREQUENCY OF ARMED SERVICES AND FOREIGN RELATIONS EXECUTIVE HEARINGS

The decline of public hearings is not the only consequence of the institutional changes at work in the Senate over the sixty-two years of the study. The frequency of executive sessions for both Armed Services and Foreign Relations

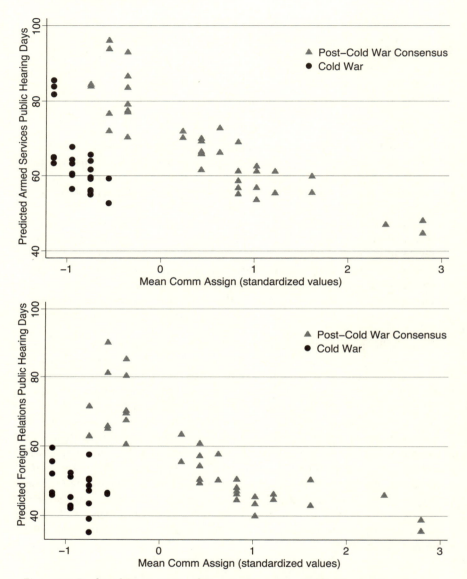

Figure 3.6. Predicted Senate National Security Committee Public Hearing Days by Cold War Consensus and Mean Committee Assignments, 1947–2008. Top: Armed Services Committee; bottom: Foreign Relations.

shows strong effects from shifts in the way senators allocated their time and contextual influences. Executive sessions are most important in creating space for committee members to delve into complex matters and to work out difficult issues with the Departments of Defense and State in private. The decline in executive sessions consequently is less about promoting regular order than creating opportunities to negotiate the boundaries between the two branches.

Figure 3.7 presents the predicted number of executive session days for the Armed Services Committee. The coefficient for Cold War Consensus is positive, but not significant, and all other variables but *New York Times* mentions are statistically significant. The mean number of committee assignments once again

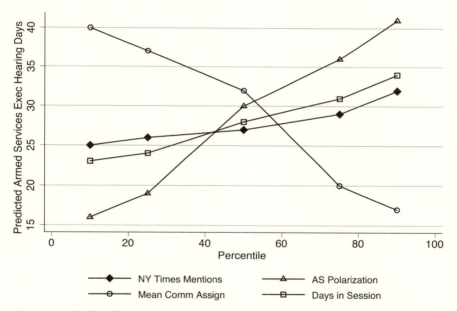

Figure 3.7. Predicted Senate Armed Services Executive Hearing Days and Institutional Change, 1947–2008.
Note: Points are predicted values for the mean number of hearings per year as each independent variable increases from the 10th percentile to the 90th percentile holding other variables at their mean and Cold War, which is not significant, constant at zero. Estimates were obtained using the Clarify procedure (Tomz, Wittenberg, and King 2003). The significant coefficients (*p* value = .05 or better) include Committee Polarity, Mean Committee Assignments, and Days in Session, which appear as hollow symbols. The predicted lines for each variable if Cold War = 1 (1947–68) have the same slopes, but are slightly higher because of the coefficient's positive sign, by roughly 1 to 2 predicted days for polarization, for *New York Times* Mentions, for Mean Committee Assignments, and for Days in Session.

exerts a strong negative effect on the frequency of secret hearings. In addition, party polarization is strongly positive, suggesting that Armed Services found meeting behind closed doors to be an attractive option under the pressure of increasing ideological divisions. This impact is not a surprise, although the magnitude of the effect is greater than expected. Finally, the frequency of executive sessions is positively linked to the length of legislative sessions. The substantive effects of all the variables are notable, indicating that senators on Armed Services had a variety of motives for cutting back on opportunities to work with administrative officials out of public view and only one stimulus, polarization, to do more.

The story is somewhat similar for Foreign Relations in Figure 3.8. The coefficient for Cold War Consensus is negative and highly significant in contrast to the relationship for Armed Services. Again, we see the dramatic effect of expanded committee portfolios on the propensity of members to meet with exec-

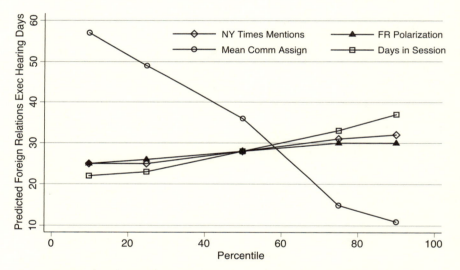

Figure 3.8. Predicted Senate Foreign Relations Committee Executive Hearing Days and Institutional Change, 1947–2008.
Note: Points are predicted values for the mean number of executive hearings per year as each independent variable increases from the 10th percentile to the 90th percentile holding other variables at their mean and Cold War constant at zero. Estimates were obtained using the Clarify procedure (Tomz, Wittenberg, and King 2003). The significant coefficients (p value = .05 or better) include New York Times Mentions, Mean Committee Assignments, and Days in Session, which appear as hollow symbols, and Cold War. The predicted lines for each variable if Cold War = 1 (1947–68) have the same slopes, but are lower because of the coefficient's negative sign, by roughly 5 to 6 predicted days for polarization, for New York Times, for Mean Committee Assignments, and for Days in Session.

utive officials behind closed doors. The length of the legislative session also has a positive and moderate impact on the predicted number of secret hearing days. Media coverage accounts for a small difference in predicted days, and unlike Armed Services, party polarization exerts little impact on the committee's propensity for meeting behind closed doors.

One final factor to consider in the frequency of executive session hearings is the level of seniority of members on the Armed Services and Foreign Relations Committees. Senior members gain experience and knowledge of a committee's business, they develop relationships with their colleagues, and they form contacts with officials in the executive branch. These characteristics may incline them to conduct more inquiries behind closed doors when they dominate their committees.

Both Armed Services and Foreign Relations have enjoyed special status within the Senate among the four "Super A" committees, signifying especially desirable jurisdictions. According to Senate rules, each senator has the privilege of membership on at least one Super A committee and is restricted from serving on more than one. In recent years, both parties have allowed senators to obtain waivers to hold seats on two Super A committees: for example, Armed Services and Appropriations or Foreign Relations and Finance. Nevertheless, a hierarchy exists within the Senate, which is defined by the patterns of transfer from one committee to another and has proved relatively stable.[18] The exception is Foreign Relations, which had been the top-ranked committee for more than a century before losing status in the mid-1970s and dropping further since 1995.[19] Indeed, today many senators shun the committee or leave quickly if they receive an assignment.

Another way of capturing the priority senators assigned to committees is the seniority ratio, a measure that takes a value below one if the committee has more junior members than would occur by chance and greater than one if the committee has more senior members.[20] In this formulation, the value of a committee depends upon senators' willingness to stay and build a career. According to Figure 3.9, Foreign Relations became much less attractive to senators according to the seniority ratio, while Armed Services remained a desirable committee for those assigned to it.

Plugging the seniority ratio into the previous models for Armed Services and Foreign Relations, the variable is a significant predictor of the frequency of

[18] Groseclose and Stewart (1998); Stewart (2012).

[19] Canon and Stewart (2002); Stewart (2012, Figure 6).

[20] Fowler and Law (2008a; 2008b). The seniority ratio is highly correlated with the index derived from transfers developed by Groseclose and Stewart (1998). It is based on yearly observations of the seniority of members on each committee, divided by the average seniority of the chamber as a whole, rather than an aggregation of transfers from multiple Congresses. Thus, it is more amenable to statistical analysis of yearly hearings. See Fowler and Law (2008a; 2008b) for detailed description of the measure's construction.

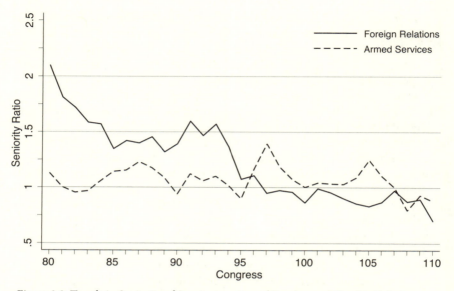

Figure 3.9. Trends in Seniority of Senators on Armed Services and Foreign Relations Committees, 1947–2008.
Source: Fowler and Law (2008a; 2008b) and updated by Law in 2009. The Seniority Ratio measures the concentration of senior members on individual committees compared to the distribution of senior members in the entire chamber.

executive sessions for both committees.[21] With Cold War Consensus set at zero and all other variables at their means, increasing the presence of senior senators on the Armed Services Committee raises the predicted number of executive hearing days from nineteen days at the 10th percentile to thirty days at the 90th percentile. In contrast, the predicted number of secret hearings drops for Foreign Relations from thirty-four predicted days to nineteen days as the committee's seniority ratio moves from the 10th to the 90th percentile. Recalling from Chapter 2 that Foreign Relations' executive sessions have been disproportionately devoted to oversight, this is a very important finding. In effect, senators who serve on the committee do not appear to be as invested in it as their peers on Armed Services.

Overall, changes in senators' expectations regarding their allocation of time, when combined with alterations in the context in which the national security committees operate, have affected the opportunities for senators to interact pri-

---

[21] I do not present the results here in the interest of saving space. The seniority ratio did not produce a significant coefficient for public hearing days for either Armed Services or Foreign Relations, and it had a negative sign for the latter committee. In effect, Foreign Relations seems to have depended on young cohorts of policy entrepreneurs to generate a public agenda.

vately with executive branch officials. Some observers might consider fewer secret meetings to be a desirable development. Yet, given the need for candid discussion and discretion in defense and foreign policy, a reduction in opportunities
for give-and-take between senators and administrators is not without cost.

The transformation of the Senate committee system has happened gradually
and without fanfare. Senators have made choices about how they allocated their
time and how they adapted their committees to changes wrought by the Cold
War, the press, and the electorate. Throughout this fitful process of evolution,
one critical moment occurred with particular consequences for the Foreign Relations, the debate and ratification of the Panama Canal Treaty in 1977–78.

The Panama Canal and the Declining Fortunes of Foreign Relations

The Senate ratification of the Panama Canal Treaty in 1979 represented a major
battle to redefine the stance of the United States toward relations with the Soviet Union and with nations grappling with postcolonial revolutionary movements. This fight sparked conflict inside both the Republican and Democratic
Parties to redefine their national reputations in foreign affairs over several decades. The dispute regarding transfer of the canal was instrumental in altering
the role of the Senate Foreign Relations Committee in important ways. First, it
cost many senior members their seats, contributing to a perception among senators that membership on Foreign Relations was not a good place from which
to cultivate advocacy groups, and embroiled members in highly visible and
contentious debates with the potential to generate primary challenges. Second,
the Panama dispute exposed the committee's failure to adapt to a new era in Senate politics. The committee followed its standard procedures, which in many
respects constituted a model of due process and deliberation in treaty making,
but at the eleventh hour Foreign Relations was rolled by a junior senator who
was not even a member. For a time, the committee continued to pursue an active agenda under the new Republican majority elected in 1981, but it was unable to recover its old luster.

Relations between the United States and Panama have been troubled since
Panamanians obtained independence from Spain in 1821. U.S. troops landed
periodically in Panama in the nineteenth century to restore order, and U.S.
treaty rights obtained in 1903 permitted Americans to defend the canal from
attack, to control the Canal Zone and its residents, and to retain its lease "in
perpetuity," provisions that were a source of continuous and profound resent-
ment in the country. The U.S. presence in Panama was a symbol, as well,
throughout Latin America of America's neglect of the interests of its southern
neighbors, its episodic interventions on the side of powerful economic organizations, and its support of authoritarian regimes.

Several presidents attempted to change the relationship with Panama as a means of addressing larger tensions in the region. The Eisenhower administration negotiated a treaty, ratified in 1955, that made modest changes, and the Johnson administration began negotiations to abrogate the treaty and replace it with a new approach. President Nixon also pursued changes to the status of the canal until his resignation.

Once President Carter took office, he completed the negotiations. Amid rumors roiling Capitol Hill, two treaties were signed by both nations on September 7, 1977, and immediately submitted to the Senate. Senators ratified the first treaty in March 1978 and the second in April 1978, both by a vote of 68–32. Together, they granted Panama sovereignty over its territory, gave the United States the right to manage and defend the canal until December 31, 1999, replaced the Panama Canal Company with the Panama Canal Commission, which included both U.S. and Panamanian members, and transferred all Canal Zone installations and equipment on January 1, 2000, to Panama without cost.

When the final version arrived in the Senate, senators on Foreign Relations found themselves in the middle of a firestorm for which their conversations in executive sessions had left them poorly prepared. The House had been agitating about the treaty for several years, including highly symbolic legislation prohibiting the use of State Department funds to fly the Panamanian flag in the Canal Zone. Although lacking a formal role in the ratification process, House members claimed authority over the disposition of U.S. property.

More important, conservatives in the GOP, long restive with the efforts of Nixon and Kissinger to establish détente with the Soviet Union and normalize relations with China, advocated a more confrontational approach to communist regimes and a more assertive U.S. foreign policy in the world, generally. They viewed the fight over Panama as a "dress rehearsal" for the larger battle over the proposed SALT Treaty, and an "excellent opportunity to seize control of the Republican Party."[22] Two right-wing lobbies formed to "save" the Panama Canal, and these groups deployed a "Truth Squad" of prominent Republican senators to challenge the treaty. In addition, Ronald Reagan delivered a half-hour televised address opposing the treaties in the winter of 1978.[23] Not all conservatives joined in, however, as Senator Barry Goldwater (R-AZ) predicted violence in Latin America if the treaty failed.[24] Moving forward with the treaty, the prominent conservative contended, would demonstrate that "the United States was serious about promoting democracy and anti-imperialism."[25]

On the other side of the aisle, the canal assumed a different meaning. For many Democrats, negotiations with Panama presented the opportunity for the

---

[22] Zelizer (2010, 279).
[23] Zelizer (2010, 279).
[24] Farnsworth and McKenney (1983, 175).
[25] Zelizer (2010, 279).

United States to repair its international reputation after Vietnam and forge a more constructive partnership with its neighbors in Central and Latin America. Foreign policy realists within the party were skeptical about the security implications of conveying the canal to a state with a long history of political instability and corruption, and Carter initially had sided with them. Indeed, he had fended off Senator "Scoop" Jackson (D-WA) and other hawks within his party during the 1976 primary by vowing that the United States would "never give up complete control."[26] He made the calculation once in office that suspending treaty negotiations would fuel left-wing movements in the region and bring even greater political instability.

The Foreign Relations Committee's actions appeared to be a model of senatorial advice and consent, according to knowledgeable observers at the time, in which "deliberations were prolonged, thorough and in the end extremely influential."[27] Its procedures, in fact, were a sterling example of regular order in carrying out its responsibilities. The committee scheduled eleven days of public sessions and one day in executive session during the months of September and October 1977, which brought the secretaries of state and defense to the witness table, along with various assistant secretaries, ambassadors, cabinet members, and top-ranking military officers. Other sessions included former Secretaries of State Dean Rusk and Henry Kissinger, retired military brass, scholars, and numerous citizen advocates.

Signs of the high political stakes involved permeated the two days of hearings in which members of Congress testified. Among the eight senators and six representatives who appeared were the chairs of relevant committees, but the witness list also included Reagan allies, Senators Paul Laxalt (R-NV), Jesse Helms (R-NC), and Strom Thurmond (R-SC), who conveyed vehement conservative opposition to the treaties. Senator Robert Dole, who had been President Ford's running mate in 1976 and who planned to run for the GOP presidential nomination in 1980, also expressed strong views opposing the treaty and subsequently voted against it.

The fall hearings aroused those foreign policy elites and citizens who disapproved of giving up the canal. In May 1977, before the treaty's signing, two-thirds of Americans had heard little or nothing about negotiations regarding the treaty, but by February 1978 fully 81 percent had read or heard something about it.[28] At the height of the debate, a slight majority in one survey supported keeping the existing treaty and in another survey opposed the transfer of sovereignty.

---

[26] Farnsworth and McKenney (1983, 154, 185).

[27] Crabb and Holt (1992, 278).

[28] http://webapps.ropercenter.uconn.edu/CFIDE/cf/action/ipoll/iPollResult.cfm?keyword =panama+canal+treaty&keywordoptions=1&exclude=&excludeoptions=1&topic=Any&organi zation=Any&fromdate=1%2F1%2F1977&todate=12%2F31%2F1978&sortby=DESC&label= &studyId=&questionViewIdB=&resultsCurrentPage=1&paging=true&historyID=2150111&key wordDisplay=panama+and+canal+and+treaty&x=7&y=5 (accessed June 15, 2011).

Nevertheless, more than 60 percent of respondents favored giving the canal back *if* the United States retained the right to defend it and to use it for warships in times of emergency.

As the controversy grew, new voices emerged. The Foreign Relations Committee scheduled an additional six days of public hearings and, in the winter of 1978, one executive session, where a long list of academics, foreign policy think tank professionals, and business and labor groups appeared. Senator Majority Leader Robert Byrd (D-WV), several Republican House members, and a handful of former public officials offered further testimony. Meanwhile, the Senate Armed Services Committee, which had not participated in oversight of the decades-long treaty process, scheduled three days of public hearings in late January and early February 1978. The senators gave the military's top brass and several retired generals opportunity to voice concerns about defense of the canal in a time of emergency.

Behind the scenes, the Carter administration engaged in intense persuasion efforts, but fell short of the necessary two-thirds majority in an informal Senate vote tally. Eventually, the president agreed to a reservation to the treaty demanded by Senator DeConcini (D-AZ) that authorized the use of U.S. troops to prevent obstruction of passage through the canal.

In hindsight, the members of the Foreign Relations Committee did a poor job educating congressional colleagues and citizens. As the canal issue rose and fell at various times on the agenda from the 1950s to the mid-1970s, the committee failed to prepare lawmakers and the public for what was coming, choosing instead to deliberate behind closed doors. Perhaps this approach facilitated statesmanlike give-and-take, but it allowed opponents to frame the issue in a way that was detrimental to the ratification process.

Once the dispute escalated, the committee failed to develop compromise language to win over the fence-sitters and provide political cover for senators who supported the treaty. Senators frequently adopt reservations to treaties, especially in matters of "high politics,"[29] and presidents often anticipate opposition from senators by including conciliatory provisions in the final version of a treaty or pre-clearing it with potential opponents. There is no evidence that the Senate Foreign Relations Committee used its secret sessions to work out such a compromise as it had done in the 1947 debate over aid to Greece and Turkey. The committee did not appear to make demands on the White House during the negotiation phase for modified language; nor did it use testimony of witnesses to suggest a means for addressing concerns about defending the canal. Instead, the reservation provision that the Senate eventually adopted was negotiated publicly at the eleventh hour between the administration and a ju-

[29] Auerswald and Maltzman (2003).

nior senator, who was not a member of the committee.[30] In effect, the committee suffered a major embarrassment, even though the treaty ultimately passed.

Perhaps the unusual level of bipartisan consensus within the committee at the time blinded members to the pitfalls ahead as they met secretly with officials from the Nixon and Carter administrations. Recall from Figure 3.1, after all, that the 90th to the 95th Congress was a period of unusual cohesiveness within Foreign Relations compared to the Senate as a whole. Perhaps the prestige of the committee, which had already begun to wane, was insufficient to move the White House and its determined opponents. Whatever the reason, the fight over Panama exposed the vulnerabilities of service on the committee and set the stage for its increasing marginalization. Noted one historian, the canal marked the end of efforts by Senate liberals "to use congressional power to remake American foreign policy" after Vietnam.[31]

The canal debate was part of a larger movement in bringing ideological leanings on foreign affairs into line with predispositions on domestic affairs.[32] The issue figured prominently in the next two election cycles, as conservatives mobilized aggressively to challenge Republicans in primaries and attack Democrats in general elections. The GOP picked up only three seats in 1978, leaving Democrats to continue in the majority with a comfortable fifty-eight-seat margin. Yet Zelizer concluded that "of the 20 senators who voted for the treaty and had to face the voters afterward, six decided to retire, and seven ran and lost."[33] The 1980 Republican sweep, in which Democrats lost twelve seats and control of the Senate, received a big boost from the canal issue as part of a larger GOP narrative promoting a more assertive U.S. foreign policy agenda. Three prominent liberals on Foreign Relations, George McGovern (D-SD), Frank Church (D-ID), and Jacob Javits (R-NY), went down to defeat. When the dust settled after a series of elections, the internationalist, cross-party alliance within the Senate Foreign Relations Committee was severely damaged. During this period of party realignment on national security, members of Armed Services generally avoided the electoral slaughter.

Over the long run, the Panama Canal Treaty marked a turning point for the Foreign Relations Committee. Democratic senators remaining on the committee grew increasingly homogeneous at the liberal end of the ideological spectrum, while Republicans who joined it were outspoken conservatives or junior members eager to transfer off the committee. By 1984, the departure of Senator Howard Baker (R-TN), the "great conciliator" and skillful majority leader

---

[30] Parenthetically, the fact that adoption of reservations is the price for obtaining Senate approval suggests that lawmakers exercise greater influence over treaty making than a simple count of presidential success rates indicates (Auerswald and Maltzman 2003).

[31] Johnson (2006, 241).

[32] McCormick and Black (1983).

[33] Zelizer (2010, 284).

(1981–85), and the electoral defeat of Senator Percy (R-IL) left Foreign Relations with few Republicans inclined toward bipartisan compromise. Indeed, Senator Richard Lugar (R-IN), who later became a respected chair of the committee, was appointed to Foreign Relations in 1979, seemingly as a reward for his negative vote against the Canal Treaty.

The marginalization of Foreign Relations reduced its attractiveness to senior lawmakers. From 1991 through 2002, twelve Republican and five Democratic senators who received initial assignments to Foreign Relations transferred off the committee. The departure of Senator Judd Gregg, a New Hampshire Republican, epitomized the declining fortunes of Foreign Relations. A former House member and governor elected to the Senate in 1992, Gregg was a moderate conservative with internationalist leanings and a reputation as a rising star in the Senate. He had a resume similar to that of past Republicans who had served on the committee, but he left after two years of service.[34]

When Republicans took control of the Senate in 1995, the firebrand conservative Jesse Helms became Foreign Relations chair. At the time, five GOP freshman senators received appointments to the committee, and by the end of their first term, all had left. Over the last two decades of the study, only one senior Republican senator transferred onto the committee, ultraconservative James Inhofe (R-ID), while some of the GOP's most promising newcomers, such as Bill Frist (R-TN), Lamar Alexander (R-TN), and Olympia Snowe (R-ME), departed as quickly as they could.[35]

The Democratic representation on Foreign Relations differed significantly. A number of senior lawmakers stayed with the committee, and several senators with presidential aspirations, such as John Kerry (D-MA), Joe Biden (D-DE), and Barack Obama (D-IL), used the committee to burnish their foreign policy credentials. The Democratic membership became increasingly unrepresentative of the Senate as a whole, however, with a heavy bias toward the Northeast.

The turnover was a source of several problems for Foreign Relations. Fewer senators had the length of service to acquire expertise or develop back-channel contacts within the State Department or the White House. In addition, the frequent need to fill vacant seats made it difficult for the parties to exclude irre-

---

[34] Bob Hohler, "NH Freshman Gregg Named to Senate GOP Inner Circle," *Boston Globe*, December 7, 1994, http://www.whorunsgov.com/Profiles/Judd_Gregg (accessed December 10, 2010). Tim Weiner, "GOP Senator Frees Millions for U.N. Mission to Sierra Leone," *New York Times*, June 7, 2000, http://www.nytimes.com/2000/06/07/world/gop-senator-frees-millions-for-un-mission-in -sierra-leone.html (accessed December 10, 2010); "History of the Committee," http://www.foreign .senate.gov/about/history/ (accessed January 28, 2013).

[35] In 2012, Richard Lugar (R-IN), the Republican member with the most committee seniority, lost a bruising primary battle to a candidate backed by the Tea Party. The next most senior senator, Bob Corker (R-TN), was elected to the Senate in 2006 and served previously as mayor of Chattanooga. In the 112th Congress, several of the Senate's most conservative Republicans, such as Jim DeMint (R-SC), held seats on the committee, and no Republican senators from the Northeast, Mid-Atlantic, or West Coast had become members.

sponsible or ideologically extreme members from Foreign Relations or restore geographical balance, even if they had wanted to. Finally, the diminished participation in executive sessions, fueled in part by the loss of senior members, reduced Foreign Relations' information-gathering capacity and its informal interactions with the executive branch. A committee so unrepresentative of the full Senate and so susceptible to extreme partisanship that evolved after Panama became increasingly ill equipped to foster regular order in U.S. foreign policy.

CONCLUSION

The hearing activity of Senate committees in the aggregate fell significantly after the mid-1980s. Senators' changing expectations about their careers shifted attention away from policy specialization to coverage of more issue domains and heightened their inclinations to spend time away from Washington. The trends toward more assignments and shorter sessions, as well as the end of the Cold War Consensus, affected the chamber and the national security committees in roughly similar ways, with Foreign Relations' use of executive sessions the exception. Other long-term trends affected the Senate's national security committees, specifically. Armed Services managed party polarization by stepping up its executive session hearing days. Foreign Relations reduced its workload dramatically as its national visibility declined. In addition, Foreign Relations' inability to retain senior members had a negative impact on its frequency of executive session hearing days.

The cumulative effect of so much institutional change compromised the watchdog function of the Senate's national security committees in several ways. Fewer hearing days limited opportunities for Armed Services and Foreign Relations to engage with the executive branch, to hold the president accountable, and to educate citizens regarding defense and foreign policy decisions. By the 1990s, administration officials surely figured out that the chances of being called to testify had diminished and that it had gotten easier to stonewall without fear of being called back for additional days of questioning. Moreover, reporters and citizens had fewer opportunities to learn which topics required serious attention. Finally, the reduction in executive sessions meant that informal discussion between committee members and executive branch officials became increasingly rare.

CHAPTER 4

Committee Goals and Oversight Strategies

A MONTH AFTER LOSING HIS BID for reelection, President George H. W. Bush announced on December 4, 1992, that the United States would participate in peacekeeping operations in Somalia. Members of Congress had pushed hard for greater involvement in the chaotic East African nation, and lawmakers in both parties endorsed the Republican administration's efforts. Ten months later, eighteen elite American troops perished trying to capture a Somali warlord, an effort subsequently immortalized in the film *Black Hawk Down*. The tragic incident, in which the body of a soldier was dragged through the streets of Mogadishu, prompted a furious bipartisan response on Capitol Hill as lawmakers moved to force President Bill Clinton to withdraw U.S. troops from the area. The course of events in Somalia triggered multiple types of inquiries by the Senate Armed Services and Foreign Relations Committees, ranging from agenda setting, to implementation, to crisis. The larger patterns of oversight at work in the two committees thus were in full view as they pursued their disparate objectives.

Two aspects of the Somalia case point to the importance of member goals as drivers of committee oversight. First, both Armed Services and Foreign Relations devoted disproportionate attention to an obscure part of the world with minimal strategic importance to the United States. Second, the committees pursued their agendas seemingly without regard for unified or divided party control of the Senate and White House. President Bush, who faced a Democratic majority throughout his term, confronted substantial public pressure from members of his own party on the Foreign Relations Committee, as well as from Democrats, to engage the United States in humanitarian relief in the strife-torn nation. With Bill Clinton in the White House and the troops on the ground, the Democratic majority on Armed Services undertook multiple hearings throughout the spring and summer. Even before the Black Hawk tragedy, Armed Services and Foreign Relations began to use oversight hearings to challenge President Clinton's decision to enlarge the operation to nation building.

On both counts, the committees appear to have pursued their own goals rather than acted as agents of either party. Though wary of deploying American troops in an area with little strategic value to the United States, Armed Services was open to new missions for the Defense Department that would prevent drastic cuts in the defense budget following the collapse of the Soviet Union in 1991. After the operation shifted from guarding aid shipments to hunting down Somali militias, however, the committee adopted a protective stance toward the military that put it in direct conflict with civilian leaders in the Pentagon and White House. Foreign Relations advocated humanitarian action as a new means of asserting U.S. influence and keeping the American public engaged with the world once the Cold War had ended, but the committee quickly joined with Armed Services to demand a change of course after Clinton raised the stakes of intervention and popular sentiment shifted. Democrats on both committees, rather than shield their recently inaugurated president from congressional criticism, collaborated with their Republican colleagues in delivering a considerable blow to the administration.

In some respects, the Senate Armed Services and Foreign Relations Committees appear to have promoted the rule of law with respect to U.S. policy in Somalia. The necessary elements were all present: repeated interaction with executive branch officials, open deliberation about options, sustained attention to the outcome, and eventual assertion of congressional authority. Upon closer examination, however, neither committee put much on the line. Their disproportionate attention to a country notable for its geopolitical insignificance posed little threat to White House claims of executive prerogative. In addition, the public, while initially supportive, quickly soured on the president's changes in the mission. The committees incurred few risks, therefore, from challenging the president, first to undertake a humanitarian mission and then to end it. Overall, the Somalia case appears consistent with long-standing patterns of Armed Services and Foreign Relations to use oversight strategically to promote their respective interests of supporting the Pentagon and fostering public debate about foreign affairs.

In this chapter, I consider why divided government was not a consistent motivator for national security oversight and demonstrate how indicators of long-term committee goals influenced both committees' stance toward the executive branch. I argue that Armed Services muted partisan conflict and deemphasized oversight in order to attend to funding the Pentagon. The committee's concern with the welfare of the military stimulated oversight, however, when the president engaged in a major deployment of force. In contrast, Foreign Relations proved highly susceptible to partisan calculation because of its proclivity for debate and its authority over foreign aid. The committee was a more active overseer of foreign affairs during periods of divided government, although its actions also were conditional on the size of the international affairs budget. Moreover, Foreign Relations increased the number of public days per individual hearing when divided government prevailed. The differences between Armed Services and Foreign Relations reveal how selection biases built into the committee assignment process affected the rule of law in national security and shed light on the inconsistent findings in the scholarly literature with respect to divided government.

I apply three different lenses to the national security committees' propensity for oversight in order to assess their behavior. I begin with the committees' annual count of all types of oversight hearings to assess the effects of divided government in comparison to goal-related environmental factors. In particular, I evaluate the impact of the departmental budgets under each committee's jurisdiction and the major uses of force initiated by the president. I find that these contextual factors exerted greater influence than party rivalry on the frequency of Armed Services oversight, but divided government and environmental influences played equally important roles in Foreign Relations' oversight activity.

I unpack these findings by shifting to analysis of individual hearings to compare the allocation of committee attention to oversight and budget hearings. First, I assess the probability that an individual committee hearing was about oversight or about budget authorization. The results reveal that Armed Services' likelihood that a hearing addressed budgetary matters greatly exceeded the probability of an oversight inquiry, unless the president initiated a major use of force. Foreign Relations, in contrast, had a much higher probability that a hearing would be about oversight. Divided government did not affect the probability of either type of Armed Services or Foreign Relations hearing, however. Second, I evaluate the depth of committee inquiry by analyzing the number of days each devoted to an individual oversight or budget topic. Again, Armed Services' orientation toward expenditures became visible in the greater average length of a public budget hearing compared to a public oversight hearing. Foreign Relations, while conducting far fewer budget hearing days, tended to spend more time on those it scheduled compared to its oversight inquiries. Throughout, I evaluate the transparency of each committee's efforts by comparing open and closed oversight sessions.

In the post–World War II period from 1947 to 2008, the Senate Armed Services and Foreign Relations Committees engaged in oversight when it suited their purposes and responded to external influences in ways that furthered their predominant goals. Despite the backdrop of widespread institutional change in the Senate over six decades, the long-standing norm of assigning senators to their preferred committees generated stable, distinctive identities that defined the national security committees' approach to oversight. The operating rules illustrated in this chapter entail consequences for regular order in war and diplomacy, as well as the way scholars approach congressional inquiries more generally.

Expectations about Member Goals and Committee Oversight

Scholarly research on the motivations behind congressional oversight is full of contradictions, as noted in Chapter 1. One particularly knotty puzzle arises from the conflicting empirical results regarding the role of divided government. Rival interpretations have arisen in part from the fact that some studies looked at all types of oversight inquiries, while others focused solely on investigations. An additional source of ambiguity emerged from the practice, common among researchers, of aggregating oversight hearings across committees, as if each was an agent of the majority party and all faced the same incentives. If we accept the idea that committees have distinctive identities brought about by self-selection among senators, then we need to look to external factors beyond party control that shape their propensity for oversight.[1] In particular, we must examine the environment in which committees operated and the strategic premises they adopted for managing the interaction between member goals and outside influences. For a committee like Armed Services, oversight was a lower priority compared to its objectives of funding the Pentagon unless force was involved; for one like Foreign Relations, oversight fit well with its proclivity for policy debate subject to budgetary priorities. Whether divided government acted as a stimulus to committee oversight thus depended upon these broader concerns.

Divided Government

Contemporary scholars have applied a party lens to congressional behavior since the 1990s, when roll call voting became highly partisan and new theories emerged to reconcile the tensions between lawmakers' desire for political autonomy and their need for coordination and collective identity. Some analyses of oversight activity have confirmed the presence of party effects, while others have disputed the influence of divided and unified government. Aberbach, for example, reported a positive statistical relationship between the frequency of congressional oversight and divided control of Congress and the presidency.[2] With respect to investigations, Mayhew observed that major probes did not increase during divided government in the years 1946 to 1990, although he found signs in the 1990s that scandal inquiries were more likely when the president faced an opposing majority.[3] Extending Mayhew's data, Kriner and Schwartz uncovered evidence of the impact of divided government on congressional probes, while Parker and Dull developed different means of identifying investigations and reported that the influence of divided government was contingent on a variety of institutional factors.[4] Finally, Kriner and Schickler found that divided government varied as an impetus for investigations at different periods in congressional history between 1898 and 2006 and was more influential on inquiries in the House than in the Senate.[5]

---

[1] Fenno (1973).

[2] Aberbach (1990; 2002).

[3] Mayhew (1991; 2006). Fewer large-scale investigations occurred overall, however, in the later period.

[4] Kriner and Schwartz (2008); Parker and Dull (2009).

[5] Kriner and Schickler (2012) found that different types of party systems were important to how much impact divided government exerted on congressional investigations.

Recent research has taken committee characteristics into account in developing a link between divided government and oversight. McGrath, for example, grouped oversight hearings by committee to focus on the ideological divergence between the position of the median legislator on each committee and the president's ideological orientation. In his analysis, divided government was not a significant predictor of the number of committee oversight hearings, although the interaction between divided government and ideological distance produced a significant coefficient.[6] Parker and Dull continued to focus solely on investigations, while classifying committees according to the following typology: cartel, distributive, informational, and miscellaneous.[7] These authors demonstrated that divided government led to more and longer investigations by committees defined as cartels, while it had no impact on investigations by distributive committees. Both approaches fit with Fenno's assertion that committees differ systematically.[8]

Close examination of the Senate's national security committees demonstrates how different committee goals produced disparate patterns of oversight activity in response to external factors from 1947 to 2008. Armed Services, as noted in Chapter 2, focused on delivering economic benefits to organized constituencies and promoting public support for the Pentagon. The committee frequently engaged in advocacy oversight, battled the White House over the nation's defense posture, and engaged in struggles with other committees over the allocation of federal resources between guns and butter. To promote its spending priorities, therefore, Armed Services depended upon an outward appearance of bipartisan cooperation. The committee's optimal strategy under divided and unified government, thus, was to dampen conflict among its members and focus on budget authorizations rather than oversight.

In contrast, Foreign Relations defined itself as a policy committee. Under divided government, the committee pursued opportunities to accentuate partisan differences, to promote elite discourse about policy options, and to debate the merits of expenditures on diplomacy, international cooperation, and aid. In this respect, Foreign Relations' behavior was consistent with other behavior in the Senate in which party influence was present despite the lack of mechanisms to impose it.[9]

---

[6] McGrath (2013). McGrath derived his counts of oversight from the Policy Agendas Project, which does not provide a separate code for oversight. His approach differs from those of Parker and Dull and of Kriner and Schickler in two ways. First, he used search parameters of the hearing description listed in the Policy Agendas data set, rather than the full hearing abstract. He also seems to have included budget hearings.

[7] Parker and Dull (2012) base their distinctions on two factors: whether committees provided uniform, narrowly targeted, or mixed benefits; and how much distance occurred between the ideology score of the committee median and the party or chamber median.

[8] Fenno (1973).

[9] Smith (2007); Den Hartog and Monroe (2011).

To provide a feel for how divided government operated on the national security committees, Figure 4.1 plots the frequency of public oversight hearing days for the Senate Armed Services and Foreign Relations Committees against the total number of hearing days for each committee.[10] The patterns highlight how both Armed Services and Foreign Relations engaged in more oversight when senators devoted greater attention to committees business. Particularly striking, however, is the contrast between the two committees in the distribution of public hearings according to divided and unified party control of the Senate represented by hollow circles for divided government and black Xs for unified government.

As a general rule, Armed Services, as shown in the top panel, did not spend a large amount of time on public oversight, with a few notable exceptions. The frequencies clustered around twenty oversight hearing days per year, with slightly higher rates when the committee was at its highest level of activity. The two outliers of over sixty days per year occurred when Armed Services conducted an exceptional amount of hearings and oversight as President Truman initiated the Korean War with a Democratic majority in the Senate. The highest incidents of Armed Services oversight under divided government took place in 1947, 1956, 1987, and 1989 and generated more than thirty-five public hearing days. Nevertheless, the graph confirms expectations that the committee was not motivated to engage in public oversight as a result of partisan rivalries.

In contrast, Foreign Relations devoted considerable time to public oversight activity. The frequencies clustered at or above thirty oversight hearings per year, and the four highest cases of nearly sixty or more hearing days were all under divided government, 1975, 1976, 1991, and 2000. Moreover, one can detect an upward slope in the trajectory of circles when the committee was more engaged with hearings. During unified control of the Senate and White House, the three years in which public oversight exceeded fifty days were 1982, 2003, and 2004. Notably, the latter two years occurred at the beginning of the Iraq War, a time when the national security committees were perceived as having "checked out." The seeming anomaly resulted from the committee's penchant for state of the world reviews, however, rather than scrutiny of the Iraq conflict.

Environmental Factors

Given the stability of their identities, the environmental factors shaping each committee's activity undoubtedly persisted over a long period. To account for their strategies with respect to oversight, then, the goal-related environmental

[10] Recall from Chapter 3 that total hearing activity declined for both national security committees during the 1990s, as senators altered their career expectations. This variable serves as a control for all the statistical analyses in the chapter to avoid incorrect inferences about the source of variation in oversight activity.

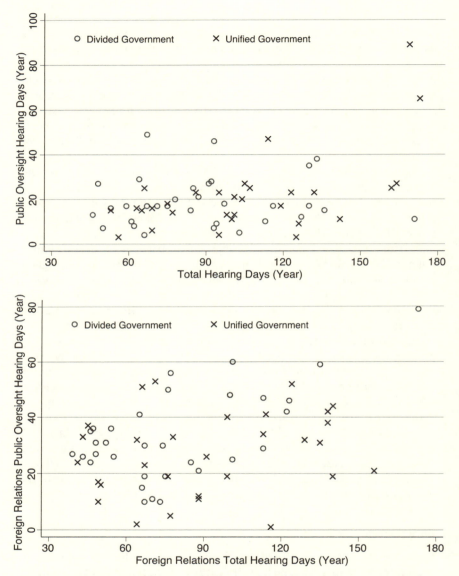

Figure 4.1. Committee Public Oversight Hearing Days, by Divided Government and Total Hearing Days (Year). Top: Armed Services; bottom: Foreign Relations.

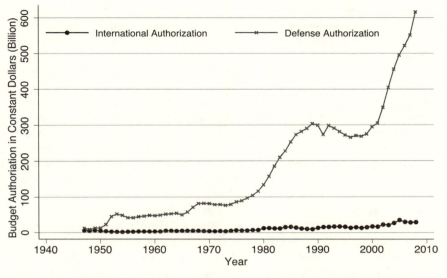

Figure 4.2. Budgets for Defense and International Affairs, 1947–2008 (in Constant 2009 Dollars).
Source: http://www.whitehouse.gov/omb/budget/Historicals, Table 3.1 (accessed June 2009).

measures should directly relate to the committees' operating premises and extend throughout the sixty-two-year period of the study. In addition, the indicators should differentiate between the behavior of Armed Services and Foreign Relations and vary sufficiently to explain changes in the frequency of oversight hearings. Two variables meet these criteria: (1) budget authorizations for defense or foreign policy and (2) initiation of major use of force by the president.

The funds authorized for defense and international affairs reflect investment in a variety of programs to promote national security. While important in their own right, the dollar amounts also represent the relative weight elected officials assigned to military might and diplomacy in implementing U.S. strategy since 1947. Figure 4.2 indicates that in the early days of the Cold War, the imbalance between defense spending and international programs, which we take for granted today, was considerably less.[11]

---

[11] I considered the possibility that the committees would be more attuned to the percentage of the total federal budget allocated to their respective programs or that they would respond to year-to-year changes in program authorizations. For Armed Services, there was some evidence that the committee increased oversight when the percentage of funds for defense declined. For Foreign Relations, there was so little variation in alternative measures that they were useless as predictors. In the interests of consistency, I opted to use the size of the budget authorization in constant dollars.

Obviously, senators who sought assignments to Armed Services followed the money, but the relationships between expenditures and oversight proved complex. As expenditures grew, we might expect the committee to have increased oversight activity to ensure that the Pentagon directed funds to members' intended targets. Expanded programs, however, put pressure on the committee calendar to ensure sufficient attention to budget hearings by incorporating oversight activity into the fiscal year authorization process.[12] A related constraint imposed by Armed Services' preoccupation with defense expenditures was the budget process itself, which demanded the committee's attention in the first and second quarters to deal with the president's January budget requests in time for the Appropriations Committee to allocate the necessary funds and get its bills through the Senate. Both the committee's proclivities and the constraints of its calendar thus suggest a relatively weak relationship between the size of the defense budget and the frequency of oversight hearings.

The opposite dynamic was at work in Foreign Relations, however. In the early years of the Cold War, expenditures on statecraft were nearly 20 percent of the total federal budget because of the Marshall Plan. When federal resources for diplomacy and aid were comparatively high, Foreign Relations had reason to engage in public oversight to educate citizens and elites about the importance of nonmilitary options in achieving the nation's security objectives. Over time, the huge disparity in authorizations for Defense and State highlighted in Figure 4.2 signaled the extent to which diplomacy lost out to force after the end of the Vietnam conflict. Low expenditures depressed committee budget hearings, however, exemplified in the poignant photograph of Senator Claiborne Pell (D-RI), chair of Foreign Relations from 1987 to 1994, which showed him presiding over an empty hearing room and lamenting the "profound lack of interest" among senators to consider the $4.5 billion dollar authorization bill for FY 1990–91.[13]

Nevertheless, foreign aid and international organizations constituted one of the more controversial items in the federal budget and symbolized larger divisions between the parties regarding America's emphasis on unilateral versus multilateral action abroad. Although committee members were unwilling to devote much attention to items in the budget authorization, they were attuned to seemingly modest program changes and what the nation achieved from the investment. Moreover, the committee's diminished interest in budget authorization freed up time for oversight activity. As federal dollars stimulated debates about diplomacy and aid, then, even small increases likely promoted Foreign Relations' oversight hearings.

A major function of oversight is to hold the president accountable for national security decisions. The use of force, therefore, was a probable impetus for committee action. Howell and Pevehouse showed that a president's initiation of major military engagements was conditional on having a favorable majority

---

[12] Deering (2005).
[13] "Another Day, No Quorum," CQ Weekly, June 3, 1989, 1338.

in Congress, and Kriner established that the duration of significant hostilities depended upon the size of the president's party coalition in the legislative branch.[14] In effect, these authors demonstrated that presidents acted *as if* they were less constrained by fear of congressional backlash when fellow partisans controlled House and Senate committees.

The response of the national security committees to the president's decisions did not necessarily depend on party strength, however. Armed Services members' hawkish policy preferences led to frequent support of the use of force, but they also triggered concerns about the interests of the military and the welfare of uniformed personnel. Consequently, the committee often aligned with military commanders rather than their civilian bosses and endeavored to ensure that troop deployments received public backing and adequate resources. Both concerns invited Armed Services oversight, irrespective of party rivalries, once the president launched a major commitment of U.S. forces.[15] The Foreign Relations Committee did not need the additional impetus of a major commitment of U.S. forces to spark its already strong inclination for oversight and its sensitivity to party control of the White House. Thus, the president could not assume that the size of his party's majority would insulate his administration from scrutiny by Armed Services, while he could expect partisan incentives to influence inquiries by Foreign Relations.[16]

Control Variables

Several factors were potential influences on the overall climate in which the national security committees operated. For example, national visibility, measured as the frequency of mentions of Armed Services or Foreign Relations in the *New York Times*, declined steadily from 1947 to 2008. Although media coverage was not a major determinant of Armed Services' overall workload, as we saw in Chapter 3, the committee's strong inclination to maintain public support for the Pentagon may have led to greater oversight during periods of greater media visibility. Foreign Relations, as we learned in Chapter 3, reduced

[14] Howell and Pevehouse (2007); Kriner (2010).

[15] There were twenty principal uses of force in the Howell-Pevehouse (2007) data set as modified by Kriner (2010). I altered their measure in the following way: I coded the variable as 1 if the action coincided with the date of the hearing for as long as it continued, and 0 otherwise. The chief difference is that I coded major conflicts, such as Korea, Vietnam, Desert Storm, Iraq, and Afghanistan, as a major engagement throughout their duration rather than their initiation date. Such military exercises did not necessarily involve casualties, for example, the Berlin Airlift or the deployment of aircraft carriers to the Strait of Hormuz, although they frequently involved the risk of escalation. In the next chapter, I look specifically at casualties. Appendix D contains alternative versions of the force variable that I considered.

[16] A possible influence on the frequency of total oversight activity is the ideological distance between the national security committees and the president. Although McGrath (2013) obtained leverage in explaining variation in aggregate committee oversight using ideological difference interacted with divided government as an independent variable, I did not find the measure useful.

its overall hearing effort dramatically when reporters diminished their attention to committee activity. Its effects, therefore, are likely captured already by controlling for the total number of days the committee spent on hearings.

Some scholars who study oversight include presidential approval ratings in their analyses on the grounds that committees would be less inclined to challenge popular presidents. The empirical results have been mixed, however. In Parker and Dull's model of investigations, public approval was not a significant variable, but in a paper about scandal inquiries by Kriner and Schickler, fewer investigations by committees in the aggregate occurred when the president's popularity rose.[17] With respect to the national security committees, approval affected the climate in which they decided how much oversight to conduct, although neither committee depended directly on the president's national standing in the polls to achieve its goals.

The institutional changes in the Senate that reduced members' investment in committee business directly affected the frequency of oversight, as demonstrated in Figure 4.1. The compression of committee agendas reduced opportunities for hearings about oversight and budgets, irrespective of goal-related factors. Failure to control for this constraint would lead to incorrect inferences about the influence of the key explanatory variables.

Calendar Effects

The congressional calendar imposes constraints on how much oversight committees can schedule. The two committees typically undertook budgetary hearings upon receipt of the president's budget in January with the intent of having program priorities in place for the April budget resolution and finalized in time for the Appropriations Committees to act by the start of the fiscal year. An important but subtle limitation arose from the rhythm of the authorization and appropriations process itself.

In recent Congresses, lawmakers have failed to adhere to this timetable and have resorted to a variety of gimmicks to fund governmental activities. Armed Services, however, has followed a consistent routine of budget authorization hearings from January to April or early May throughout the entire study period. Since 1985, Foreign Relations has frequently failed to submit a fiscal year authorization bill. However, it has a long tradition of beginning a new session or Congress with state of the world hearings and administration testimony about its foreign policy agenda. As a result, Armed Services had limited time to devote to oversight until the third and fourth quarters, while Foreign Relations was able to engage in oversight throughout the year.

In addition, election years and early adjournments frequently cut into the schedules of both committees, particularly in the fourth quarter of a session.

---

[17] Parker and Dull (2012); Kriner and Schickler (2014).

The result is a large number of quarters, especially between October and December, in which no oversight took place in one or both committees. In the statistical models, therefore, it is important to account for pronounced quarterly effects on the committees' oversight activity, particularly for Armed Services. Although I am not interested in the substantive influence of quarterly effects, I need to control statistically for the fact that unobserved features of the legislative calendar influence the relationship between one or more of the explanatory variables and the frequency of oversight. Further discussion of this issue is in Appendix D.

Public and Executive Sessions

Both Armed Services and Foreign Relations devoted a considerable portion of their hearing agendas to executive sessions. As we learned in previous chapters, the frequency of meetings behind closed doors declined noticeably after 1990, although the proportion of secret hearings devoted to oversight increased. Secrecy is an unavoidable facet of national security, but it also has the potential to serve the member goals of the individual committees. Public hearings created opportunities for Armed Services to promote military expenditure, while executive sessions offered an arena for dealing with contentious issues that otherwise would disrupt public support for the military. Open meetings were made to order for Foreign Relations' policy debates, while closed hearings did little to promote the committee's dominant goal.

In summary, both national security committees had incentives to respond to external stimuli over the sixty-two years of the study. Their differing motivations likely led to distinctive responses beyond divided government to include budget priorities and the president's use of major force. Table 4.1 summarizes the expectations with respect to environmental factors and their relationship to each committee's oversight activity.

Table 4.1. Expectations for Public and Executive Total Oversight Hearing Days

Type of Influence	Armed Services	Foreign Relations
Public Hearings		
Divided Government	No effect	Increase
Federal Budget (billions)	No effect	Increase
Major Use of Force	Increase	No effect
Executive Sessions		
Divided Government	No effect	Decrease
Federal Budget (billions)	No effect	Decrease
Major Use of Force	Increase	No effect

COMMITTEE DIFFERENCE AND NATIONAL SECURITY OVERSIGHT

Sixty-two years of national security oversight reflected the disparate approaches taken by the Armed Services and Foreign Relations Committees. The analysis begins with the yearly counts of all types of committee oversight and employs negative binomial regression to assess the impact of divided government, federal expenditures for defense and international affairs, and major uses of military force on the frequency of oversight hearing days. The focus then shifts to observation of individual hearings. Logit analysis with quarterly effects determines how much external factors influenced the probability that a hearing topic was about oversight. Negative binomial regression with quarterly effects assesses how many days each hearing lasted. Unpacking the data in this way and comparing results with models for budget hearings reveals how expenditures and the use of force shaped each committee's behavior.

Control variables include presidential approval, national media visibility, and total number of hearing days for Armed Services and Foreign Relations. Separate analyses for public and executive sessions indicated the strategic value of secrecy, especially for Armed Services. Appendix D discusses the choice of method and level of analysis, along with other issues. Summary tables of the statistical results are presented as Tables D1, D2, D3, D4, and D5.

Overview of Influences on Yearly Oversight Activity

Overall, the committee's oversight behavior fits with my expectations. Divided party control of the Senate and White House presented Armed Services with a challenge and Foreign Relations with an opportunity. Similarly, federal budget authorizations appeared to matter less to Armed Services than Foreign Relations with respect to public oversight sessions, while the reverse was true for closed-door hearings. Finally, the president's use of force stimulated increased public oversight by the former but not the latter, although both committees engaged in more inquiries behind closed doors. The statistical results are shown in Tables D.1 and D.2 in Appendix D.

The first stage of analysis is a simple model of the influence of divided government on the national security committees' public and executive oversight hearing days, with controls for *New York Times* mentions, presidential approval, and total annual hearing days. A striking difference between the committees emerges in the predicted yearly counts, as shown in Figure 4.3 in the upper panel for Armed Services and the lower panel for Foreign Relations. Armed Services typically conducted fewer oversight hearings than Foreign Relations, either in public or in secret. Both committees were more likely to schedule oversight hearings in public than in private, but the predicted differences between the two under divided government were greater for Foreign Relations.

The positive coefficients for divided government differed between the two committees in terms of statistical significance. For Armed Services the positive

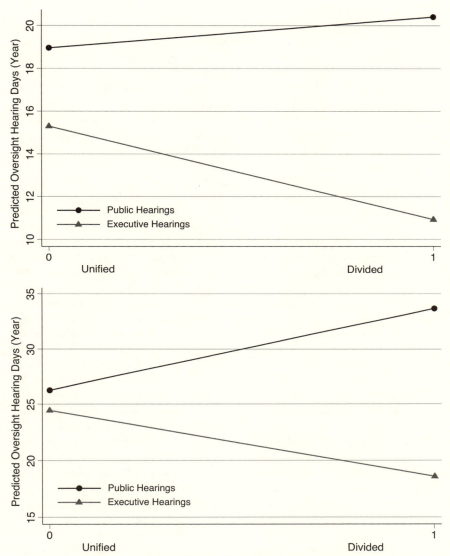

Figure 4.3. Predicted Mean Public and Executive Oversight Hearing Days, by Divided and Unified Government (Year). Top: Armed Services; bottom: Foreign Relations. Note: Points are predicted values for the mean number of public and executive hearing days per year as party control of the Senate and president moves from Unified at 0 to Divided at 1, holding control variables of *New York Times* Mentions, Presidential Approval, and Total Hearing Days at their means. Estimates were obtained using the Clarify procedure (Tomz, Wittenberg, and King 2003). For Armed Services, Divided Government is not statistically significant for public hearing days, but is significant (*p* value = .05 or better) for executive sessions. For Foreign Relations, Divided Government is almost significant for public hearings and is highly significant for executive sessions.

coefficient was not significant for public oversight and had a substantive effect of a little more than one additional public hearing day per year. In contrast, the positive coefficient for divided government for Foreign Relations was just shy of significance and raised the predicted number of oversight hearing days from roughly twenty-six annual public days under unified government to just under thirty-four annual days with divided control. Clearly, the committees had different motivations in dealing with the partisan implications of oversight.

Divided government yielded a significant, negative coefficient in predicting executive oversight days for both committees, however. Slightly more than fifteen secret Armed Services oversight hearing days per year were estimated under unified control, compared to eleven per year under divided government. Given the importance of secrecy for military operations and their potential controversy, this is a somewhat surprising result. The annual total for Foreign Relations also dropped by about five-plus hearing days per year from nearly twenty-five to roughly eighteen executive oversight days. The reduction in closed sessions under divided government makes sense given Foreign Relations' emphasis on public debate, although the committee's diminished total still exceeded that of Armed Services under either condition. Overall, the results for executive sessions seem to suggest that divided government inhibited cooperation between either committee and the White House, thus reducing the likely payoff from private face-to-face discussion about major foreign policy decisions.

In a more complex model that introduces goal-related, environmental variables, divided government behaves in roughly similar ways, although its coefficient for Foreign Relations becomes highly significant. Figure 4.4 presents a graph of the relationships for oversight hearing days and the key variables of frequency of the use of force and budget authority. For Armed Services, both factors operate in the hypothesized direction, but defense expenditure is not significant for public oversight hearings and had virtually no substantive impact, as predicted values moved from the 10th to the 90th percentile. The use of force by the president, however, was almost significant and produced a rise in public oversight days from seventeen to twenty-three per year, an increase of more than a third.

Armed Services stepped up oversight in executive sessions as budget expenditures rose, however, especially from the 50th to 75th percentile. Overall, the budget variable was statistically significant and produced a mean predicted rise of four oversight hearing days per year. Most important, the committee bolstered its inquiries behind closed doors during years in which U.S. troops were engaged in major operations, although the substantive effect was a modest mean increase of two days per year and the variable did not quite attain statistical significance.

I do not present the effects of the control variables, but it is worth mentioning that media visibility, while statistically significant in both Armed Services models, exerted a barely discernible change in predicted hearing days. Furthermore, presidential approval was neither significant nor substantively interesting

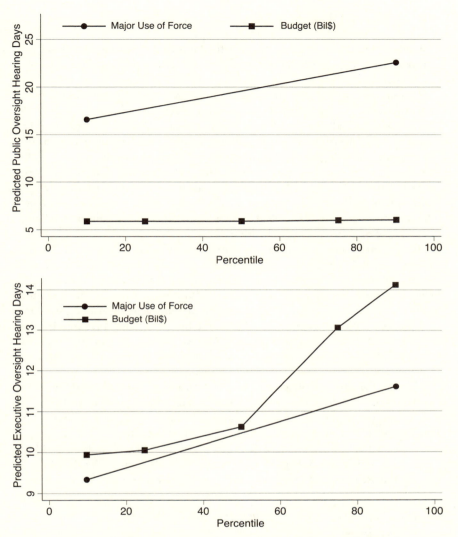

Figure 4.4. External Influences on Armed Services Oversight Hearing Days under Divided Government, by Public and Executive Session (Year). Top: Public Oversight Hearings; bottom: Executive Oversight Hearings.

Note: Points are predicted values for the mean number of public and executive Armed Services hearing days per year as each explanatory variable increases from the 10th percentile to the 90th percentile holding control variables at their mean and Divided Government constant at 1. Estimates were obtained using the Clarify procedure (Tomz, Wittenberg, and King 2003). For public hearing days, Divided Government, Budget, and Major Force fall just outside the p value of .05 for public hearings; for executive sessions, Divided Government and Budget are significant, but Major Force falls just outside the p value of .05.

for either public or closed sessions. The total number of hearing days, however, produced a strong, positive impact on the committee's public and secret oversight agendas.

Foreign Relations, while motivated to engage in oversight during divided government, also stepped up its public hearing activity at higher levels of federal expenditure all else equal. The steep increase in Figure 4.5 from twenty-nine oversight hearing days at the 50th percentile to nearly sixty days at the 90th percentile is highly significant, and it is especially striking in light of the small size of the actual expenditure increases (in constant dollars) for international affairs. Foreign Relations was less likely to engage in public oversight when major military operations were under way, but the variable was not significant and its substantive effect shown in Figure 4.5 was a mean predicted decrease of only two oversight hearing days.

Although modest boosts in international expenditures increased Foreign Relations' public scrutiny of the executive branch, the opposite effect held with respect to executive sessions and the relationship was statistically significant. Unlike Armed Services, Foreign Relations did not increase executive session monitoring during times of heightened military engagement. Among the control variables, media visibility was significant, but minimal in affecting the predicted number of hearing days. As with Armed Services, presidential approval exerted little influence in the model, while the total number of hearing days substantially increased secret oversight hearing activity.

In sum, the effects of divided government varied by committee and the venue of the inquiry in the yearly oversight activities of Armed Services and Foreign Relations. The former committee did not adjust its oversight with changes in the Pentagon budget, while the latter proved quite sensitive in its oversight efforts to relatively small changes in expenditures for aid and diplomacy. Most important, the president triggered greater oversight by Armed Services by initiating the use of force, but did not have a similar impact on Foreign Relations.

External Influences on the Probability That an Individual Hearing Is about Oversight

Turning to individual hearings, strategic calculations by each committee emerge that clarify the aggregate statistical patterns shown above. In this section, the conditional logit model for each committee uses the same variables from the preceding analysis to predict the probability that an individual hearing was for oversight or budget. For this analysis, I introduce quarterly random effects to control for the constraints of the legislative calendar.[18] The statistical results appear in Appendix D as Tables D.3 and D.4.

---

[18] Models in Stata are clogit grouped by quarter to produce separate estimates for the probability that a hearing is either for oversight or budget, as explained in Appendix D. The estimated

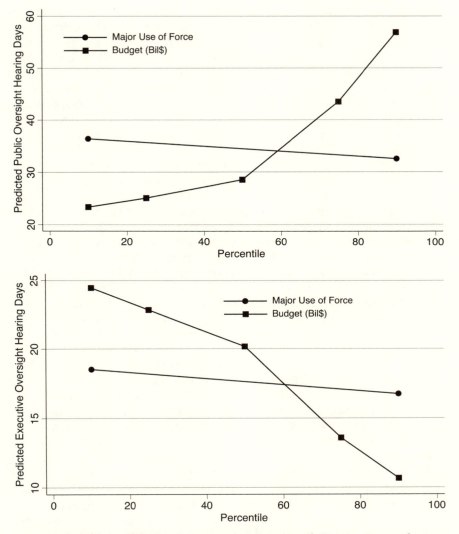

Figure 4.5. External Influences on Foreign Relations Oversight Hearing Days under Divided Government, by Public and Executive Session (Year). Top: Public Oversight Hearings; bottom: Executive Oversight Hearings.

Note: Points are predicted values for the mean number of public and executive Foreign Relations hearing days per year as each explanatory variable increases from the 10th percentile to the 90th percentile holding control variables at their mean and Divided Government constant at 1. Estimates were obtained using the Clarify procedure (Tomz, Wittenberg, and King 2003). For both public and executive hearing days, Divided Government and Budget are highly significant, while Major Force is not.

Figure 4.6 presents the predicted probabilities that Armed Services scheduled an individual public hearing about oversight or budget. The upper graph shows the distribution of the predicted probabilities of each hearing type by percentile in order to highlight the differences in content when U.S. forces were engaged in a major military operation. I represent a hearing's predicted oversight content by circles and its budget content by triangles. Hearings that occurred when U.S. forces were engaged in a major operation or war appear as black markers connected by solid black lines, while those that took place without a significant mobilization of troops appear as gray markers with dashed gray lines.

The frequency of force had a major impact on the content of Armed Services hearings and was statistically significant for oversight hearings, both public and secret sessions. When U.S. troops were in harm's way, the committee had a much higher probability of scheduling a public oversight hearing than when U.S. forces were not engaged. At the highest predicted values (the 90th percentile) for oversight under each force condition, the difference was 25 percentage points. Put another way, when force was involved the probability that an Armed Services public hearing would be about oversight never fell below 50 percent. In contrast, force was not significant in predicting the likelihood of a public budget hearing, and there was little difference in the pattern for budget inquiries whatever the status of military action. Although the predicted values are from two separate models, the graph nevertheless conveys the sense that Armed Services modified the content of its hearings in favor of oversight when U.S. troops were at risk. Parenthetically, divided government had no impact on the probability of either type of Armed Services public hearing.

The size of the defense budget was significant in predicting the probability of a public oversight hearing, but not an executive session oversight inquiry. The same was true for the likelihood that a hearing would be about Pentagon expenditures. Turning to the bottom panel of Figure 4.6, we see the predicted probabilities of a public oversight or budget hearing arrayed against the levels of funding for defense when major use of force was involved. The predicted probability of a public oversight hearing appears as an open circle in black, and the predicted probability of a public budget authorization hearing appears as an X in gray.[19] The gaps in the budget sequences result from the fiscal years in which no U.S. forces were engaged in a major military mission, with the largest occurring when defense budgets were in the interval of 90 billion and 175 billion

---

relationships between the dependent and independent variables are curvilinear, but I present only the point estimates of the probabilities at the 10th, 25th, 50th, 75th and 90th percentiles to simplify the graphs. Because the predictions arise from separate models, they are not strictly comparable.

[19] The Clarify software does not apply to models with random or fixed effects, so I used the Stata predict command with the option that sets the quarterly effect at zero, pu0. Further details are in Appendix D.

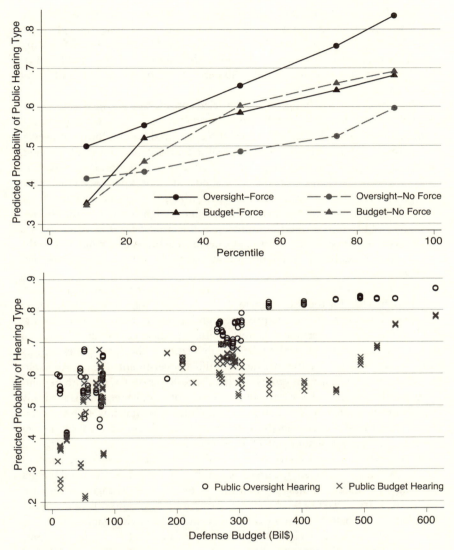

Figure 4.6. Predicted Probability of Armed Services Public Oversight or Budget Hearing. Top: Predicted Values of Hearing Type by Use of Force in Percentiles; bottom: Predicted Values for Use of Force by Defense Expenditures.

Note: Points in the upper panel are predicted probabilities that an individual public hearing type is for oversight or budget at different levels of force, shown in black and gray. Major force was highly significant for Armed Services' oversight type, but not for budget type. The predicted probabilities are graphed in the lower panel against the Defense Budget, which was significant for both types of public hearings.

dollars. This period coincided with the years of the Carter administration. For the lowest levels of defense spending, the probability of a public oversight hearing varies from roughly 40 to 70 percent, given the mobilization of U.S. troops. At the higher levels of spending, however, the probabilities of a public oversight hearing are consistently above 80 percent under the condition of major use of force.

The probability of a budget hearing varied considerably in the decades leading up to the Carter administration, even during periods of military engagement. Once defense expenditures rose above three hundred billion dollars, however, the probability of a budget inquiry remained consistently above 50 percent. Coincidentally, as defense budgets increased above three hundred billion, in only two years, 1985 and 1986, did the United States *not* experience a major use of force.[20] Despite its proclivities for prioritizing budgetary matters, then, Armed Services was drawn into more frequent oversight activity by the chronic state of mobilization of the U.S. military in the last twenty-five years. Such a shift was made possible, not by dramatic declines in budget hearings, but by the committee's reduced public attention to hearings about nominations, treaties, and statutes.

The results for Foreign Relations in Figure 4.7 produce no statistically significant coefficients for the uses of major force, but they help to unpack the effect of divided government on the predicted probability of an oversight hearing. Although divided government almost attains significance, the distribution of predicted values from the 10th to the 90th percentile in the upper panel appears almost identical under either divided or unified government. The overall likelihood of a budget hearing is quite low, just above 40 percent at the 90th percentile, and neither divided government nor the use of force generates a statistically significant relationship. International expenditures, however, were highly significant for oversight hearings (both public and secret), but were not significant in influencing the probability of a budget hearing.

One factor in this counterintuitive result is apparent in the lower panel of the figure. I have calculated the predicted probabilities for oversight and budget hearing type under conditions when the United States is engaged in military operations. The cluster of black, hollow circles at the left-hand side of the figure is similar to the pattern for Armed Services, and indicates a great deal of variation in the predicted probability that a hearing will be about oversight. The committee's approach diverges sharply, however, when the budget for international affairs surpassed ten billion dollars, an event that occurred in 1980. By the time expenditures on diplomacy and aid passed the twenty-billion mark, the probability that a Foreign Relations hearing would be about oversight had steadied at 90 percent or better. In contrast, the probability that a hearing would address

---

[20] In 1990 the FY expenditures were $303 billion and in 1991 they were $299 billion and did not exceed $300 billion again until 2001.

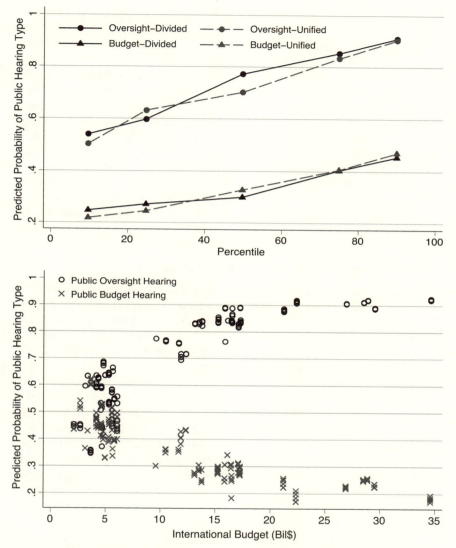

Figure 4.7. Predicted Probability of Foreign Relations Public Oversight or Budget Hearing with Divided and Unified Government or Major Force, by International Expenditures. Top: Divided and Unified Government; bottom: International Budget. Note: Points in the upper panel are predicted probabilities that an individual public hearing type is about oversight or budget under divided (black) or unified (gray) government with Major Force, which was not significant for either type, set at 1. The lower panel graphs predicted probabilities for oversight (black circle) and budget (gray x) against the International Affairs budget, which was significant for oversight but not budget.

budget authorization settled into the range of 15 to 25 percent by the mid-1980s.

In summary, the Senate Armed Services and Foreign Relations Committees demonstrated consistent biases in their approach to oversight. Armed Services displayed a decided preference for budget hearings unless the Pentagon was actively engaged in missions overseas. Since mobilization of U.S. forces was nearly continuous in the last two decades under study, we can now appreciate the increasing pressures on the committee that were evident in Chapter 1 to step up oversight activity, despite its inclinations to focus on expenditures. Foreign Relations revealed such a strong inclination for oversight that party control of the White House didn't seem to matter in shaping the probable type of an individual hearing. At the same time, the committee's propensity for oversight appears strongly linked to relatively modest changes in the budget for diplomacy and aid, a change made possible in the last three decades because of its avoidance of budget hearings.

External Influences and the Depth of Committee Hearings

As I began close examination of the hearing data from the Senate Armed Services and Foreign Relations Committees, I made the surprising discovery that the number of hearing topics had remained relatively stable over time. What had changed was the number of days devoted to each hearing. In other words, the big shift in the frequency of hearing days documented in Chapter 1 represented a serious loss of depth for each inquiry. An Armed Services review of the performance of military personnel, for example, might have consumed three or four days in the 1960s or 1970s. By the 1990s, however, the same oversight inquiry was more likely to consume a single day. Similarly, Foreign Relations devoted multiple days to examining the foreign policy challenges posed by developments in the Soviet Union or popular demonstrations against the United States in Latin America. In more recent years, however, the committee would be more likely to seek testimony from administration officials in a single public session. Thus, the frequency of days per hearing offers an informative perspective on the adaptations both committees made to their changing institutional and political environment.

In the analysis that follows, I use negative binomial regression with quarterly effects to evaluate the impact of external factors on the depth of inquiry in each committee's hearings. The dependent variable is the number of days per hearing, while the independent variables include the same external influences and controls used throughout this chapter. I employ dummy variables for oversight and budget hearings to capture differences attributable to the type of hearing. Consequently, it is possible to directly compare the coefficients and predicted values for each type of hearing. The statistical results for public and executive sessions for both committees appear in Table D.5.

Beginning with Armed Services, divided government exerts no significant effect on the length of either public or executive hearings. The uses of major force exercise a positive and significant influence on the length of each inquiry, while the size of the defense budget exerts a modest, statistically significant impact. The dummy variables for the content of the hearing are strongly significant for both oversight and budget inquiries, compared to the depth of other types of Armed Services hearings. In this respect, we get confirmation that Armed Services has been able to maintain focus on budgets, despite the pressure of having to do more oversight during periods of major mobilization. In other words, it has traded off in-depth consideration of nominations, statutes, or treaties for more days per hearing on oversight and expenditures.

Figure 4.8 graphs the predicted number of public days per hearing for each committee against the budget authorizations for defense and international programs. The black hollow circles represent predicted days for each public oversight hearing, while the gray Xs capture the predicted days for a public budget hearing. Throughout the period of study, Armed Services (shown in the upper panel) gave greater weight in terms of its allocation of time to individual budget topics. In the early decades of the Cold War, for example, the typical budget hearing lasted more than two days and in later years never fell below a day and a half. In contrast, oversight hearings were of lesser duration, typically a full day shorter than the average budget hearing. The disparity in depth of inquiry remained fairly consistent during most of the time series, although the gap narrowed a bit when the defense budget rose to over 350 billion dollars after the 2001 attack on the World Trade Center. Since the war on terror began, the most striking pattern for Armed Services is the fact that its predicted public budget hearing dropped to below two days, and its typical oversight hearing has consumed roughly a day.

For much of its history, Foreign Relations (shown in the lower panel) allocated more public days for each hearing than Armed Services, a pattern that held for both oversight and budget hearings with a modest blip in the days per hearing under conditions of divided government. Beginning in 1980, when the budget for international affairs exceeded ten billion dollars for the first time, the predicted length of both types of hearings dropped below two and a half days and continued to decline steadily. After 9/11, authorization for international programs jumped by 24 percent to twenty-two billion dollars, and the predicted number of days per hearing remained consistently higher for budgets than for oversight. The differences were relatively slight, however: no more than a quarter of a day. In practical terms, Foreign Relations compensated slightly for its preference for oversight hearings by allocating more days to its relatively infrequent budget hearings.

The analysis reveals that the national security committees pursued their goals through complex strategies in allocating their time and attention. With respect to the overall pattern of oversight, Armed Services was more attuned

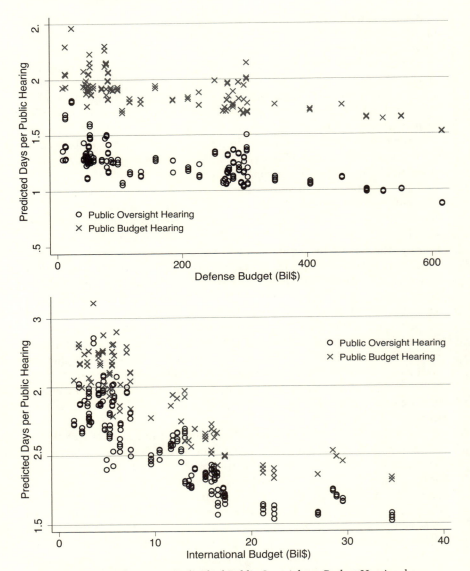

Figure 4.8. Predicted Days per Individual Public Oversight or Budget Hearing, by Budget (Billions of Dollars). Top: Armed Services; bottom: Foreign Relations. Note: Predicted values are the number of days per hearing calculated using Stata's predict command. The dummy variables identifying oversight (black hollow circles) and budget (gray Xs) hearing length are highly significant, as is the program budget for each committee. Major Force is significant and positive for Armed Services, but not for Foreign Relations.

to the president's use of force than his party affiliation, while Foreign Relations geared its inquiries into administration performance to divided government without responding to major military operations with increased oversight. In addition, Armed Services' yearly oversight hearings did not vary much with the size of the Defense Department budget, while Foreign Relations' yearly agenda became more skewed to oversight as small incremental increases in the international affairs budget prompted greater committee scrutiny. These results are consistent with the expectations laid out at the beginning of the chapter.

Upon closer examination of individual hearings, the two committees' decisions about oversight appeared to be dependent upon the relative importance they attached to budget inquiries. Armed Services had a higher probability of scheduling budget hearings when the U.S. military was not engaged in major missions abroad, but shifted its attention to oversight when the president initiated and continued the use of significant force. Given the fact that the United States has been at least partially mobilized on a nearly continuous basis since 1988, the committee has adapted by scheduling more oversight hearings. Nevertheless, it averaged more days per hearing when it examined the defense budget.

Although Foreign Relations provided clear evidence of the link between divided government and its yearly public oversight activity, its individual hearings revealed a more complicated calculation. Unlike Armed Services, the committee was less likely to schedule budget hearings regardless of divided government or unified party control. Thus, it had a much more flexible schedule in which to pursue oversight. Moreover, when the committee did conduct budget inquiries, it tended to compress its attention into a smaller number of hearings that lasted several days. With less constraint from budgetary concerns, then, the committee could pursue the opportunities for oversight offered by divided government.

In summary, the national security committees adapted their hearing schedules to suit their members' objectives. Armed Services' commitment to budgetary activity conformed to regular order by following routines in predictable sequence. Moreover, its heightened attention to public oversight when the president engaged the nation in a major military operation suggests adherence to practices of executive accountability. Nevertheless, the committee's skewed schedule reduced opportunities for oversight, especially during the first half of the year, and its preoccupation with support for the military during times of stress did not necessarily lead to tough questioning about performance.

In some respects, Foreign Relations compensated for the biases of Armed Services through its own skewed objectives. The committee's predilections for oversight ensured that administration witnesses were likely to be interrogated about its policies, particularly during times of divided government. Yet the committee did not adjust its oversight behavior during times of military mobilization, and it adopted a cavalier stance toward the process of authorizing international programs. Its partisan orientation casts doubt, furthermore, on how effectively it was able to educate the public. Foreign Relations showed a propensity for relatively lengthy hearings, but over time the committee shifted to inquiries of relatively short duration. In examining the trends for all types of national security oversight, then, neither committee satisfied the criteria of regularity, depth, and transparency consistent with the rule of law.

Black Hawk Down: Somalia and Party Elites in Congress

Operation Restore Hope, the humanitarian effort in Somalia that President George H. W. Bush launched in December 1992, exemplified the importance of congressional activity in providing an arena for dialogue about U.S. use of force. Both the Senate Armed Services and Foreign Relations Committees launched multiple types of inquiries in public and secret venues. Initially, Foreign Relations led the way, using hearings to attract media attention to an emerging foreign policy problem. As events unfolded, the committees undertook inquiries into the implementation of the humanitarian effort and eventually shifted into crisis mode, which transformed Somalia from tragic error into full-blown confrontation with the executive branch. As the senators redefined the purpose of the hearings, moreover, they shifted back and forth between public and executive sessions. Throughout the roughly eighteen months of congressional scrutiny of U.S. policy toward Somalia, the committees' strategic premises were evident in the topics, venues, and intensity of their oversight activity. At first glance, the pattern of hearings conformed to the procedural regularity that is essential for the rule of law. Upon closer examination, the case revealed the limitations of oversight when it is driven primarily by committee goals.

Somalia in the 1990s was the archetypal failed state. It started to disintegrate with the brutal Ogaden War with Ethiopia in 1978 and spiraled into devastating violence after a military coup in 1991. The dislocation of the civilian population, along with severe drought, led to massive starvation that eventually attracted the intervention of the United Nations. Widespread killing and chaotic administration impeded international relief efforts, ensuring that much of the aid ended up in the hands of warlords and thieves. Eventually, the United States joined with the United Nations in an attempt to ease the suffering of the hapless civilians with Bush's announcement that twenty-six thousand U.S. troops would lead an international force to allow aid efforts to resume. The purpose of the operation was "to establish a secure environment in Somalia," with "no intent to get involved in hostilities."[21] Most lawmakers expressed support of the president's actions, although some Democrats and Republicans urged caution.[22]

---

[21] Fisher (1995, 153).

[22] Clifford Krauss, "Mission to Somalia; A Few in Congress Advising Caution, or Vote, on Somalia," *New York Times*, December 7, 1992, http://www.nytimes.com/1992/12/07/world/mission-to-somalia-a-few-in-congress-advising-caution-or-vote-on-somalia.html (accessed January 2008).

Political observers have offered various interpretations about Somalia. Some have seen U.S. involvement there as an example of the imperial presidency,[23] while others have interpreted it as a rare case of congressional assertiveness in contemporary foreign affairs.[24] Still other scholars have framed the case in terms of the "CNN effect" and the power of the media to arouse public opinion to compel a president toward a foreign policy he would otherwise reject.[25] All of these explanations have overlooked the role of Senate committee oversight in putting the crisis on the national agenda and shaping its eventual outcome.

In the spring of 1991, well before Bush's commitment of troops, the Senate Foreign Relations Committee held two days of public hearings on problems with the relief effort in Somalia. The committee raised the Somali crisis on the public agenda with more public hearings in March and May 1992. After a trip to the region in July 1992, Republican committee member Nancy Kassebaum (R-KS) introduced a resolution urging President Bush to organize a multinational effort to provide security for food aid operations. The committee held an additional public hearing in October 1992.

Foreign Relations was not the only congressional advocate for U.S. involvement in Somalia. A number of senators and House members made public statements and sent letters to the White House. Despite the enthusiasm on Capitol Hill, Armed Services did not participate in the debate about joining the UN peacekeepers.

Public opinion, buoyed by the extraordinary American and allied victory in the Gulf War in 1991, backed the idea of U.S. troops engaging in multinational peacekeeping. Indeed, in the aftermath of the Cold War, a rough bipartisan consensus among citizens had emerged in favor of peacekeeping, at least in principle.[26] Bush's announcement sparked a frenzy of media activity, including TV crews with special night-vision cameras positioned on the Somali beach to film the landing of Marines and Special Forces units on December 9, 1992.

Despite high levels of congressional and public approval, the president's actions unleashed a major debate in Congress about the War Powers Act and the need for a formal authorization by Congress. Historically, presidential discretion to use military force in another country had involved the safety of American citizens, protection of U.S. property, treaty obligations, or vital strategic interests. None of those conditions applied to Somalia, and President Bush, meanwhile, had been replaced by President Clinton. Nevertheless, the Senate approved the commitment of troops on February 4, 1993 after they had begun operations, and the House followed suit with a more limited grant of discretion in May. The two chambers never resolved their differences about the timetable, so the mission proceeded without formal legislative approval.[27]

---

[23] Fisher (1995); Rudalevige (2006).
[24] Carter and Scott (2009); Kriner (2010).
[25] Edwards and Wood (1999, 329); Carter and Scott (2009, 38).
[26] Holsti (2004, 181).
[27] Brown (2003).

With troops engaged, oversight of Operation Restore Hope shifted in the Senate to the Armed Services Committee, which undertook a series of hearings. The committee questioned representatives of the new Clinton administration publicly in January and March and met privately for a classified briefing with military and DOD officials, also in January.

The president, having decided to continue the mission, expanded its scope beyond delivery of relief supplies and protection of refugees that spring. Efforts to contain the clan rivalries perpetuating the nation's instability generated controversy, which increased with the ambush and death of twenty-six Pakistani peacekeepers in June 1993.

Critics on Capitol Hill from both parties pressed for a deadline to withdraw troops once the Clinton administration began talk about "nation building."[28] Republicans were unhappy about the close command relationship with the United Nations and the change in the nature of the mission, and prominent Democrats, such as Senator Robert Byrd (D-WV) and House International Relations Chair Lee Hamilton (D-IN), initial skeptics, had become even more wary of the costs. Foreign Relations held a public session in July, and Armed Services devoted a day of inquiry to the mission in August after eight soldiers lost their lives. In reaction to the deaths of the American soldiers, words like "fiasco," "quagmire," and "debacle" circulated on Capitol Hill. "As the body bags pile up," declared Senate Minority Leader Robert Dole (R-KN), "the confusion in the U.S. increases. Enough Americans have died in Somalia."[29]

The military's failure to capture the leading warlord, Mohammed Farrah Aidid, who was responsible for much of the violence in the capital, further fueled congressional opposition to the American presence in Somalia. Public support for the mission waned over the summer, and by September the House passed a nonbinding resolution directing the president to remove troops by January 31, 1994. The Senate added an amendment to the FY 1994 defense authorization bill requiring the president to seek congressional authorization by November 15 for continued deployment.[30]

The grisly episode with the downed helicopter on October 3 prompted President Clinton to announce an additional deployment of U.S. troops to restore some semblance of order and then withdraw fully by March 31, 1994. In response to growing congressional and public opposition, Armed Services scheduled four days of public testimony between October 4 and 13 and an executive session on October 19. Foreign Relations heard witnesses for two days on October 19 and 20. The Senate and House passed resolutions approving the president's plan in mid-October and early November, respectively. The president

---

[28] Fisher (1995).

[29] Judy Keen, "Public Feels 'Confusion' about Goals," *USA Today*, October 5, 1993, http://global.factiva.com (accessed September 5, 2012).

[30] Brown (2003).

kept his commitment to withdraw the troops the following March, and Armed Services continued to monitor the situation in Somalia in 1994 and 1995 with three public hearings and two executive sessions.

Somalia was unusual in numerous respects. Two different presidents, operating under both divided and unified government, deployed troops and became targets of criticism from both parties. In addition, Armed Services and Foreign Relations generated a great deal of information at all stages of the crisis, from the initial hearings, to the expansion and subsequent failure of the mission, to the eventual agreement by President Clinton to disengage militarily. During the eighteen months between the troops' landing and their final withdrawal, the two Senate committees held a total of twenty-three hearings, some lasting more than a day, which ran the gamut from agenda setting to policy implementation and crisis. Lawmakers passed various resolutions and endeavored to amend legislation authorizing defense programs for FY 1994 to enforce their will. Overall, the Senate national security committees appeared to go to considerable lengths to hold the executive branch accountable for its decisions regarding Somalia.

Generally, the Somalia case fits with the larger picture regarding committee goals and strategic premises that emerged from the statistical analyses in this chapter. Armed Services left the issue of peacekeepers in the Horn of Africa to Foreign Relations until the boots were on the ground. The committee followed its usual practice in the winter and spring of 1992, when the issue first arose, of concentrating on the budget authorization for the next fiscal year. Once major force was deployed in early 1993, the committee engaged, despite the fact that unified government prevailed with Democrats continuing their majority in the Senate and gaining control of the White House. The public hearings revealed a protective tone reflecting senators' concerns that the Pentagon would become mired in an untenable position that citizens would eventually repudiate. The frequent use of executive sessions enabled the committee to voice its concerns in private. Overall, Armed Services' emphasis on budgetary matters kept it out of the initial debate over joining the peacekeeping mission, while its concern for the well-being of the military trumped partisan calculation, as it had throughout the post–World War II period.

For the Senate Foreign Relations Committee, partisan rivalry figured throughout the debate over Somalia. In 1991 and 1992, a popular Republican president up for reelection confronted a Democratic majority in the Senate. After Bush's extraordinary success in the Gulf War, the Democrats on Foreign Relations sought to dent the president's reputational advantage for competence in foreign affairs by seizing on his failure to act in Somalia. Republican Senator Kassebaum subsequently countered with her trip to Somalia and a resolution calling for U.S. intervention.

Despite the presence of a newly elected Democrat in the White House in 1993, Foreign Relations continued to direct attention to Somalia but was more involved with other parts of the world. Clinton had campaigned on domestic issues and, as a former governor of Arkansas, had limited credentials for statecraft. Democratic senators understood that the party needed to improve its reputation in foreign affairs, and the inexperience of the president offered an opening for the committee to shape discourse among policy elites. As the public eventually soured on "nation building" and then grew irate after the Black Hawk debacle, Democrats turned to oversight hearings to contain the damage.

The larger issue is why, with so many security problems to choose from and a dramatic shift under way in the global balance of power, both Senate committees concentrated so much attention on an impoverished state with little strategic value to the United States. Many political commentators held up Somalia as an example of the CNN effect, media-driven foreign policy in which the press generated pressure for U.S. intervention in a particular country or region.[31] Others cited Somalia as an example of the public's tying the hands of the president because of its antipathy to casualties.[32] Neither of these interpretations makes sense without considering the role of congressional oversight in shaping elite discourse. With respect to the CNN effect, it is instructive to remember that at the time the overall salience of international affairs among the general public was extraordinarily low in terms of respondents listing international affairs as the "most important problem." If citizens embraced peacekeeping in Somalia, it was a "top of the head" response typical of a public exposed to elite cues in the press.[33]

Discourse on Capitol Hill, which focused on the risks of nation building even before casualties became an issue, signaled elite concern about the mission and appeared to have influenced the public's perceptions about Operation Restore Hope.[34] Senators grew worried when the Pakistani soldiers were killed in June and eight Americans died in August, long before the mayhem in Mogadishu. Consequently, public support had already declined substantially by the time the Black Hawk crashed. Overall, U.S. operations in Somalia experienced a dramatic decline in public support from 72 percent in favor prior to the engagement of U.S. troops to 52 percent after the Battle of Mogadishu, which produced a total of twenty-nine casualties.[35] Parenthetically, Somalia was viewed more favorably than the Lebanon peacekeeping operation, which had 256 casualties, or the interventions in Bosnia and Kosovo, which had zero casualties.

---

[31] Edwards and Wood (1999, 329); Carter and Scott (2009, 38).

[32] Parallels with the bombing of the Marine barracks in Lebanon in 1983 and with Rwanda and Bosnia are common in the literature (Burk 1999; Holsti 2004; Luttvak 1994).

[33] Zaller (1992); Zaller and Chiu (1996); Brody (1994); Berinsky (2007; 2009); Groeling and Baum (2008); Howell and Pevehouse (2007); Kriner (2009; 2010); Voeten and Brewer (2006); Berinsky (2009).

[34] Burk (1999); Kriner (2010); Henderson (2002).

[35] Eichenberg (2005, 169).

With the advantage of hindsight and access to the hearing record, it appears that there would not have been a CNN effect had the national security committees not played their part. Ordinarily, Armed Services' skepticism about peacekeeping would have aroused its members' concern, but in the case of Somalia the committee did not publicly raise objections to it. A closer look at the committee's agenda in 1991 and 1992 reveals serious preoccupation with Desert Storm and its aftermath, and in 1993 it showed repeated hearings about the "build down" of U.S. forces, base closings, and the reconfiguration of the U.S. defense posture in the aftermath of the Cold War. Members of the Armed Services Committee doubted that the United States could reduce its military establishment in favor of peacekeeping, and they worried about exposing the military to a lengthy conflict or, worse, an ill-considered mission, such as that in Lebanon. Yet, even the skeptics saw that humanitarian operations provided a rationale for avoiding the dramatic cuts that had occurred after Vietnam and a means for maintaining public support after the Soviet Union posed less of a threat.

The Foreign Relations Committee, in contrast, saw U.S. intervention in places like Somalia as a welcome shift in U.S. policy toward multilateral cooperation and a softer projection of power. Peacekeeping was a mission that could be done relatively cheaply by a smaller army, and it fit nicely with the instincts of Foreign Affairs members who favored international cooperation. The committee was adrift under the weak leadership of Chairman Claiborne Pell, who, we noted earlier, had little luck engaging members in budget matters. Somalia thus offered an opportunity for a larger debate about the future direction of U.S. foreign policy that fit remarkably well with the goals of its members. Clinton's UN ambassador, Ryan Crocker, for example, viewed the operation as a limited success because it created enough stability to limit the number of deaths from starvation to several hundred thousand instead of a million.[36] Among Republicans, too, there was an appreciation of the political value of using the military for humanitarian purposes.

Among GOP members on the national security committees and Republican policy elites more generally, Somalia was part of a larger narrative regarding conservative ascendance over U.S. foreign policy.[37] The successful U.S. intervention to drive Iraqi troops from Kuwait, along with President George H. W. Bush's sky-high approval numbers in its aftermath, suggested opportunities for the GOP to retain its edge as the party perceived to be stronger in foreign affairs. A small group of isolationists was content to let the world fend for itself with the Soviet Empire in tatters, while other Republicans contended that U.S. hegemony reduced the U.S. need for international cooperation. Some staunch

[36] Crocker (1995).
[37] Zelizer (2010).

neoconservatives, such as John Bolton, who was hostile to multilateral organizations and considered the Somalia mission a disaster, granted the usefulness of humanitarian interventions.[38] Although peacekeeping was not a natural fit for Republican senators on either Armed Services or Foreign Relations, as an alternative to reductions in the defense establishment it enjoyed some support among foreign policy hawks.

Somalia generated a disproportionate amount of attention at the time of its collapse, and its aftermath sparked considerable debate about its implications for U.S. foreign policy. In 1993, for example, Armed Services conducted a total of twenty-five days of public oversight hearings and eighteen days of secret oversight hearings. That same year, Foreign Relations devoted seventeen days to public oversight and fourteen days to closed-door sessions. From one perspective, the committees appeared to be following an orderly process to review the executive's policy agenda, its implementation of the humanitarian mission, and its performance following a crisis. The scrutiny of Somalia consumed a disproportionate amount of each committee's hearing days, thus constraining their ability to engage the administration on other policies of greater importance to the rule of law in U.S. foreign policy.

Despite the minimal stakes in terms of national security, the intervention in Somalia enjoyed high levels of public approval, with a majority continuing to support the mission after the Black Hawk went down. Indeed, popular consensus about the value of humanitarian missions in cooperation with other nations and the United Nations persisted after U.S. troops were withdrawn.[39] The disproportionate attention to Somalia, however, came at the cost of activity to educate the public about the challenges of a post–Cold War world. Overall, the case demonstrates the interplay of factors that stimulated oversight and provides a concrete example of how strategic premises shaped the Senate national security committees' response to their environment.

Conclusion

The patterns of oversight activity of the Senate's national security committees have consequences for democratic politics and for the study of Congress. Lawmakers and citizens require information to evaluate how the president exercises the executive's vast discretion over national security, but they depend upon specialized congressional committees to gather it. Senate committees have their own agendas as a result of the committee assignment process that promotes internal consensus about priorities and the means of achieving them. Over the sixty-two years of the study, the Armed Services and Foreign Relations Committees

---

[38] Bolton (1994).
[39] Holsti (2004, 157); Kull and Destler (1999).

pursued consistent strategies in using oversight to attain their respective goals of support for the military and public debate about foreign policy. The frequency of oversight, the record of public and closed sessions, the comparison with budget inquiries, and the lack of depth for individual hearings by Armed Services and Foreign Relations thus indicate a mismatch between the incentives that guide committee behavior and the needs of both Congress and the public.

The theoretical expectations based on the distinctiveness and relative autonomy of Senate committees do a good job of explaining variation in national security oversight over time and between committees. Substantively, the results indicate that divided government did not impact the public hearing oversight activity of Senate Armed Services, but did influence its propensity for hearings behind closed doors, while the opposite pattern occurred for Foreign Relations. In addition, the president's initiation of the use of force prompted the former to increase oversight, while exerting little effect on Foreign Relations. Moreover, the findings demonstrate substantial differences in the committees' propensity for budget hearings, which constrained the likelihood of oversight by Armed Services and facilitated review by Foreign Relations. Overall, the analysis confirms the importance of committee workloads discussed in Chapter 3 in accentuating competition for space on the committees' calendars.

Critics of Congress frequently have pointed to inadequate oversight as a major failing of the institution, particularly with respect to matters of war and diplomacy. Several different factors raise concerns about both the quantity and the relevance of the Senate Armed Services and Foreign Relations Committees' oversight activity during the sixty-two years of the study. Together, the results in this chapter highlight deficiencies in national security oversight, not just in terms of quantity, but also in terms of the types of presidential decisions that committee members subjected to public review.

CHAPTER 5

Police Patrols and Fire Alarms in U.S. Foreign Policy

Lt. Gen. Kevin Kiley, surgeon general of the Army, sat at the witness table in the hearing room of the House Oversight and Government Reform Committee on March 5, 2007, confronting irate lawmakers. The general, who had been commander at Walter Reed Army Hospital from 2002 to June 2004 and briefly served as acting commander in early March 2007, was attempting to explain why convalescent soldiers at Walter Reed were housed in appalling conditions and subjected to a stunningly unresponsive bureaucracy. Beside Kiley was Maj. Gen. George W. Weightman, who had held the post for six months and been fired the week before as a result of an exposé that appeared in the *Washington Post* on February 18.[1] The generals' fellow witnesses included soldiers with devastating injuries, records of heroism, and sad stories about administrative neglect as outpatients following their discharge from Walter Reed's main hospital into Building 18, suddenly notorious for cockroaches and despair. When one lawmaker asked General Kiley how he could have remained ignorant of conditions in the facility opposite his residence, he replied, "I live across the street, but I don't do barracks inspections at Walter Reed."[2]

Walter Reed was typical of many Washington scandals in the sense that problems at the facility had been hiding in plain sight. The subject of complaints from soldiers and their families for years, Walter Reed's dismal outpatient conditions invoked a long history of inadequate treatment of soldiers and veterans dating back at least to the Gulf and Vietnam Wars. After the story broke, some lawmakers claimed they had tried but failed to get help for their wounded constituents. Advocates noted that they had repeatedly drawn attention to the inadequacies of care for injured military personnel. Indeed, a cursory search of the *New York Times* and *Washington Post* revealed numerous articles that depicted problems with the Army's health care delivery system. Similarly, the investigative reporter, Dana Priest, had filed a number of hard-hitting stories

---

[1] Dana Priest and Anne Hull, "Soldiers Face Neglect, Frustration at Army's Top Medical Facility," *Washington Post*, February 18, 2007, http://www.washingtonpost.com/wp-dyn/content/article/2007/02/17/AR2007021701172.html (accessed October 20, 2010).

[2] MSNBC, "Lawmakers Visit Walter Reed," March 7, 2007, http://www.nbcnews.com/video/nightly-news/17470863#17470863 (accessed October 20, 2010).

about Bush administration errors in the conduct of the Iraq War that put soldiers at risk. General Kiley's detached comment that he did not "inspect barracks" extended beyond the Army to Congress. Apparently, legislators did not inspect barracks either.

The scandal not only represented an administrative breakdown, but also signaled a failure of legislative oversight. Citizens cared about the welfare of soldiers and their families, even if they did not understand the geopolitics of the conflict. By 2006, almost 40 percent of Americans had designated defense and international affairs as the nation's most important problem, approaching levels seen during the Vietnam War. In House districts with high levels of casualties, public support for the Iraq mission eroded as their representatives made speeches on the floor.[3] Voters eventually took their concerns about casualties to the polls during that year's congressional election.[4] Yet citizens did not get the kind of cues from formal hearings that had shaped their understanding of previous conflicts. In the absence of systematic public review, the public lacked information about an aspect of the Iraq War that mattered most to them and that they could use to hold the president accountable for foreign policy decisions.[5]

The Walter Reed case thus raises larger questions: What factors, if any, motivated the Senate's national security committees in the decades leading up to Iraq to generate information that citizens cared about? How did past stimuli for oversight of major events and crises differ from routine inquiries into bureaucratic performance in the Departments of Defense and State? Both the Senate Armed Services and Foreign Relations Committees geared the content of oversight hearings to influences that were directly or indirectly related to the reputations of the national parties. The committees thus appeared more attuned to the informational needs of organized constituencies rather than the general public.

The familiar typology of "police patrols" and "fire alarms" provides a useful framework for analyzing the content of national security oversight, because it captures the costs and benefits to lawmakers associated with different types of hearing content. Recall from Chapter 1 that police patrols entailed regular inquiries that monitored an agency's compliance with congressional intent and its implementation of programs. Fire alarms, such as Walter Reed, were event-driven and arose from outcry by citizens, political activists, experts, and journalists about executive incompetence or wrongdoing.[6] Patrol hearings involved matters of lesser salience than alarm inquiries and consequently were less disruptive to the status quo. The two types of hearings served different goals and

---

[3] Kriner and Shen (2014).

[4] Grose and Oppenheimer (2007); Gelpi, Feaver, and Reifler (2007); Gartner and Segura (2008); Kriner and Shen (2007).

[5] Ornstein and Mann (2006). The findings in Chapter 4 confirmed the critics in demonstrating that the Senate Armed Services and Foreign Relations Committees held fewer oversight hearings than for previous wars.

[6] Balla and Deering (2013).

led to distinctive behaviors by Armed Services and Foreign Relations in generating information about critical issues of war and peace.

This chapter examines committee choices regarding the content of national security oversight hearings by comparing routine inquiries to reviews of major crises and scandals. I first exploit the unique characteristics of the study's fine-grained coding of hearings to develop measures for police patrol and fire alarm oversight.[7] I then turn to expectations about committee behavior before examining the distribution of patrols and alarms for each committee, particularly as they relate to changes in military casualties from 1947 to 2008. I next analyze the influence of the president's party and casualties on each committee's choice between routine and event-driven hearings, as well as their venues. Finally, I focus solely on crisis oversight as a form of committee review that is particularly important to democratic accountability. I conclude with the Walter Reed case, which reveals a common connection between scandals and crises and illustrates Armed Services' efforts to juggle the nationalizing effect of military conflict with its constituency-related goal of supporting the Pentagon.

One criterion for the rule of law in international affairs is the provision of information that citizens can use to hold public officials responsible for policy choices. By this standard, crises and scandals should figure prominently on committee agendas, yet the average number of days per quarter spent by the Senate's national security committees on alarms was low. Many quarters between 1947 and 2008 had no hearings of the type most salient to the public, despite the near constant state of mobilization of the United States. In addition, the committees' concerns with the reputational consequences of oversight colored the distribution of patrol and alarm hearings. The frequency of each type of hearing for Armed Services and Foreign Relations depended on which party held the presidency and how high battle deaths rose. Public opinion, as measured in national surveys, had very little effect on the type of oversight during the study period. The committees' concerns about party reputations regarding foreign policy indirectly generated episodes of accountability, but their overall record of providing information for the public at large proved uneven.

Defining Police Patrol and Fire Alarm Oversight

The distinction between police patrols and fire alarms appears deceptively straightforward; it requires simply that we tell the difference between the routine and the unusual, between the ongoing program and the problematic event. When lawmakers conducted patrols of agencies, for example, they checked to make sure that bureaucrats followed congressional intent and administered a statute effectively. When they launched alarm inquiries, in contrast, they suspected

---

[7] McCubbins and Schwartz (1984).

that something had gone wrong, that it needed to be fixed, and quickly. Applying these commonsense understandings to oversight turns out to be complicated, however, by the subjective nature of many policy issues, partisan politics, and the dynamic aspect of international events.

In distinguishing between types of oversight, I treated police patrols as reviews of ongoing administration and fire alarms as inquiries about specific and potentially controversial events.[8] Recalling the descriptions of hearing content in Chapter 1, police patrols included hearings that involved implementation of a specific program, progress on noncontroversial treaty negotiations or administration of a low salience treaty, overviews of the state of the world or a region, and efforts to put a foreign policy issue on the president's agenda. Generally, Armed Services spent a considerable amount of time on program implementation, while Foreign Relations devoted the bulk of its routine oversight hearings to state of the world assessments. In effect, the intent of patrol inquiries for each committee was similar, even though the substance differed.[9]

The greater challenge arose in classifying fire alarms. I grouped the following types of hearings together: military and international crises, authorizations and resolutions regarding the use of force, negotiation or implementation of major treaties, and mismanagement and scandals. Crises, of course, did not necessarily lead to investigations, but they often created the conditions for scandals, particularly in periods involving lengthy conflicts. The choice to combine the two was consistent with the event-driven, and often divisive, nature of fire alarms. I analyze crises separately, however, at the end of the chapter.

My approach differs from that of other scholars who have studied oversight on two counts. First, some analysts have defined oversight as any type of review,[10] while I distinguish between patrol and alarm hearings. The only study in which scholars separated police patrols from fire alarms demonstrated that routine inquiries occurred frequently.[11] The distinction thus appeared to be a meaningful one, and it turned out to be particularly relevant to the monitoring of national security.

Second, other analysts have focused solely on investigations, which constituted a subset of fire alarm hearings.[12] These authors identified scandal or incompetence by: (1) salience in the news media; and (2) computerized keyword searches of congressional hearing abstracts.

---

[8] Balla and Deering (2013) used a similar approach.

[9] See Appendix A for details of the many procedures I used to ensure the reliability of the coding.

[10] Aberbach (1990; 2002); McGrath (2013) also includes budget hearings as "review."

[11] Balla and Deering (2013) looked at different Congresses and four pairs of House and Senate Committees only. One pair of committees they examined was the Senate Armed Services and House Armed Services Committees.

[12] Mayhew (1991; 2006); Kriner and Schwartz (2008); Parker and Dull (2009; 2012); Kriner and Schickler (2012; 2014).

The criterion of media salience, first adopted by Mayhew, and subsequently employed by Kriner and Schwartz, defined major investigations as having stimulated at least twenty front-page articles per Congress in the *New York Times*.[13] Media-based definitions of investigations raise problems of simultaneity, however, if reporters covered a problem once members of Congress started looking into it and members scheduled additional hearings once the press found them newsworthy. Furthermore, the declining news coverage of Congress and the national security committees, noted in Chapters 2 and 3, meant that over time fewer examples of executive wrongdoing qualified as publicity probes. The mistreatment of veterans at Walter Reed would not have made the cut, for example, although it was undeniably a major scandal.

Other studies identified investigations by coding Congressional Information Service (CIS) abstracts of congressional hearings using computerized searches of keywords, such as "mismanagement," "scandal," or "abuse."[14] Selection bias is a potential concern when defining investigative oversight through keywords. Scandals over executive performance have occurred at predictable times in a president's tenure and involved events for which the evidence of wrongdoing was problematic.[15] Furthermore, hearing titles and abstracts often reflected the political orientation of the committee chair or staff.[16] For example, Senator Jesse Helms (R-NC), chair of Foreign Relations from 1995 to 2000, alleged scandal in the title of a hearing investigating President Clinton's granting of clemency to Puerto Rican separatists convicted of terrorism in the 1970s

[13] Mayhew (1991; 2006); Kriner and Schwartz (2008). These scholars were looking for evidence that divided government stimulated investigations, but neither analysis found strong support for the idea. Mayhew's initial study reported no difference in "publicity probes" between divided and unified government, although he qualified his results in a later version by noting that the few major probes occurring after 1990 took place under divided government. Kriner and Schwartz's results echoed Mayhew's, but the authors found an effect for divided government after they controlled for the ideological distance between Congress and the president and the ideological homogeneity of the majority party. Notably, their findings were less robust for the Senate than the House, and they had no cases that made the threshold of major investigation for the 108th and 109th Congresses.

[14] Parker and Dull (2009; 2012); Kriner (2009); Kriner and Schickler (2012; 2014). Parker and Dull developed this research strategy to examine congressional inquiries into controversial executive performance. Their first analysis indicated that divided government had a strong effect on the frequency of investigations solely in the House, and became somewhat important in predicting Senate investigations after 1975. In a later study solely of House investigations, Parker and Dull demonstrated that divided government and committee characteristics increased investigatory behavior. Kriner reported that attacks on the Bush administration's conduct of the war were closely linked to the incidence of divided government. It does not appear that the oversight hearings in this study were solely confined to scandal. Kriner and Schickler found that divided government from 1896 to 2006 predicted investigations for the House, but not the Senate; and it increased the relative frequency of high-profile inquiries, but only when the House parties were polarized.

[15] Nyhan (2014).

[16] The lack of systematic standards prior to the Congressional Information Service's assumption of responsibility in 1970 for cataloguing and publishing committee hearings added to the problem of bias in committee titles and abstracts.

and 1980s.[17] In addition, committees controlled the salience of an inquiry by determining how many days a hearing lasted and whether it took place in public. Finally, many investigative hearings were the work of specially created select subcommittees, which required authorization by a chamber majority that often had an obvious political agenda.[18]

In effect, congressional committees typically did not undertake investigations unless they intended to find a scandal. The processes by which committees labeled an inquiry as scandal or mismanagement and decided to launch an investigation were essentially the same. Media salience and keyword searches as means of classifying investigative hearings thus were vulnerable to selection bias. For this reason, I coded directly from the hearing abstract and cross-checked the content with other sources.

As a result, my data likely have more observations regarding committee concerns about mismanagement that did not rise to the level of scandal. Both committees showed interest in administrative problems and executive errors in judgment, but they exercised restraint in how they framed their inquiries in order to minimize damage to key programs under their jurisdictions. In a few cases, Armed Services undertook inquiries about procurement and operational readiness that probably should have become public scandals, but were described in committee documents with neutral language. Such hearings targeted problems for which the committee wanted remedy but not controversy, and they are the ones my method picked up that a keyword search might have missed. For Armed Services, such hearings typically involved the performance of a particular weapon or weapons systems or the training of military personnel. For Foreign Relations, the hearings targeted the State Department's handling of particular events or relationships with key allies.

The special character of international affairs is the primary reason for my decision to define fire alarm oversight to include crises rather than concentrate solely on investigations of executive wrongdoing. Both crises and scandals in foreign affairs involve executive actions that citizens care about, and both speak to big questions of democratic control. From my examination of the hearing record for Armed Services and Foreign Relations over sixty-two years, wars, international crises, and investigations frequently went hand in hand. To be sure, hearings about crises and scandals occurred independently in both committees, but during major conflicts, they clustered together.

Scholars who studied oversight hearings made no distinction, however, between legislative inquiries into domestic and foreign events, and for most committees they would not have needed to. Yet major conflicts historically have

---

[17] CIS No. 2000-S381–8, September 14, 1999. This was a policy disagreement, not a scandal, since there was no evidence that Clinton had been influenced improperly.

[18] Roughly half of the major investigations Mayhew (1991) analyzed were conducted by specially created committees.

created opportunities for waste, fraud, and abuse because authorized funds typically received less scrutiny during emergencies than might otherwise have been the case. Furthermore, opponents of a U.S. military operation sometimes challenged the president indirectly by looking for evidence of incompetent execution rather than raising public ire by attacking the president's strategy head on. Finally, states and nonstate actors precipitated emergencies that opened administration officials to criticism for failing to anticipate the dangers of an unfolding situation. Such errors in judgment did not necessarily constitute malfeasance or even incompetence, given the uncertainties of the international arena, but they justifiably aroused committee scrutiny.

To review descriptions of hearing content from Chapter 1, both committees spent about a third of their total oversight hearing days on crises or scandals and the remainder on police patrols. Armed Services split its attention to crises about evenly between public and executive sessions, while Foreign Relations reviewed crises more frequently behind closed doors. In addition, Armed Services was more likely to launch scandal inquiries than Foreign Relations, although the differences were not great. Both committees invested a great deal of time on crisis oversight at the onset of the Korean War, in the period of escalating U.S. involvement in Southeast Asia, and to a lesser extent during the conflicts in Iraq and Afghanistan. Armed Services pursued crisis inquiries more actively than Foreign Relations in the 1990s because of Desert Storm and the collapse of Yugoslavia, while Foreign Relations was exceptionally active during the first term of the Reagan administration.

Overall, the trends for both committees suggest that what people cared about, scandals and crises, received a moderate level of attention compared to routine inquiries. Armed Services devoted an average of seven public days per year to fire alarms and thirteen public days to police patrols. Its executive sessions were similarly skewed with six days per year allotted to fire alarms and seven days to patrols. Nevertheless, the range of hearings varied widely for both types of hearings, indicating that Armed Services tried to make room on its agenda when events demanded attention. The committee's highest number of public patrol days per year reached eighty-five, while its maximum number of fire alarms per year was sixty-five. The figures for executive session patrols and alarms were forty-four and thirty-one, respectively.

Foreign Relations averaged six public hearing days per year on alarms and twenty-six public hearing days per year on patrols. In contrast to Armed Services, the committee allocated more of its executive calendar on average to alarm days than patrols, with fourteen and eleven closed hearing days per year, respectively. Again, the variation was substantial, with the greatest number of public alarms attaining forty-four days per year and the highest number of public patrols rising to seventy-six days per year. For executive sessions, the maximum value for each type of hearing content was thirty-five alarm days per year versus forty-two patrol days.

For both committees, then, the trends in the content of oversight and the venues for fire alarm and police patrol hearings suggest strategic calculation in the way Armed Services and Foreign Relations responded to routine administration and international events. Given their disparate goals, this should not be surprising, but the variation raises questions about whether the committees sought the type of information that served the interests of the public. Did they increase fire alarm inquiries when the public expressed concern about national security issues or mounting casualties? Was their oversight activity timely and transparent?

Expectations for Police Patrols, Fire Alarms, and Committee Strategies

By definition, fire alarms involved events that sparked widespread public attention, while police patrols implied routine matters with a smaller, but more attentive audience. In the realm of national security, crises and scandals tapped into the power of the presidency to nationalize policy issues, while routine monitoring tended to engage organized interests and policy elites. In addition, the president's handling of important defense and foreign policy events figured in the overall reputations of the Republican and Democratic Party, while administrative decisions in the Pentagon and State Department mattered most to narrow constituencies. Alarm hearings thus spoke directly to large questions of democratic accountability, while patrols contributed to ongoing review processes that constitute regular order. Together, both types of oversight fostered the rule of law in international affairs, but their dissimilarities led to different perceived gains and losses from each type of hearing. The high frequency of patrols compared to alarms suggests that both Armed Services and Foreign Relations found the former less costly.

The theory of police patrols and fire alarms predicts the conditions under which lawmakers resorted to one or the other. Lawmakers engaged in "patrols" of bureaucratic activity when they could obtain reliable information without much cost. They wrote statutes to stimulate third-party "alarms" about wrongdoing, however, when information was difficult to obtain.[19] If Congress set up the statutory triggers for fire alarms correctly, bureaucrats would not stray. The theory thus predicts that legislators could cut back on oversight inquiries secure in the knowledge that important abuses of bureaucratic discretion would come to light.

This underlying cost-benefit logic is applicable to the content of national security oversight hearings, with two caveats. First, statutory constraints on executive discretion in foreign affairs are comparatively weak and rarely engage the

[19] McCubbins and Schwartz (1984).

judiciary in enforcement. Second, third parties setting off alarms included international actors.[20] In effect, the committees opted for patrols when gathering information was inexpensive and produced little fallout. They did not necessarily respond to alarms, however, unless failure to monitor the executive became costly. Given the constraints on senators' time, the committees frequently reduced patrols in favor of alarms when events demanded their attention. Both committees thus attempted to optimize short-term gains and losses across hearing types in accordance with their dominant goals.

Three types of influences were potentially relevant to distinguishing among types of national security oversight from 1947 to 2008, and all were connected to varying degrees with party reputations. First was the party label of individual presidents whose handling of foreign affairs affected the Republican or Democratic brand in the minds of voters. Second was the salience of defense and foreign policy issues among the general public. Third was the loss, as measured by the number of battle deaths, from the use of force to accomplish U.S. foreign policy goals. Each of these dimensions—president's party, public salience, and casualties—posed challenges that the Senate Armed Services and Foreign Relations Committees met in different ways with respect to the content of oversight hearings.

The President's Party

The American presidency has a unique capacity to nationalize issues and make them salient to the public.[21] This characteristic is particularly strong in the realm of foreign affairs, where the symbolic power of the office, the constitutional mantle of commander in chief, and the vast discretion delegated by Congress to the executive all come together. The decisions by the Senate Armed Services and Foreign Relations Committees to undertake fire alarm oversight thus were fraught with political implications. The effect of the president on national security oversight was asymmetric, however, with respect to both his party label and the individual committee.

Republican administrations have held long-standing reputational advantages for greater competence in foreign affairs.[22] In addition, higher expectations for Republican presidents prompted voters to judge them more harshly than Democratic presidents for perceived policy mistakes.[23] The imbalance in party reputations meant that oversight would be more costly to Republican presidents, while the payoffs from calling Democratic presidents to account for their management of crises might be relatively modest. All else equal, we would expect

---

[20] See the graphs in Chapter 1 and the article by Balla and Deering (2013).
[21] See, for example, Skowronek (1993) and Howell, Jackman, and Rogowski (2013).
[22] Petrocik (1996); Petrocik, Benoit, and Hansen (2003–4).
[23] Trager and Vavreck (2011).

Democratic committee majorities to engage in more police patrols and fire alarm hearings when a Republican occupied the White House; we would anticipate little to no effect on either type of hearing content when Democratic presidents confronted Republican-dominated committees.

All else was not equal, however, because of the disparate ideological stances of the national parties toward defense and foreign policy. Republican presidents after Eisenhower adopted a proactive stance toward the conduct of U.S. foreign policy compared to Democrats. Since Reagan, they also placed less emphasis on international cooperation when determining the nation's strategic interests. The hawkish disposition of the contemporary Republican Party made GOP presidents natural allies of the Senate Armed Services Committee, a relationship that set up cross-pressures between party benefits and goal-related payoffs for the members with respect to oversight.

The Armed Services Committee had several options for balancing the gains and losses of oversight content arising from the asymmetry of party ideology: (1) it could have protected Republican presidents, even during times of divided government, by scheduling fewer patrol and alarm hearings; (2) it could have increased the frequency of executive sessions to deflect attention about difficult issues away from a like-minded Republican in the White House; or (3) it could have altered the mix of police patrol and fire alarm hearings during times of increased public concern about defense policy. Under various conditions, Armed Services appears to have employed all three strategies. No doubt, the resulting variation in hearing content accounts for the findings in Chapter 4 that divided government was a poor predictor of the committee's total oversight activity.

At first glance, the Foreign Relations Committee had a more straightforward calculation to make. The partisan orientation of the committee encouraged it to engage in greater oversight during periods of divided government, and GOP presidents sometimes needed prodding toward diplomacy. Nevertheless, the committee had to reckon with the costs of public backlash if it challenged a president during times of crisis when the public demanded national unity. The remedy to this dilemma was to engage in more patrol hearings about the overall direction of U.S. policy without directly challenging the president's handling of specific events or crises. The committee's heavy reliance on state of the world hearings enabled it to be partisan, therefore, while conforming to popular norms of support for the president during an emergency. Nevertheless, the committee still found it beneficial to substitute fire alarm hearings for police patrol inquiries when a Democratic majority on the committee could obtain low-cost information to undermine the credibility of a Republican president.

Public Opinion

The American public is notoriously ill informed about the rest of the world. Many scholars contend, therefore, that policy elites influence the public's attitudes toward national security rather than respond to shifts in citizen opinion. If this condition held between 1947 and 2008, we would expect to see little popular influence over the frequency and content of either type of oversight hearings. The Gallup measure of the "most important problem" facing the country demonstrates that attitudes varied considerably over the period of study, but the source of that variation is unclear.

In Figure 5.1, for example, we see peaks of concern in 1958 and 1959, from 1965 to 1969, and from 2005 to 2007. The last years of the Eisenhower administration were not necessarily more dangerous than the Kennedy years, with threats to Berlin and dangers of confrontation over Soviet missiles in Cuba, yet twice as many people expressed concern about international affairs under Ike. Moreover, we know that peak hearing activity in both Armed Services and Foreign Relations Committees occurred during the 1970s, but public anxiety dropped precipitously after Nixon resigned and showed little upward movement until 1983. Overall, the number of people citing defense and international issues as most important averaged about 16 percent, hardly a powerful motivator in most years for committee oversight.

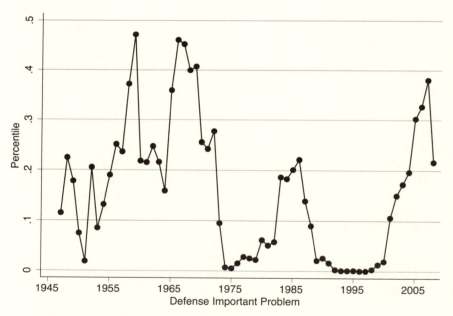

Figure 5.1. Salience of National Security Issues, 1947–2008.
Note: Percentage of public selecting defense, national security, or foreign policy as the "Most Important Problem" in Gallup surveys.
Source: iPOLL, http://www.ropercenter.uconn.edu/data_access/ipoll/ipoll.html (accessed June 2005 and June 2009).

Periods of moderate to strong concern about national security issues provided incentives for increased patrols, however, despite the sometimes puzzling levels of public concern abut national security. Armed Services could engage in advocacy oversight to highlight the needs of the military at times of serious international pressure, while deflecting performance issues to executive sessions. Foreign Relations could find a more receptive audience for its reviews of the state of the world during periods of public anxiety. Nevertheless, the committees' public police patrol hearings appeared more useful in keeping attentive constituencies informed about the administration of key programs than in responding to the general public.

War Casualties

The costs of war required attention from both the Senate Armed Services and Foreign Relations Committees throughout the post–World War II period. Rising battle deaths involved constituents from senators' home states and dampened "rally round the flag" effects, particularly for lengthy military operations. For Armed Services, the loss of life inevitably led to questions about the welfare of the troops and the need for greater fire alarm hearings. The committee could exercise discretion, however, over the amount of public exposure to give its reviews and shift its inquiries into executive session.

Figure 5.2 presents data on battle deaths by quarter from 1947 to 2008 and shows considerable variation during the period of study. The level of casualties was zero in relatively few years, while the loss of life in Iraq and Afghanistan was moderate compared to that in Korea and Vietnam. Given the public salience of war casualties, the Senate Armed Services and Foreign Relations Committees had a potentially large role to play in educating citizens about national security issues through alarm hearings throughout the post–World War II era.

Berinsky's comprehensive analysis of public opinion in wartime indicated that partisan and group orientations structure the attitudes of citizens during major conflicts, just as they do in domestic politics. He noted, "During war, people judge the correctness of military actions through the lens of their partisan predispositions."[24] Both committees had to weigh the costs of oversight, therefore, when casualties began to rise. Some inquiries had to be public to satisfy citizens and attentive publics that the national security committees took the loss of life seriously. Yet much of the increased scrutiny would require executive sessions out of the need to protect sensitive information about military operations. Such closed-door hearings also enabled the committees to manage the political costs of a particular conflict, which was particularly useful to the consensus-minded members of Armed Services. Finally, increased attention to a crisis (and its attendant scandals) presented the committees with a

---

[24] Berinsky (2009, 9).

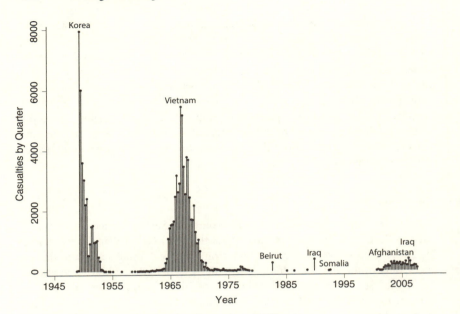

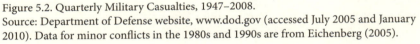

Figure 5.2. Quarterly Military Casualties, 1947–2008.
Source: Department of Defense website, www.dod.gov (accessed July 2005 and January 2010). Data for minor conflicts in the 1980s and 1990s are from Eichenberg (2005).

trade-off: ramp up the committee workload or cut back on the number of po-lice patrol hearings. Thus, as the motivation to engage in fire alarm hearings rose, police patrol inquiries likely diminished.

Figure 5.3 presents the distribution of quarterly public police patrol and fire alarm hearings according to the frequency of casualties. Following common practice among scholars who use casualty data, I took the natural log of the quarterly data in Figure 5.2 to smooth out the extreme values. I then created a version lagged by quarter, which provided the best fit in the statistical models in the next section. At the extreme right of the x-axis one finds the adjusted quarterly casualty figures for the Korean War. Moving left along the axis one finds a mix of adjusted quarterly observations from Korea and Vietnam, some of which mingle with data from the Iraq and Afghanistan wars around the in-terval between 3.5 and 4.5. At the far left are the adjusted casualty figures from the Marine barracks attack in Beirut, Desert Storm, Somalia, and smaller-scale events involving loss of a few troops.

The top panel shows the mix of quarterly public fire alarms, depicted as black Xs, and quarterly public police patrols, marked as gray hollow circles, for the Senate Armed Services Committee from 1947 to 2008. One striking feature of the figure is the incidence of alarm hearings when casualties were at zero,

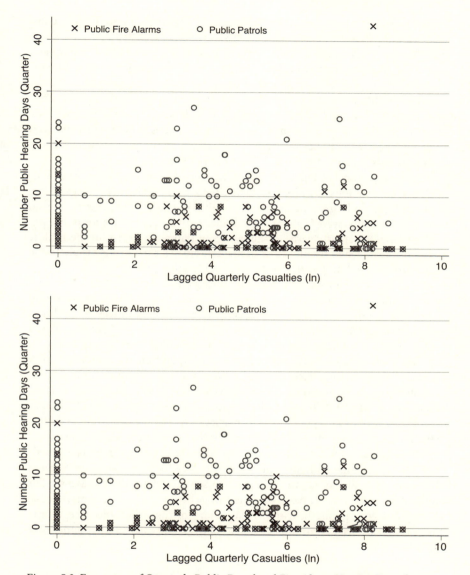

Figure 5.3. Frequency of Quarterly Public Patrol and Fire Alarm Hearing Days, by Quarterly Casualties. Top: Armed Services; bottom: Foreign Relations.
Note: The top panel demonstrates that Armed Services shifted emphasis on police patrol hearings at low levels of casualties to fire alarms at higher levels. The bottom panel shows that Foreign Relations focused on patrols, regardless of casualty levels, and kept its infrequent inquiries into scandal and crises very short.

which indicates committee attention to major crises that did not involve combat operations. Given the sensitivity to the use of force revealed in the last chapter, this pattern is not surprising. Nevertheless, such hearings were infrequent, relatively speaking, and typically consumed fewer than ten days of public inquiry per quarter. More common was the prevalence of quarters with no public hearings of either type. Empty quarters were most common in the middle range for casualties, but were present, as well, at the highest levels of adjusted battle deaths. Finally, the graph provides evidence of a substitution effect between hearing types, with public patrols showing a decline as casualties increased and public alarms becoming more frequent with rising loss of life.

The bottom panel of Figure 5.3 presents a very different pattern for the Senate Foreign Relations Committee. Again, we see some alarm hearings at low casualty levels and a great many quarters with zero hearings of either type, even when battle deaths were high. The committee's strong preference for police patrol hearings emerges clearly in the figure and appears to rise in the middle range of the adjusted frequency of casualties. No clear pattern is visible in the distribution of public alarms with respect to casualties, however.

Overall, police patrols and fire alarm hearings served different constituencies and disparate committee needs in the post–World War II era. Thus, we would expect to see a strategic use of hearing content by both committees under different scenarios. With respect to public oversight hearings, Armed Services would be more protective than Foreign Relations of Republican presidents and more inclined than Foreign Relations to take advantage of citizen concerns about defense and international issues to build support for its programs through public police patrols. In addition, Armed Services would decrease patrols in favor of fire alarms when U.S. troops experienced rising casualties. Foreign Relations, in contrast, would find public patrols particularly useful in wartime to deflect damaging confrontations with the president that result from alarm hearings.

With respect to executive sessions, Armed Services likely would have scheduled more hearings with Republican administrations compared to Foreign Relations. In addition, we would expect to see each committee make similar trade-offs between secret patrols and alarms when casualties were on the rise, as they did with public hearings. A summary of the expectations regarding the national security committee's choices of oversight hearing type appears in Table 5.1.

PARTY REPUTATION EFFECTS AND POLICE PATROL AND FIRE ALARM OVERSIGHT

The education of the public is a prime function of congressional oversight, particularly in the realm of foreign affairs. From citizens' perspective, some types of information are more salient than others. People care more about the costs

Table 5.1. Expectations for Public and Executive Police Patrol and Fire Alarm
Oversight Hearing Days

Type of Influence	Armed Services		Foreign Relations	
	Police Patrols	Fire Alarms	Police Patrols	Fire Alarms
Public Hearings				
Divided-Dem. Pres.	No effect	No effect	Increase	Increase
Unified-Rep. Pres.	Decrease	Decrease	Increase	Increase
Divided-Rep. Pres.	Decrease	Decrease	Increase	Increase
Public Opinion	Increase	Decrease	No effect	No effect
Casualties	Decrease	Increase	Increase	Decrease
Executive Sessions				
Divided-Dem. Pres.	No effect	No effect	Decrease	Decrease
Unified-Rep. Pres.	Increase	Increase	No effect	No effect
Divided-Rep. Pres.	No effect	No effect	No effect	No effect
Public Opinion	No effect	No effect	No effect	No effect
Casualties	Decrease	Increase	Increase	Decrease

of war and bureaucratic wrongdoing than about routine program administration. Thus, I pay particular attention to the stimuli for fire alarm oversight, which reviews the executive's performance in managing crises and the vast resources of the national security state.

I begin with the number of days each committee devoted to police patrols and fire alarms. The data are organized by quarter, producing 248 public observations and 248 executive observations for each committee. I chose to look at the data by quarters because I was especially interested in the responsiveness of Armed Services and Foreign Relations to changes in quarterly casualties. As in the case of total oversight activity analyzed in the last chapter, the congressional calendar was a factor in the committees' hearing schedules and appeared vividly in Figure 5.3 because of so many quarters without a patrol or fire alarm hearing. I dealt with the unobserved factors responsible for this pattern through random quarterly effects, as discussed in Appendix E.

The statistical analysis employs negative binomial regression, a method appropriate for count data.[25] With this model I test for the influence of the president's party, public salience of defense and international issues, and casualties on the frequency of oversight hearing content. To assess the effects of the president's party, I created three dummy variables: (1) divided government with a

---

[25] Poisson regression requires that the mean and variance be equal, an assumption that the distributions for budget, police patrol, and fire alarm hearings did not meet. The high incidence of zeroes led me to consider using zero-inflated negative binomial regression. In Appendix E, I explain the tests and reasoning that indicated that negative binomial regression was the superior technique.

Democratic president (2) unified government with a Republican president, and (3) Republican president and Democratic Senate. Thus, the excluded base category was Democratic presidents under unified government. As controls, I included the size of the budget for the Defense and State Departments, which proved to be a strong predictor of total oversight in the last chapter, quarterly changes in presidential approval, and total hearing days. I also employed dummy variables for specific committee chairs. Tables E.1 through E.6 contain the statistical results for the analyses for each type of hearing by committee and by public and executive session.

Beginning with the Armed Services Committee and patrol hearings, the results partially confirm expectations about how the committee would behave. On the one hand, the influence of the president's party was not significant in explaining public patrols, although the signs for Republican presidents were negative, as anticipated. On the other hand, the salience of public opinion was positive and significant, as Armed Services engaged in more police patrols during periods of high public concern about national security. In addition, the adjusted casualties variable was negative and significant, confirming the need for the committee to reduce patrol hearings as the human costs of warfare increased. Among the control variables, only total hearing days was significant in the full model, and it was positive.

The first panel of Figure 5.4 presents the predicted number of police patrol hearing days by quarter as adjusted casualties increased from zero to their maximum. The values for Republican presidents appear as hollow black circles and those for Democratic presidents as hollow gray squares. Although the coefficients differentiating presidents by party were not significant, there is a clear pattern in the figure once we take account of casualties. At almost every point on the casualties scale, Armed Services scheduled less routine program oversight for Republican administrations compared to Democratic administrations. Moreover, the positive influence of public opinion in stimulating greater numbers of quarterly patrol hearings turns out to have been a peacetime phenomenon. Once casualties approached the adjusted value of 4, which was the level of Iraq and some early and late quarters of the Korean and Vietnam Wars, inquiries into program implementation took up no more than two or three days per quarter.

The effects of the president's party show up dramatically in the models of public fire alarm quarterly hearing days. The coefficient for Republican administrations under unified control is large, negative, and strongly significant, as hypothesized. The other dummy variables dealing with the president's party label are not significant, and the combination for Republican administrations and Democratic committee majorities has the wrong sign. The public's assessment of defense as an important problem has a negative coefficient, as anticipated, but is not significant. The effect of casualties produces an increase in public alarm days and is highly significant, consistent with expectations. Of the control variables, only budget authorization is significant and positive.

The impact of the Armed Services Committee's protective stance toward Republican administrations and its responsiveness to rising casualties present a dramatic picture in the second panel of Figure 5.4 on page 150. Again, Republican administrations are represented with black hollow circles and Democratic administrations with gray hollow squares. Once casualties rose above zero, the difference in predicted quarterly fire alarm hearings is stark. At modest and high levels of casualties, Republican presidents were less likely to be the targets of fire alarm oversight. The exceptions, marked by the circles in the middle of the casualties scale, include George W. Bush at the hands of a Democratic committee majority in 2007, and especially in 2008 when the average was close to six days per quarter.

The results for police patrols in executive session reveal the expected cooperation between Armed Services and Republican presidents quite strongly with

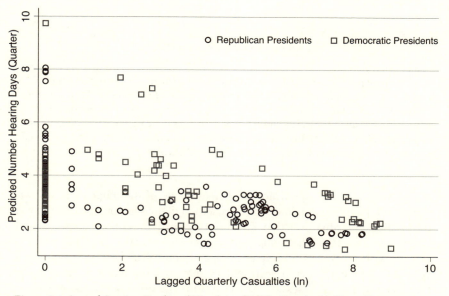

Figure 5.4. Armed Services Predicted Number of Public Patrol and Alarm Hearing Days, by President's Party and Casualties. First panel: Public Police Patrols; second panel: Public Fire Alarms.

Note: The above panel shows the predicted number of Armed Services public police patrol hearing days for Republican and Democratic presidents at different levels of casualties with all continuous variables set at their mean and other variables at their medians. The distribution of the black circles indicates that the committee was less inclined to conduct public patrol hearings under Republican presidents than under Democratic presidents, although the predicted values tend to convergence at very low levels when casualties were at their highest.

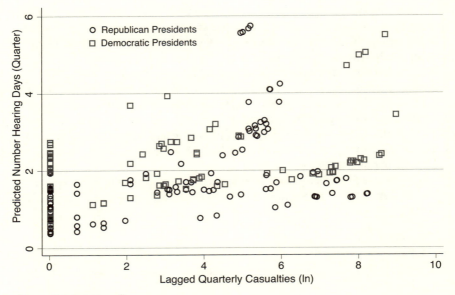

Figure 5.4. (*continued*)

The above panel shows the predicted number of Armed Services public fire alarm hearing days for Republican and Democratic presidents at different levels of casualties. The distribution of black circles and gray squares indicates a rising propensity to engage in oversight of scandals and crises as casualties increased under presidents of either party. Nevertheless, Republican presidents' handling of crises generally received less scrutiny than that of Democratic presidents, all else equal.

a large, positive, and significant coefficient. None of the other variables was significant other than total hearing days, although the sign for casualties was in the predicted negative direction. The results confirm the adverse consequences of the reduced workloads among Senate committees for the frequency of executive sessions analyzed in Chapter 3. Once I controlled for the effects of the committee's total number of hearing days, there was not much variance in the frequency of executive session patrols left for the other variables to explain other than the Republican label of the president.

The results for secret alarm hearings reveal a positive response by Armed Services to rising casualties. This finding seems to confirm the fact that the committee made trade-offs between hearing types as security conditions demanded. When casualties rose, secret alarm hearings increased, while secret police patrols decreased. Considering public and secret patrols together further confirms the protective bias within Armed Services toward Republican presidents, which was masked by the committee's use of executive sessions to deal with routine program administration.

The graph in Figure 5.5 shows the frequency of predicted executive session patrols and alarms at different levels of casualties under Republican administrations only. The hollow circles represent patrols and the hollow squares signify fire alarms. The point estimates are from different models and are not strictly comparable, but the overall pattern is interesting. When casualties were at zero, Armed Services conducted a lot of patrols and quite a few fire alarm

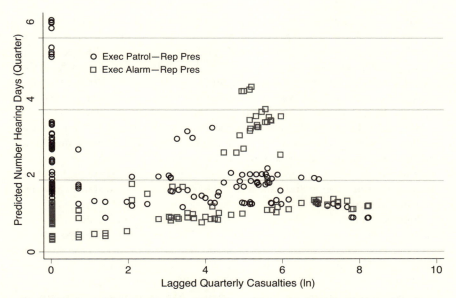

Figure 5.5. Armed Services Predicted Number of Executive Patrol and Alarm Hearing Days, by Casualties.

Note: This figure displays the predicted quarterly values for Armed Services executive session hearing days from two different negative binomial regression models (xtnbreg) with random quarterly effects for fire alarm and police patrol hearing days under Republican presidents at varying levels of casualties with all continuous variables set at their mean and other variables at their medians. Given the different models, the point predictions are not directly comparable, but the comparison of the overall patterns is still informative.

The Casualties variable is not significant in the model for executive patrols, which are represented by hollow black circles and follow no consistent pattern. The high frequency of circles at zero casualties occurred during the Reagan presidency, when the committee cooperated with the president to build up U.S. defense capabilities. The Casualties variable has a positive sign and is highly significant for executive alarm oversight hearing days, which appear as hollow gray squares and follow an upward trajectory. The high frequencies of squares at medium levels of casualties coincided with efforts of a Democratic committee majority in 2007–8 to increase oversight of the Iraq War, although the first quarter of 2006 had a relatively high count.

hearings, all else equal. The very high values for patrols in the leftmost column represent the first term of Reagan's presidency, as the committee joined with the administration in building up U.S. military capabilities. Differences in hearing type emerge under other presidents once battle deaths occurred, however, with secret patrol hearings dominating until the adjusted variable moves beyond 4, when crises and scandals became the more frequent type of closed-door oversight hearing. Recalling that the values at or above 4 reflect losses from Iraq, as well as some quarters of the wars in Korea and Vietnam, the committee appeared to substitute one type of secret oversight for another during wartime.

The chair of the Armed Services Committee has considerable discretion to decide what type of hearing to schedule and where to hold it. I tested for the influence of individual chairs by creating dummy variables for each of the eleven senators who have chaired the committee from 1947 to 2008. I then included each individual, one at a time, in the models for patrols and fire alarms, both public and secret. I discovered that when Senator John Stennis (D-MS) chaired Armed Services, the committee reduced both public and secret fire alarm sessions. Similarly, when Senator Barry Goldwater (R-AZ) led the committee, public fire alarm sessions went down. To my surprise, the variables controlling for the tenure of two of the committee's most influential chairmen, Senators Richard Russell (D-GA) and Sam Nunn (D-GA), did not yield statistically significant coefficients.

Figure 5.6 depicts the predicted frequency of quarterly public alarm hearing days under all presidents compared to the predicted number of such days during the tenure of Senator Stennis, who chaired the committee from 1969 through 1980 under both Republicans (Nixon and Ford) and Democrats (Carter). Recall from Chapter 3 that Stennis was an ardent champion of the Pentagon and presided over the committee during a period of intense warfare, a relatively peaceful interval, and an atmosphere of growing alarm about the Soviet Union. As one can see from the solid black circles representing his terms as chair, Stennis depressed the level of public oversight of scandals and crises, regardless of the president's party or the level of casualties.

Overall, the way in which Armed Services allocated its time suffered from a substantial lack of transparency during the period of the study. There is no obvious reason other than committee self-interest in supporting the Pentagon to have insulated Republican presidents from scrutiny. Nevertheless, the lower rates of public monitoring through police patrols and fire alarms and the tendency to beef up secret patrols under Republican administrations suggest a decided partisan bias. Moreover, the committee's public scrutiny of the Defense Department was lower than normal under the tenure of Senator Stennis, and to a lesser extent under Senator Goldwater. The committee's interest in promoting the interests of the military establishment partially offset its reticence, however, when public interest in defense issues was high and, more important, when casualties rose. One should not lose sight of the fact, however, that casualties

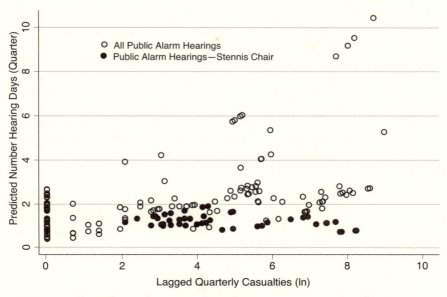

Figure 5.6. Effects of Armed Services Chair John Stennis on Quarterly Public Fire Alarm Hearing Days, by Casualties.
Note: Predicted values are from negative binomial regression (xtnbreg) of quarterly public fire alarm hearings with random quarterly effects and with all continuous variables set at their mean and other variables at their medians. The solid black circles in the graph demonstrate how Stennis, who was chair from 1969 to 1980, decreased the Armed Services Committee's public inquiries into crises and scandals, even when casualties were very high.

attained high levels before the committee's public scrutiny of crises and scandals increased. Even then, the added hearings amounted on average to no more than a few days per quarter.

Shifting to the Senate Foreign Relations Committee, we see very different patterns of police patrol and fire alarm oversight. Beginning with routine inquiries, the committee proved to be moved almost exclusively by presidential politics. For public patrols, the party coefficients were highly significant for all presidents, and negative for Republican administrations confronting a Democratic committee majority, when compared to the base category of unified government under Democrats. The public opinion and adjusted casualties variables were not significant and did little to improve the overall fit of the models, although all of the control variables proved to be significant and positive.

The first panel of Figure 5.7 presents the predicted quarterly public patrol hearing days under Republican and Democratic presidents, as casualties move from zero to their maximum adjusted value. Again, the hollow black circles represent all Republican presidents, and the hollow gray squares represent all Democratic presidents. The casualty variable is not statistically significant for public patrols, and the pattern as casualties move from low to high does not reveal a consistent relationship for either type of presidential administration. Abnormally high values for Republican presidents occurred during Ford's tenure and Reagan's first year in office, periods of divided and unified government, respectively. Nevertheless, one feature of the graph stands out; regardless of the level of casualties, Republican presidents inspired more police patrol inquiries by the Senate Foreign Relations Committee over the period of study.

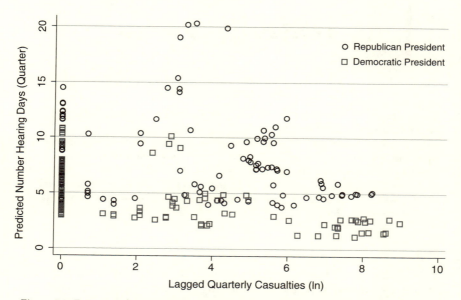

Figure 5.7. Foreign Relations Predicted Number of Public Patrol and Alarm Hearing Days, by President's Party and Casualties. First panel: Public Police Patrol Hearing Days; second panel: Public Fire Alarm Hearing Days.
Note: This figure depicts the distribution of the Foreign Relations Committee's predicted public patrol and alarm hearing days from negative binomial regression (xtnbreg) with quarterly random effects and with all continuous variables set at their mean and other variables at their medians. The above panel shows the predicted values for patrols as casualties increase.

The casualties variable is not significant for public patrol days, but the various dummy variables for the president's party have highly significant coefficients. The hollow black circles represent Republican presidents and show no consistent pattern with respect to casualties, although the coefficient is positive. The hollow gray squares represent all Democratic presidents and are consistently lower at all levels of casualties except 1947 and 1977.

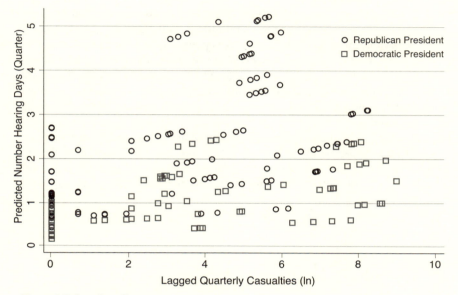

Figure 5.7. (*continued*)

The above panel presents the predicted values for public fire alarm days for which Casualties is a highly significant variable. The pattern of hollow circles for Republican presidents follows a sharp upward trajectory as casualties increased; the distribution of inquiries for Democratic presidents also rose, but at a more modest rate.

The results for Foreign Relations' fire alarm inquiries are not very informative. The coefficient for divided party control with a Republican president and Democratic committee majority is positive and almost significant, and the other theoretically important variables do not attain significance, although the sign of the casualties variable is in the correct direction. Basically, the control variables of State Department Budget and total hearing days explain most of the variance in the model for public crises and scandal oversight.

The graph of the predicted number of quarterly fire alarm hearing days in the second panel of Figure 5.7 above indicates some difference between the committee's treatment of Republican and Democratic presidents, however. Once casualties passed the adjusted value of 2, fire alarm scrutiny of Republican presidents went up sharply. These results were most pronounced for the Nixon and Ford presidencies and the early years of the Reagan administration. The scrutiny of Democratic presidents showed a slight upward trend as casualties increased. Generally, the most important feature of the graph is that Foreign Relations monitored crises and scandals under Republican administrations more closely than under Democratic administrations at all levels of casualties. Still, one should not attribute too much import to the differences, which are relatively slight in terms of the number of predicted quarterly days involved.

The most important insight about Foreign Relations from the two panels of Figure 5.7 is the imbalance of the committee's public hearing agenda toward police patrols. Since 1947, the committee appears to have made comparatively little effort to shape public discourse about international crises or scandals. It appears that with the exception of 1966 and 1971 under Fulbright's chairmanship the committee satisfied the members' inclinations toward policy debate without getting into visible confrontations with the president over his handling of crises and scandal.

Figure 5.8 graphs the predicted values for police patrols and fire alarms from two separate models of executive session hearings. Although the individual point estimates are not comparable for the different types of oversight, the graph underscores the committee's penchant for patrols over alarms even behind closed

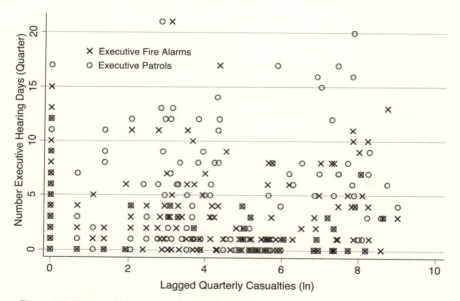

Figure 5.8. Foreign Relations Predicted Number of Executive Alarm and Patrol Hearing Days, by Casualties.
Note: This figure represents the predicted values for all presidents from two different models of Foreign Relations executive patrol and alarm hearing days from negative binomial regression (xtnbreg) with quarterly random effects and with all continuous variables set at their mean and other variables at their medians. The Casualties variable is negative for executive fire alarms and patrols and not significant in either model. The distribution of the predicted fire alarm values, represented by black Xs, shows a modest upward rise, yet it also reveals a substantial number of quarters with zero fire alarm hearings even when casualties are very high. The pattern for police patrols, depicted with hollow gray circles, captures Foreign Relations' propensity for secret patrol hearings that examine the "state of the world" even under conditions of high casualties.

doors. Despite the high number of quarters with zero hearings at all level of casualties, Foreign Relations had many quarters with more than five executive session hearing days and twenty-eight quarters with ten or more days of secret hearings. With the exception of several quarters at the highest level of casualties, which occurred during Korea and Vietnam, the bias toward secret patrol hearings over alarms appears at most levels of casualties.

The final lesson from the analysis of the content of Foreign Relations hearings is the substantial impact of the committee's diminished workload over the last two decades of the study period. Total hearing days is a powerful influence on both patrol and alarm inquiries in all of the statistical models for the committee. The graph in Figure 5.9 depicts the predicted values for Republican presidents only, since they were the more frequent target of public patrol and alarm monitoring. Although the point estimates are not directly comparable, the patterns of predicted values for each hearing type differ.

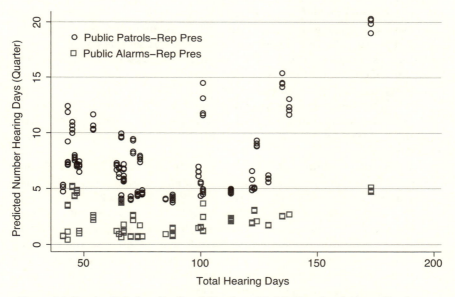

Figure 5.9. Foreign Relations Predicted Number of Public Patrol and Alarm Hearing Days, by Republican Presidents and Total Hearing Days.
Note: This figure presents predicted values for public police patrols (hollow black circles) and fire alarms (hollow gray squares) during Republican administrations calculated with the two models depicted in Figure 5.8, but graphed this time against total hearing days. The distribution for both indicates that, all else equal, the level of Foreign Relations workload has been a prime factor in the content of the committee's oversight hearings. A lower level of overall hearing activity, typical of the last two decades, appears to have had a particularly strong effect on the frequency of patrol hearings.

Public patrols reveal a U-shaped pattern with a substantial cluster of hearings at the extreme left-hand side of the graph. In other words, when Foreign Relations was relatively inactive, it still made room for public reviews of the state of the world; when it was very busy, it added many more patrols. In contrast, the predicted frequency of fire alarm hearings did not vary much with the distribution of total hearing days. In years of relatively short hearing dockets, then, the committee would have had to diminish its public deliberations about other topics, including statutes, nominations, treaties, and most of all budgets, in order to schedule alarm hearings.

CRISES AND WAR AS A SPECIAL CASE?

Grouping crises and scandals into a single dependent variable raises an issue about the robustness of the results. Would the asymmetrical patterns of oversight for Republican and Democratic presidents hold up if we looked solely at crises? Would the differences in Armed Services and Foreign Relations responsiveness to rising casualties continue? On the one hand, major conflicts created pressures for committees to avoid criticizing the president in the interests of presenting a unified front to the nation's enemies. On the other hand, wartime offered opportunities for the political construction of scandals to challenge the president's policies indirectly. The statistical analyses of Armed Services' crisis hearings alone yielded results that were similar to the findings for combined alarm hearings. The models solely for Foreign Relations' crisis hearings, in contrast, changed with respect to both the president's party and casualties.

Recall that crisis oversight was a significant activity for both the Senate Armed Services and Foreign Relations Committees between 1947 and 2008. Armed Services devoted about a quarter of its total hearing docket to crisis oversight, according to Figure 1.6, split almost evenly between public and executive session oversight. It allocated about an eighth of its hearing agenda to scandals, with about two-thirds of those days devoted to public inquiries. Foreign Relations, too, spent about a quarter of its hearing days on crises, but scheduled more than two-thirds of them behind closed doors. Its attention to scandal was modest, about 8 percent, split nearly equally between open and closed sessions. Thus, we might expect that removing observations of scandal hearings mattered more in statistical models for Armed Services.

The pattern of results for crisis hearings Armed Services, however, proved consistent with the earlier results for fire alarms. The committee's propensity to shield Republican administrations shows up clearly in the negative and highly significant coefficients for both public and secret hearings. The casualties variable is positive, although not quite significant for public crisis hearings, and it is positive and highly significant for executive session crisis hearings.

Figure 5.10 presents the predicted values for Armed Services' public crisis hearings over the range of adjusted casualties from zero to their maximum value. As in previous graphs, the point estimates for Republican presidents are represented as black hollow circles and for Democratic presidents as gray hollow squares. For most levels of casualties, Democratic administrations received more scrutiny of their handling of crises than did Republican administrations. The exceptions occurred in the middle range of the scale, where we see two clusters of circles at roughly four predicted days of hearings per quarter. All

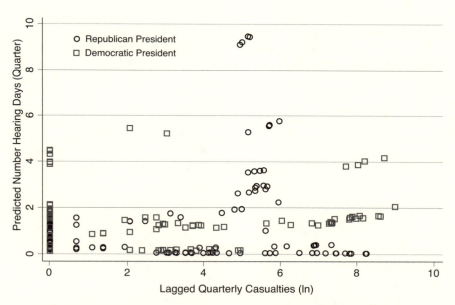

Figure 5.10. Armed Services Predicted Number of Public Crisis Hearing Days, by President's Party and Casualties.
Note: The predicted number of Armed Services public crisis hearing days in this figure from negative binomial regression (xtnbreg) with random effects and with all continuous variables set at their mean and other variables at their medians indicates that Democratic presidents, shown as hollow gray squares, received more scrutiny than Republican presidents, represented by hollow black circles, at the lower and upper ends of the casualties spectrum, although only one of the variables for president's party was significant. The committee was also more likely to have quarters with zero crisis hearing days under Republican presidents. The Republican exceptions lay in the middle range of the Casualties variable, which was not statistically significant, and included all of 2007–8, when President Bush faced a Democratic majority determined to increase oversight of the Iraq War. The Democratic president outlier in which predicted hearing days exceeded four per quarter occurred at the beginning of President Clinton's term and involved the Somalia crisis.

of these occurred in 2007–8, when Democrats took control of the Senate and the committee's consensus regarding Republican presidents broke down.

The results for Foreign Relations' crisis hearings show some differences in approach compared to the models that include scandals. For public crisis hearings the coefficient for the president's party is no longer significant, although it remains positive. The casualties variable is significant and positive, however, when scandals are no longer included in the dependent variable. The model for executive session crisis hearings is essentially the same.

According to Figure 5.11, however, Republican presidents received more scrutiny than Democratic presidents during times of crisis from Foreign Relations, particularly at the lower and middle ranges of casualties. The highest predicted values were for the Republican president during 2005 and 2007. Nevertheless, the predicted number of days per quarter was no more than five at its highest level, and the hearing record reveals that the topics primarily addressed crises

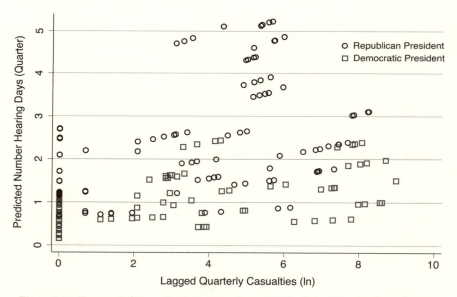

Figure 5.11. Foreign Relations Predicted Number of Public Crisis Hearing Days, by President's Party and Casualties.

Note: The predicted number of Foreign Relations public crisis hearing days from negative binomial regression (xtnbreg) with random effects and with all continuous variables set at their mean and other variables at their medians shown in this figure indicates that Republican presidents (hollow black circles) received more scrutiny than Democratic presidents (hollow gray squares), particularly at the lower and middle ranges of the casualties spectrum. The values near five per quarter for Republican presidents occurred during 2005 and 2007.

other than Iraq, most notably Iran and North Korea. This was a classic example of the committee's habit of trying to influence public opinion during wartime while avoiding direct challenges to the president's conduct of war.

Overall, the national security committees' efforts to deal with the nationalizing impulses of foreign policy on party reputations had asymmetric effects on the content of their oversight hearings. The president's party and the costs of war impacted the scrutiny of administration policies, albeit in different ways for the Senate Armed Services and Foreign Relations Committees. For most of the study period, the Republican Party enjoyed a consistent advantage among voters for handling international affairs, while Republican presidents after Eisenhower tended to take a more aggressive stance toward the use of force. Together, these factors motivated the Armed Services Committee to shield Republican administrations from public patrol, alarm, and crisis inquiries. In contrast, Republican presidents invited more attention from Foreign Relations, although the additional hearings usually were patrols of various regions or the state of the world and did not involve direct challenges to the White House over specific conflicts.

Similarly, war casualties exerted a substantial influence on the oversight behavior of Armed Services, but had a relatively weak effect on Foreign Relations. For Armed Services, popular concerns about defense offered an opportunity to build support for the military through additional patrol hearings, but rising battle deaths demanded greater committee attention to the crises that produced them. To preserve secrecy and reduce the appearance of disunity, the committee sacrificed transparency by moving crisis hearings behind closed doors. When the costs of war became particularly pressing, moreover, Armed Services cut back on patrols in favor of alarm hearings.

For Foreign Relations, rising casualties created conditions that stimulated the committee's interest in public debate, but only up to a point. Foreign Relations chose to emphasize patrol hearings generally, and its preference for this type of oversight had little relation to the level of casualties or public salience of foreign policy issues. The committee did step up crisis oversight during the period of study as battle deaths rose, but the predicted increase in hearings was modest and the content was not necessarily directed at the conflict producing the casualties. Foreign Relations appears to have been constrained by public norms about national unity during times of crisis, but also was handicapped in its ability to deal with major events in the last two decades by the reduction in its overall workload.

Overall, the statistical results confirm the effects of party on the content of national security oversight, as mediated through the goals of the Senate Armed Services and Foreign Relations Committees. The record from 1947 to 2008 was not as dismal as congressional critics asserted, but it raised legitimate concerns about the committees' ability to educate the public regarding issues that mattered most for democratic accountability. The scandal over outpatient services at Walter Reed Hospital illustrated Armed Services' troubled efforts to balance its protective instincts toward the Pentagon and Republican presidents with popular concerns over the treatment of military personnel.

Fire Alarm at Walter Reed Hospital

The wounded warriors of the Iraq War posed a challenge for the Senate Armed Services Committee. Members were reluctant to publicly criticize the Pentagon at a time when the military was overtaxed and underprepared for the civil war in Iraq. Yet the extraordinary pressures on American troops, which included multiple deployments, heavy casualties from roadside explosive devices, suicide bombers, and inadequate equipment, were impossible to ignore. The *Washington Post*'s story in February 2007, with its graphic details of the appalling conditions at Walter Reed's Building 18, exposed the committee's dilemma. Having pursued a path of low visibility in dealing with oversight of the Iraq War behind closed doors, Armed Services was suddenly swamped by rival House and Senate committees eager to claim headlines and credit for supporting the troops at home. Democratic members were in the particularly uncomfortable position of supporting inquiries that would fuel a partisan narrative in the 2008 election or maintaining committee solidarity. Executive sessions, a frequent solution to this dilemma, had only postponed the inevitable divisions fueled by the increasingly unpopular war. Armed Services eventually abandoned its reticence under a Democratic majority because the Walter Reed scandal suited the larger partisan purpose of supporting the troops, although it indirectly discredited the Bush administration's prosecution of the war.

After his initial March 5 appearance before the House Armed Services Committee, General Kiley appeared the next day before the Senate Armed Services Committee, this time accompanied by the Army chief of staff and two high-ranking Department of Defense officials. He testified once more on March 8 before the House Armed Services Committee, also with top Pentagon brass by his side. The Senate Armed Services and Veterans Affairs Committees followed up with joint hearings on April 12 and 13, 2007, regarding the efforts of the Veterans Administration and the Department of Defense to coordinate health care, transitional services, and disability procedures for returning soldiers. Despite chronic neglect, Walter Reed's outpatient services finally commanded the full attention of many lawmakers.

Events had moved rapidly after the *Post* published its article, although Congress was in recess the week after the story broke. The House held its first inquiry on March 5, and the Senate followed suit the next day. Judging from newscasts, lawmakers turned out for the testimony rather than make their usual brief appearances at hearings. By the time members launched their inquiries, Secretary of the Army Francis J. Harvey had already fired General Weightman, appointed Kiley as acting commander, and then abruptly resigned. The recently confirmed Secretary of Defense Robert Gates reportedly had fired Kiley, whose retirement from the Army took place on March 12, 2007, and had named Maj. Gen. Eric B. Schoomaker commander at Walter Reed.

Meanwhile, President Bush had issued an executive order on March 6 to create a Pentagon task force and to establish the President's Commission on Care for America's Returning Wounded Warriors, chaired by former Senate majority leader and Republican presidential nominee Robert Dole, a wounded veteran of World War II, and former secretary of health and human services in the Clinton administration Donna Shalala. The task force issued a report in mid-June, and the commission issued findings and recommendations on July 25, 2007,[26] which coincided with the Senate's approval of legislation to improve screening for brain injuries, reduce red tape for soldiers requiring care, and increase pay for military personnel. Such is the power of "fire alarms" to stimulate oversight and prompt remediation.

Once the scandal became a national issue, many committees claimed jurisdiction over Walter Reed. In addition to the armed services committees in both chambers, the list included the special oversight committee in the House, the committees responsible for appropriations and veterans' affairs in both chambers, and even a subcommittee within the House Energy and Commerce Committee. In total, seven different congressional committees held thirteen separate hearings during 2007 that examined the care of soldiers at Walter Reed and around the country. Additional hearings occurred in 2008.

The overlapping jurisdictions of so many committees could have increased the likelihood that some entrepreneurial lawmaker would ask questions about how the troops were doing when they returned home. Yet no one scheduled hearings until the story made it impossible to turn a blind eye and created an irresistible opportunity for Democrats to challenge a Republican president's conduct of the war in Iraq. Thus, Congress produced too little information leading up to the scandal and too much once the scandal came to public notice.

In fairness, lawmakers at the various hearings had reason to believe this war was different. High-ranking officials had paid many well-publicized visits to Ward 57, the Army's state-of-the-art unit for amputees. President Bush had declared the nation's commitment to care for its soldiers in a visit before Christmas 2006, noting, "We owe them all we can give them. Not only for when they're in harm's way, but when they come home to help them adjust if they have wounds, or help them adjust after their time in service."[27] Yet there is little evidence that members of the Senate Armed Services Committee looked beyond the official line. With a Republican president and Senate majority, the

---

[26] National Public Radio, "Panel Calls for Changes in Military Medical Care," July 25, 2007, http://www.npr.org/templates/story/story.php?storyId=12227958 (accessed October 10, 2010).

[27] Priest and Hull, "Soldiers Face Neglect."

committee had little inclination to embarrass the White House or its allies in the Pentagon or to feed growing public alarm about the Iraq War by uncovering ineptitude at Walter Reed.

In these circumstances, Armed Services might have posed questions about the treatment of soldiers behind closed doors, as they had done so often in the past, once casualties mounted. The committee's calendar of executive sessions between 2004 and 2008, however, revealed no sign that senators had scheduled hearings regarding medical treatment of soldiers. Individual members very likely made informal inquiries, but their close ties to the military establishment might have inclined them to trust assurances that everything was under control.[28]

Walter Reed had lost out to other pressing military matters on the Senate Armed Services Committee's crowded calendar in 2007. From January through March, for example, members held twenty-five days of public hearings that dealt with a variety of issues: abuses in contracting at the Defense Department, errors in intelligence gathering and interpretation leading up to the Iraq War, readiness of Marine and Army personnel for combat, impact of the START treaty on the U.S. nuclear defense posture, interaction with NATO in prosecuting the war in Afghanistan, and requests to authorize a variety of defense programs for the next fiscal year.[29] Clearly, the Armed Services Committee addressed matters of grave importance. Yet its hearing agenda amounted to an average of 1.5 hearing days per week for the first quarter of the legislative session, hardly an impressive informational effort, given the Iraq War's deep difficulties and the new Democratic majority's pledge to improve oversight of the conflict. The inadequate review of the condition of American soldiers thus appears to have been a casualty of senators' declining attention to committee business.

The pattern of inquiry into the Walter Reed situation, as we observed earlier in this chapter, was consistent in many respects with Armed Services' past approaches to crises and scandals. Republican presidents, besides Bush, typically received less committee oversight from police patrols and, especially, from fire alarm hearings. Moreover, the committee's reliance on secret hearings was also a practice that prevailed prior to the Iraq War. Throughout the post–World War II period, the committee demonstrated bias in the selection of hearing topics and lack of transparency about the costs of war. The last two years of the

---

[28] Committee members at the time who had served in uniform, either on active duty or in the reserves, included Republicans Warner, Graham, McCain, Inhofe, and Sessions and Democrats Webb, Akaka, and Reed.

[29] The Senate Foreign Relations Committee in the same period had a similarly full plate with fifteen days of public hearings that included many issues also of interest to Armed Services: review of the "surge" strategy in Iraq, civil war in Somalia, proliferation of weapons of mass destruction, human rights abuses in the Philippines, diplomatic initiatives toward Iran, military strategy in Afghanistan, and authorization of the following year's foreign assistance program. Again, this is an impressive list, until one does the math to arrive at 1.25 hearings per week.

Bush administration represented an anomaly, however, when the committee's predicted public fire alarm inquiries in 2007–8 and public crisis hearings exceeded the norms for Republican and Democratic presidents.

Armed Services had allocated its limited time to activities perceived as more valuable than oversight of Walter Reed. Once scandal was in the air, however, the committee could not ignore such a glaring example of incompetence. More important, the case captures the ways in which wars and scandals often coincide. The shocking conditions in Building 18 gave the newly empowered Democrats a nonideological way to discredit the Bush administration's war effort and to tarnish the Republicans' reputation in the eyes of the public for competence in international affairs.[30]

The plight of the soldiers at Walter Reed was such a powerful issue for Democrats because it brought the war home to the public in a way that few other events could match. Citizens cannot form "pictures in their heads" about events in far-off places,[31] and so they depend upon political elites—elected officials, interest group and party advocates, experts, bureaucrats, and journalists—to construct meaning about unfamiliar situations abroad.[32] In 2007, after more than five years of warfare, Americans still lacked knowledge about Iraq and Afghanistan and had little exposure to the soldiers and military families who bore the cost. They could understand the televised warriors' missing eyes and ears, however, and grasp the halting speech that resulted from brain trauma. The intensely human drama made the Walter Reed story fit the news values of the media, and thus freed congressional opponents to raise larger questions about the Iraq War's strategic goals and probable success.

In addition, Walter Reed became a vehicle for raising issues that were unrelated to Iraq. Democrats used the difficulties of caring for so many severely injured personnel to pose larger doubts about constraints on the military's ability to fight another war and on U.S. relations with the rest of the world. Bush's opponents in Congress did not have to talk about grand strategy, when they could point to the condition of wounded soldiers as a reason for a more restrained approach. Public support of the war already had waned by the time the scandal hit the newswires,[33] and Walter Reed gave lawmakers an easily accessible way to warn citizens about the risks of future conflicts.

Finally, the situation at Walter Reed bolstered Democratic aims in the larger ideological battle with Republicans about the size and role of government. Maintenance at Walter Reed had been turned over to a private firm in 2004 in keeping with the GOP's commitment to privatizing many of the services

---

[30] Walter Reed is a good example of how fire alarms that trigger oversight can be endogenous rather than exogenous to the decision to launch an inquiry.

[31] Lippmann (1922).

[32] Zaller (1992; 1994); Bennett (1990).

[33] Karol and Miguel (2007); Berinsky (2009); Kriner and Shen (2007); Grose and Oppenheimer (2007).

provided by the federal bureaucracy. The contractor's poor performance and lack of accountability discredited the idea of outsourcing governmental services, especially the use of private contracts in the military.

The larger lesson of Walter Reed pertains to the overall workload of the Senate Armed Services Committee. Inquiries into scandal constituted a small percentage of all congressional committee activity,[34] not just national security committee hearings. Senators increased the risk of overlooking important matters, however, as their efforts to gather information declined. Time is always a constraint on how much oversight a committee conducts, but wars have traditionally demanded—and received—greater scrutiny from Armed Services. As time pressures impelled the committee to make use of scarce hearing days in the most advantageous manner, its reluctance to engage with issues that did not fit the goals of the committee became more problematic. The efforts to balance the costs and benefits of oversight led to the neglect of America's wounded warriors and demonstrated why the soldiers fell through the cracks.

Conclusion

The Senate's national security committees had major responsibility over the period of the study for furthering the rule of law in U.S. foreign policy by educating the public. Critical to this effort was gathering and disseminating information that people cared about and could use to evaluate the president's performance. Armed Services and Foreign Relations conducted numerous patrol and alarm hearings, but they fell short with respect to the quantity of oversight, the bias in content selection, and the lack of transparency. It seems safe to conclude, after surveying sixty-two years of police patrol and fire alarm, that failures of oversight, such as the Walter Reed scandal, likely were commonplace rather than exceptional.

The difficulties evident over the period of study reflected a number of constraints on how the committees conducted their business. Changing norms in the Senate regarding committee work mattered, especially to Foreign Relations, and they were exacerbated by the complexity of the post–Cold War environment. The committee agendas became very crowded, because of budget and statutory issues, technological change, and the proliferation of actors on the international stage. Trade-offs under increasingly severe time limitations were inevitable.

Yet the committees also confronted political pressures that hindered their capacity to adequately educate the public. Armed Services shielded Republican presidents, apparently to protect its relationships with potentially useful allies in the White House. It also utilized public patrol hearings to build public sup-

---

[34] Kriner and Schwartz (2007).

port for the military. Foreign Relations concentrated on state of the world inquiries that satisfied its partisan leanings without violating norms about national unity, but its lack of focus undoubtedly reduced the impact of its hearings on the public and the press. The end result for both committees was information gathering that was geared to policy elites and not particularly useful to ordinary citizens.

The record of Armed Services and Foreign Relations with respect to casualties is the most disturbing aspect of the analyses in this chapter. Monitoring the costs of war must be a priority for national security oversight to ensure accountability of the president's decisions. The frequency of quarters in which no alarm or crisis hearings took place, even at high levels of battle deaths, indicates a lack of urgency throughout the post–World War II Congress that seems inappropriate for a democratic society. In addition, the tendency within Armed Services to pursue alarm hearings behind closed doors, while perhaps necessary from the perspective of military operations, undermined transparency about whether the loss of life was commensurate with the nation's strategic objectives. Finally, the lack of response to public opinion and casualties by the Foreign Relations Committee was at odds with the basic function of oversight to educate citizens. In summary, the public's greatest need from the Senate's national security committees was for frequent, consistent, and visible oversight of crises and scandals. Citizens did not receive it with Walter Reed, nor apparently with many other crises and scandals. The behavior of the Senate Armed Services and Foreign Relations Committees thus raises serious questions about who was guarding the guardians over the past six decades.

PART III

Reclaiming Congressional War Powers

Foreign policies demand scarcely any of those qualities which are peculiar to a democracy ... a democracy can only with great difficulty regulate the details of an important undertaking, persevere in a fixed design, and work out its execution in spite of serious obstacles. It cannot combine its measures with secrecy or await their consequences with patience.

—Alexis de Tocqueville, *Democracy in America*, 1835

CHAPTER 6

Return to the Rule of Law in International Affairs

WHY SHOULD AMERICANS CARE about a topic as arcane as oversight hearings in the Senate Armed Services and Foreign Relations Committees? We could speculate about whether the frequency, content, and openness of committee inquiries contributed to the nation's safety between 1947 and 2008. We could debate whether the Senate's national security watchdogs needed to conduct more or fewer hearings. We should focus, however, on the larger issue of whether the findings in Part II revealed a review process that furthers the rule of law in international affairs. The results, as I have presented them, strongly suggest reason for concern about the regularity, transparency, and education of the public that took place in the Senate's committees responsible for defense and foreign policy.

Some observers of U.S. foreign policy take the opposite view, that lawmakers ask too many questions and damage the nation's interests abroad with untimely inquiries. Such opinions reflect pessimistic assumptions about citizens, lawmakers, and administration officials, however, that are inconsistent with democracy over the long run. The performance of the Senate Armed Services and Foreign Relations Committees thus raises broader issues about whether public accountability in international affairs is desirable or even possible in the twenty-first century.

The debate about the competence of democracies in foreign affairs is a very old one, as the quote from Tocqueville attests. Among skeptics, some hold that citizens are neither interested nor informed enough to evaluate the president's conduct of war and diplomacy. Others contend that legislators are too parochial and preoccupied with reelection to be trusted with the weighty matters of international affairs. And still others, including many members of Congress and executive branch officials, assert the constitutional primacy of the commander in chief in foreign affairs or make pragmatic claims about the president's superior capabilities to design and execute global strategies.

Each argument contains a large element of truth, but together they devalue the procedural regularity and public discourse so essential for the rule of law in foreign affairs. They consign citizens to the role of subjects in international affairs, governed by the superior wisdom of technocratic elites. They upset the constitutional design of the U.S. system by undermining the logic of checks and balances and separation of powers in favor of presidential dominance. They assume a capacity for unitary decision making and competence in the executive branch, despite the frequency of discretionary wars that severely damaged the reputations of the presidents who made them. Settling for the status quo, then, means accepting a very impoverished view of the American polity and a blindness to the risks posed by executive miscalculation. In a forceful critique of congressional abdication of its responsibilities, Senator Jim Webb (D-VA), who has since retired, cautioned, "Practical circumstances have changed, but basic philosophical principles should not."[1]

In this chapter, I examine the underlying premises of the skeptics' view. I argue that the public, while preferring national unity on matters involving national security, makes sensible use of information when public officials provide it. I then turn to expectations among lawmakers that perpetuate a low level of congressional engagement with the executive and use the work of constitutional theorists to highlight common misunderstandings about the logic of the Constitution. In addition, I contend that a major barrier to a more constructive role for lawmakers in international affairs is not the Constitution, but the large number serving today who have very limited legislative experience. Finally, I outline the risks to the presidency that result from asserting executive supremacy over national security. These ideas are well known in the various subfields of American politics, but I pull them together here as the underpinning for the reform proposals I address in the next chapter.

The Paradox of Public Opinion and National Security Oversight

Congressional oversight poses contradictions for how citizens understand international affairs. The public embraces bipartisan support for the president as the norm in the realm of national security. This belief is partially valid in the sense that the framers intended that American policy toward other nations would reflect widespread consensus. Citizens' desire for unity harms their own interests, however, by discouraging open deliberation about the potential risks and costs of presidential actions in the international arena. Lawmakers' questions about presidential decisions, paradoxically, often have been least welcome when they are most necessary.[2] Nevertheless, Americans manage quite well when they receive authoritative cues about how to "read" national security.

---

[1] Jim Webb, "Congressional Abdication," *National Interest*, March–April 2013, http://national interest.org (accessed March 19, 2013).

[2] Huntington framed the dilemma for the twentieth-century Congress that still applies: independence, he noted, "provokes criticism," while "acquiescence brings approbation" (1973, 6).

The public's dilemma when evaluating foreign policy is captured in Daniel Webster's famous remark during the War of 1812 that politics "ceases at the water's edge." Citizens resonate to its call for harmony, and modern presidents regularly invoke the quote to promote support for their national security policies. Evolving over time, Webster's words rank among the most misunderstood in American history and contribute to public confusion about how much information to demand from congressional watchdogs on Capitol Hill.

Webster took to the floor of the House in 1814 to oppose a bill that encouraged military enlistment in the fight against the British. He had two purposes: to dissuade Federalist lawmakers from their plans to use an expanded army as a vehicle for annexing parts of Canada; and to challenge the idea that lawmakers could authorize invasion of another country through ordinary legislation. After scolding his colleagues for demonizing their opponents, Webster reiterated the Hamiltonian principle that the nation's security depended on commerce. His reference to the water's edge was a reminder that the war's objective was protecting maritime interests from the British navy, not expanding U.S. territory. Webster summed up his views this way: "If, then, the war must be continued, go to the ocean. If you are seriously contending for maritime rights ... thither every indication of your fortune points you. There the united wishes and exertions of the nation will go with you. Even our partisan divisions, acrimonious as they are, cease at the water's edge."[3]

Webster's plea was neither a call for bipartisanship nor a means for marginalizing dissent, although his words have since evolved to serve both aims. The quote appears so widely because it fits many different political purposes. For example, Senators Henry Cabot Lodge (R-MA) and Arthur Vandenberg (R-MI), both Republicans serving under different Democratic presidents, employed it regularly to assert their points of view. Lodge's rhetoric framed his opposition to the Treaty of Versailles, which established the League of Nations. Calling for Woodrow Wilson to work with opposition senators to find compromise wording, Lodge used the phrase to highlight the president's intransigence. Vandenberg also employed the phrase frequently to justify his close collaboration with the unpopular Truman administration and to bolster his standing as a statesman worthy to be president. Both men employed the words for which they have mistakenly received credit to claim a role for the minority party in decisions about national security.

Since then, "politics stops at the water's edge" has appeared in presidential statements to silence critics and promote national unity. Journalists have used it, too, most often to frame news about the president's difficulties with troublesome lawmakers. By admonishing legislators to get in line behind the president, the "water's edge" rhetoric misleads the public and contradicts the very idea of congressional oversight.

[3] U.S. House of Representatives, Annals of the 13th Congress, 2nd Session, 1814, 940–51.

Popular desires for cohesion in foreign policy collide with Americans' mistrust of centralized authority. On the one hand, the office of the presidency combines symbolic and ministerial functions in one person, making it a source of national unity. On the other hand, the modern presidency inspires images of both "promise" and "fear," and serves as the "battering ram" of American politics, which simultaneously destroys the existing political order while reconstructing a new one.[4] During wartime, presidents invariably have asserted more influence over the legislative agenda,[5] and they have enjoyed greater legislative success on domestic policies.[6] From an institutional perspective, then, international conflict strengthened the leverage of an office that lacked well-defined boundaries and derived its authority from the development of extra-constitutional powers.[7] This jerry-built framework maintained legitimacy as long as Congress retained a credible capability to rein in the executive.

In the past, peacetime contraction of the executive branch followed wartime expansion, sparing the public the necessity of choosing between competing views of "presidentialist" and "congressionalist" views of war powers. The public no longer has the luxury of waiting for the executive branch to shrink naturally, given the ongoing state of mobilization in the United States since the start of the Cold War. Yet popular expectations about how far Congress should go in constraining executive power remain unclear in the minds of most citizens, until the president provokes a crisis or prolonged military operations wear out their patience.

Citizens undeniably operate at considerable disadvantage in determining whether the president's actions abroad are appropriate to the level of threat to the nation's interests. Scholars have demonstrated, however, that the public has developed a reasonable understanding of many major foreign policy issues.[8] Much of the learning about foreign affairs, however, depends upon political actors and the media to provide alternatives to the president's framing of international events. Particularly problematic have been voters' reactions to the nation's numerous military engagements and combat fatalities, which varied widely between toleration for high body counts in "good" wars and hypersensitivity to a few deaths in "bad" ones.[9] Without debate between the legislative and executive

---

[4] James (2005); Skowronek (1993).

[5] Milkis (2005).

[6] Cohen (1982); Meernik (1993); Wittkopf and McCormick (1998); Prins and Marshall (2001); Mayhew (2005); Howell, Jackman, and Rogowski (2013).

[7] Griffin (2013).

[8] Aldrich, Sullivan, and Borgida (1989); Bartels (1991); Page and Shapiro (1992); Page and Bouton (2006).

[9] Holsti (2004); Mueller (1973; 2005); Jentleson (1992); Jentleson and Britton (1998); Burk (1999); Feaver and Gelpi (2004); Gelpi, Feaver, and Reifler (2005; 2007); Karol and Miguel (2007); Aldrich et al. (2005); Eichenberg (2005); Boettcher and Cobb (2006); Berinsky (2007; 2009); Eichenberg, Stoll, and Lebo (2006); Voeten and Brewer (2006); Gartner, Segura, and Wilkening (1997); Gartner and Segura (1998; 2008); Baum and Potter (2008); Hill, Herron, and Lewis (2010).

branch, citizens have had difficulty in determining which battles were worth fighting.

A major trigger for the public to pay attention to hostilities has been what scholars term "elite discourse." Conflict among foreign policy elites, including public officials, experts, activists, and journalist, alerted the public to start paying attention to foreign policy issues.[10] Disagreement also stimulated the press to cover particular international events more aggressively, especially if the disputes occurred among authoritative actors, such as members of Congress.[11] Criticism from members of the president's own party received the most media attention,[12] which reinforced the message that major stakes were involved and ensured that citizens had more information than usual.

Senate committees responsible for foreign policy, as we have seen throughout this book, played a critical role in organizing, sustaining, and publicizing elite debates. In the absence of committee processes of formal review, citizens can still obtain information about the consequences of the president's policies. But they will be operating in a piecemeal, fragmented way without benefit of context or a coherent framework.

An innovative study by Kriner and Shen, for example, illustrates the diffused process by which citizens gained information about the Iraq War from individual lawmakers.[13] The authors first demonstrated that House members in districts with rising casualties were more likely to criticize the war in public speeches on the floor. They then showed that Democratic lawmakers in high-casualty districts also were more likely to cast antiwar votes than their fellow partisans. Finally, Kriner and Shen reported that public opinion regarding the war coincided with their representatives' antiwar positions. The more a lawmaker opposed the war, the more likely he or she had constituents who also opposed it.

Kriner and Shen's study ties together a number of disjointed facts regarding the Iraq War. We know from earlier chapters that misinformation about Iraq among Americans was extremely high. We also know that the Senate Armed Services conducted most of its oversight of Iraq behind closed doors and that Foreign Relations devoted relatively little of its public hearing agenda to the conflict once it commenced. Finally, we know that a considerable number of House Republicans lost their seats in the 2006 and 2008 elections because of growing hostility to the duration and cost of the Iraq conflict. It appears that citizens gradually learned of the local costs of the violence in Iraq, prompting

---

[10] Zaller (1992; 1994); Zaller and Chiu (1996); Brody (1994); Bennett (1990; 1996); Bennett, Lawrence, and Livingston (2007); Voeten and Brewer (2006); Berinsky (2007; 2009); Howell and Pevehouse (2007, chap. 6); Baum and Groeling (2010).

[11] Bennett (1990); Cook (1998).

[12] Groeling and Baum (2008).

[13] Kriner and Shen (2014).

individual members in affected distracts to react with criticism and, in turn, reinforcing public concerns.

Such local accountability was by no means trivial, but it was a very limited form of democratic control over presidential war making. The process of information dissemination was extremely uneven, because citizens got critical information from their elected representative only if they lived in areas with sufficiently high casualties. Moreover, the process cast the costs of war in terms of its effects on "friends and neighbors" rather than broad national purposes.[14]

As a thought experiment, imagine how public attitudes might have evolved had the Senate Armed Services and Foreign Relations Committee organized public, sustained attention to the deteriorating situation in Iraq that became evident in 2004. A growing recognition among policy elites had developed by then that the occupation of Iraq was proving more costly and difficult than the Bush administration had anticipated. In the absence of a formal process of review, there was no national forum for developing facts about what was happening on the ground or vetting rival proposals for dealing with the increasingly violent insurgency. For citizens who lived outside the constituencies directly affected by the war, the default informational resource was partisanship. Republicans continued to support their president, while Democrats turned against him, giving Iraq the distinction of being the only modern war in which citizens divided so cleanly along party lines.[15]

Matters of national security involve much more than local or partisan concerns, and they require a form of discourse that engages the public at large about the overarching goals of U.S. actions abroad. Congressional oversight that engages the president through an orderly process of review should provide the means for assessing the merits and demerits of administration policy. Before dismissing citizens as too ignorant to evaluate foreign policy decisions, we should ask whether committee watchdogs provided them with information they cared about and could use to hold the president accountable.

Changing the Conventional Wisdom about Congressional War Powers

The subordination of Congress in national security affairs has become so entrenched over the years that the institution's marginal status is widely accepted among many members as the norm. Legislative impotence was not a recent aberration that arose from the unique circumstances of the Bush administra-

---

[14] Scholars term this type of representation "dyadic," in which constituents articulate concerns, members respond with speeches and roll call votes, and the attitudes of both converge. It is a one-to-one version of local, geographically based congruence that does not produce collective, national accountability of the government as a whole.

[15] Jacobson (2006).

tion's efforts to prosecute the "war on terror."[16] Its seeds were sown in earlier administrations, and it continued into the Obama presidency. Recent critics on the left, for example, pointed to legislators' failure to adopt clear rules about the use of drones to assassinate suspected terrorists, while those on the right, such as Senator John Cornyn (R-TX), accused the president of acting as if Congress was "a potted plant," after Obama approved U.S. participation in the NATO bombing of Libya in 2011.[17] Representative Walter Jones (R-NC), however, laid the blame for congressional impotence squarely on lawmakers: "We're neutered as a Congress.... We have for too long ... been too passive when it comes to sending our young men and women to war."[18] While decrying the reemergence of the imperial presidency, lawmakers in both parties have been complicit in their own marginalization.

Two developments, in my view, helped perpetuate the "potted plant" status of Congress in foreign affairs. The first stemmed from a widespread misconception among lawmakers about the logic of the Constitution, especially the nature of the president's emergency powers. The second resulted from the presence of so many members with relatively little experience on Capitol Hill. Both trends stand in the way of any serious effort to restore Congress to its proper role in foreign affairs.

In recent years, some students of the Constitution have promoted a theory of the unitary executive and attempted to draw a bright line of separation between those powers on the congressional side of the divide and those that fall within the sole purview of the executive branch. The Supreme Court's *Chadha* decision in 1983 reflected legitimate concerns among judges about lawmakers' tendency to delegate authority to the president and then selectively rescind it through legislative vetoes. Congress could delegate or not, the justices reasoned, but if they chose to give presidents responsibility to do something, they could not engage in second-guessing after the fact.

Some have pushed the unitary executive theory further than the Constitution warrants, however, especially by asserting war powers to be the sole province of the commander in chief. In weighing claims about presidential authority, it is important to remember that the framers defined tyranny as the concentration of power in a single branch. In addition, they devised the system of separated powers as a self-regulating mechanism in which the "ambitions" of members of Congress would be in constant tension with the "ambitions" of presidents.[19]

---

[16] Griffin (2013); Fisher (2013).

[17] See, for example, Felicia Sonmez, "Libya Conflict Sparks War Powers Debate in Senate," http://www.washingtonpost.com/blogs/2chambers/post/libya-conflict-sparks-war-powers-debate-in-senate/2011/05/19/AFpb8I7G_blog.html (accessed May 20, 2011).

[18] Jonathan Allen and Marin Cogan, "Did Obama Lose Congress on Libya?," *Politico*, March 2, 2011, http://www.politico.com/news/stories/0311/51687.html (accessed May 15, 2012).

[19] *Federalist* 48 is the most explicit statement about the framers' definition of tyranny, while the constraining effects of ambition are addressed in *Federalist* 51. Hamilton, Jay, and Madison (1962).

To accomplish the goal of self-correction, then, each branch was given "a will of its own," as well as shared functions with other branches. Thus, Article I of the Constitution gave the legislature a formidable list of specific powers for regulating diplomacy and war, such as establishing the military code of justice. Moreover, it conferred joint powers that enabled the legislature to retaliate if threatened with encroachment by the president. The Senate's advice and consent requirements over nominations and treaties, along with provisions that both chambers approve declarations of war, exemplified the idea of shared powers. Given these numerous provisions of exclusive and overlapping powers, congressionalists, such as Fisher, reject the idea that the Constitution has an ambiguous meaning that enables the president to claim wide latitude for action.[20]

Many lawmakers today carry copies of the Constitution in their pockets, and House Republicans in the 112th Congress required members to cite the relevant passage in the document when sponsoring new laws. These behaviors among some current members reflect the relatively new doctrine of "originalism," which holds that the meaning of the Constitution lies in specific language, as the framers understood it in 1787. Neither the provisions of Article II nor the framers' discourse at the time of ratification contain explicit language supporting the prerogatives claimed by modern presidents under the rubric of commander in chief. Madison's *Notes* from Philadelphia, for example, reveal a deep suspicion of executive aggrandizement; George Mason, in particular, "was all for clogging the [path] to war."[21] The *Federalist Papers*, too, indicate wariness about a too-powerful president. In an effort to disarm critics of the single executive, for example, Hamilton compared the war powers enjoyed by the governor of New Hampshire to those in the hands of the president of the United States and concluded that citizens had more to fear from the governor.[22] Writing at the height of the war on terror more than two centuries later, Justice Sandra Day O'Connor noted tartly in the *Hamdan v. Rumsfeld* case that the Constitution does not give the president "a blank check."[23]

A near permanent state of emergency contributed to the marginalization of Congress in foreign affairs since the beginning of the Cold War. The architects of the Constitution recognized that presidents would act during emergencies, particularly to repel attack. The debate at the Constitutional Convention over whether Congress should "make" war (the original verb) or "declare" war (the final version) reflects such thinking. The delegates were aware of the great powers threatening America's borders and the likelihood that Congress might not be in session when an urgent situation arose.[24] They also had read Locke and Blackstone regarding the prerogative powers of the executive.

[20] Fisher (2006; 2008; 2009, 2013).
[21] Madison (1987, 476).
[22] Hamilton, Jay, and Madison (1962, *Federalist* 69).
[23] *Hamdan v. Rumsfeld*, 548 U.S. 557 (2006).
[24] Madison (1987, 475–77).

Under the doctrine of *salus populi*, emergency actions are consistent with constitutionalism, if executive discretion furthers "the welfare of the people." In other words, legal provisions should not prevent the executive from acting in order to attain "the publick [*sic*] good, without the prescription of the Law, and sometimes even against it."[25] Since Jefferson dispatched the navy to deal with Barbary Coast piracy and then acquired the Louisiana Territory from France, presidents have employed this rationale for extra-constitutional decisions. Congress permitted such latitude because presidents sought congressional approval for their actions after the fact. Until the Cold War, they never claimed *inherent* powers for unilateral action.[26]

Nevertheless, the final judgment about the wisdom of executive decisions under *salus populi* lay with the people and their representatives.[27] The exercise of discretion was valid only if it produced results that truly furthered the public interest; consequently, executives who acted outside the Constitution would have to submit to review and possible sanction after the consequences of their deeds became apparent. Good intentions were not enough; nor could presidents be permitted to assess their own handiwork. As Madison noted, "Those who are to conduct a war cannot in the nature of things be proper or safe judges whether a war ought to be commenced, continued or concluded."[28]

Typically, the people's elected representatives arbitrated between citizens and the executive about the appropriate use of discretion, because the public was constrained in its ability to evaluate matters of diplomacy and military strategy.[29] Lawmakers were not simply de facto judges of presidential discretion, moreover, but also embodied the people's will in their own right. Presidents, beginning with Theodore Roosevelt, have asserted a superior claim for deference in international relations, because they are elected by the entire nation and therefore represent its unity of purpose.[30] Despite presidential assertions, lawmakers, too, reflect the popular will. The framers, well aware of democracies' propensity for demagoguery and mob rule, would have been highly suspicious of the idea that presidents enjoy a direct, plebiscitary relationship with the people or hold a monopoly on defining the public good. Madison, in particular, favored a republican form of government in which representatives from diverse constituencies

---

[25] James (2005, 6).

[26] Silverstein (1997).

[27] Kleinerman (2007); Fatovic (2004).

[28] Quoted in MacKenzie (2009).

[29] I develop this argument more fully in Fowler (2011).

[30] Progressives supported this idea because they viewed an executive at the head of a technically proficient administrative state to be the source of sound public policy untainted by the corruption of patronage politics. Advocates of responsible party government backed it because they considered presidents, working in concert with disciplined legislative parties pledged to a common platform, as the best means to attain democratic responsiveness and accountability. Contemporary conservatives have embraced a dominant executive recently as a means of pursuing an aggressive foreign policy agenda.

would "refine and enlarge the public view." In other words, Madison saw the national interest as a construction from multiple viewpoints rather than a truth known solely to security experts in the executive branch.[31]

In the aftermath of past emergencies, members typically moved to rebalance the powers of the legislative and executive branches. The urge to revitalize Congress and rein in the president usually occurred when legislators realized their influence as individual politicians waned with the power of the institution in which they served.[32] Typically, the opportunity to act on this realization coincided with disturbances in the congressional party system, serious scandals, or the end of major wars. The need for members to restore public respect for Congress added oxygen to the reformist fires.

Few lawmakers serving in the Senate and House today have any recollection of what it means to assert institutional ambition in foreign affairs, however. Only a minority of representatives and senators has served in the institution prior to the trauma of 9/11. For most, the powers exercised by both Presidents George W. Bush and Barack Obama appear routine rather than extraordinary. Thus, when Senator Rand Paul (R-KY) held the floor with a thirteen-hour filibuster in March 2013 to protest President Obama's use of a "kill list" to target American citizens who collaborated with terrorists for assassination,[33] several senators defended the role of the president as investigator, prosecutor, judge, jury, and executioner, despite the absence of any legal framework other than a secret memo.

Added to lack of perspective on how a system of separated powers should work in practice has been the high percentage in recent years of inexperienced lawmakers who gained their seats in Congress by running as outsiders. Hamilton and Madison worried about the tendencies toward amateurism and shortsightedness in democracies, a view subsequently echoed by Alexis de Tocqueville.[34] For Hamilton, the problem for the fledgling U.S. state was continuity and competence in administration. He likely would have viewed with alarm the transient "government of strangers," the deep layers of political appointees, and the revolving door between executive agencies and lobbying organizations that characterize the modern executive branch. More to the point, these patterns undermine presidents' claims to superior understanding and capabilities that justify the delegation of so much power to the executive.

---

[31] Hamilton, Jay, and Madison (1962, esp. *Federalist* 10). The Madisonian view contrasts with the "realist" model of statecraft in which the national interest is both unitary and the result of external competition.

[32] Dodd and Schott (1979); Sundquist (1981).

[33] http://www.washingtontimes.com/news/2013/mar/6/rand-paul-filibusters-brennan-nomination-cia-direc/?page=all (accessed April 2014).

[34] Tocqueville (1945) was highly critical of the quality of political leadership in the United States.

For the founders, however, capability in the legislature also was a prime concern. Refuting the arguments of the Anti-Federalists for short terms between elections in *Federalist 53*, Madison and Hamilton argued that high turnover in Congress would render the nation vulnerable to the sway of demagogues. More important, they contended that the legislature needed "members of longstanding ... who will be thoroughly masters of the public business."[35] Such superior knowledge and experience, they added, were especially important for conducting foreign affairs. One consequence of fewer senior members, we saw in Chapter 3, was fewer executive sessions with administration officials. As a recent critique of Congress concluded, the expertise and stature found previously on the national security committees has eroded, particularly in the Senate Foreign Relations Committee. The report's author, an experienced political player on Capitol Hill, noted tactfully that the middle and lower ranks on these committees were especially "thin."[36]

Citizens do not value congressional participation in foreign affairs until their innate fears of executive power come into play. Any change within the institution, therefore, will have to come from a small number of lawmakers who gain political rewards from becoming "masters" of national security. Chapter 7 explores incentives for elevating the Senate's watchdog functions.

BRINGING THE PRESIDENT ON BOARD

A particularly daunting obstacle to generating space for lawmakers to implement the rule of law in international affairs is resistance to change within the executive branch. Contemporary debates over congressional and presidential prerogatives in foreign affairs treat the relationship as a zero-sum game, as if one branch's gain in power diminishes the other branch's influence. This mentality was especially pronounced among former Republican officials from the Ford and Reagan administrations, who experienced the frustrations of dealing with combative Democratic Congresses under divided government.[37] Their remedy during the George W. Bush presidency was to assert an expansive interpretation of executive powers under the rubric of the "war on terror."[38]

A much stronger case exists for the president to share power in light of the shadowy enemies the nation confronts today. Yet every American president since World War II has operated under the influence of Franklin Roosevelt,

---

[35] Hamilton, Jay, and Madison (1962, esp. *Federalist* 53)

[36] Kay King, "Congress and National Security," Special Report No. 58, Council on Foreign Relations, November 2010, 19, http://www.cfr.org/congress/congress-national-security/p23359 (accessed March 2013).

[37] Crovitz and Rabkin (1989); Cheney (1990).

[38] Kassop (2003); Yoo (2005).

"Doctor Win the War," whose strength of purpose sustained the nation through the dark days after Pearl Harbor, the military setbacks during the war's first two years, and the long grind through Italy, France, and the Pacific islands that established the momentum for victory after his death. Desirous of the same lofty place in history, presidents have sought to adopt the mantle of wartime leader. They have gotten into trouble, however, when they have led the country into military conflicts that lost legitimacy in the eyes of the public and made claims of authority that were not commensurate with the risks to the nation's security.

Harry Truman is now lionized for his policy of containment of the Soviet communism, so it is easy to forget that the Korean War brought down his presidency. His unilateral maneuvers in 1950 to send troops to Asia under UN auspices set the precedent for subsequent presidents to assert sweeping prerogatives to initiate military action that have little basis in the Constitution, but have become widely accepted as the norm.[39] The president was supported at the time by many of his former colleagues in the Senate, but his war proved so costly and unpopular that he was unable to seek reelection in 1952 and left office with an abysmal standing in the polls no president matched until George W. Bush retired in 2008.

Truman's many other accomplishments elevated his standing in the eyes of historians, but those successors who embraced his unilateral view of presidential war powers were not so fortunate. Lyndon Johnson's escalation of U.S. engagement in Vietnam from military aid and advisors to full-fledged war is, in my view, one of the great tragedies of the American presidency. A gifted politician, with an extraordinary record of landmark legislation in civil rights and social policy, LBJ would have been remembered as one of the greats had his presidency not imploded over his conduct of the war in Southeast Asia. As the casualties mounted and the president's efforts to conceal the truth about the situation in Vietnam became increasingly divisive, he cancelled his reelection bid in 1968 and left office under an oppressive cloud of public disapproval that, by many reports, broke his heart.

Richard Nixon, another adherent to an overly expansive view of executive power, was not forced from office because of his claims of war powers, although they were "imperial" in the eyes of his critics. After all, he was reelected with a resounding majority in 1972, and his National Security Advisor, Henry Kissinger, won the Nobel Peace Prize in 1973 for negotiating the Paris Peace Accords. Doubtless, some of the foes who pursued him over the Watergate scandal were spurred on by their hostility to his war policies. Nevertheless, Nixon's signature foreign policy achievement, the Paris Peace Accords, was undone by his failure to consult Congress in the deal to end the war or to use a formal treaty that would have required Senate ratification. To induce South Vietnam to sign the accord, Nixon and Kissinger gave secret assurances that American bombers

---

[39] Koh (1990); Silverstein (1997); Fisher (1995; 2006); Griffin (2013).

would come to the aid of the South in the event that the North resumed hostilities.[40] These consummate strategists could not anticipate that their clandestine strategy freed lawmakers of legal or moral responsibility to honor the pledge to the Saigon regime. After Nixon's resignation, lawmakers ignored President Ford's pleas for further military assistance, setting the stage for the chaotic airlifts from the roof of the U.S. embassy in 1975.

George W. Bush was the most recent example of the perils awaiting presidents who overestimate their power in foreign affairs. He enjoyed extraordinary popular support after 9/11 and a Congress more than willing to go along with his agenda. But he was unwilling to give a respectful hearing to the few legislators who counseled caution, who raised hard questions about the aftermath of the invasion of Iraq, and who turned out to have been remarkably prescient about the difficulties of occupation. Those few administration officials who provided candid testimony at congressional hearings were severely sanctioned to drive home the message that Congress should be kept in the dark as much as possible. Whatever the eventual outcome of these two long and costly conflicts, Bush's presidency collapsed under their weight, as did his party's reputation for competence for its conduct.

Presidents would profit from sharing power with reinvigorated national security committees in the long run. Lawmakers provide political cover for presidential initiatives, and they generate useful intelligence about the political risks of particular strategies. The principles famously articulated by President Reagan's secretary of defense, Caspar Weinberger in 1984, spoke to both benefits of congressional involvement. His fifth criterion for the use of military force, for example, stated that the United States would commit troops to defend "vital interests" only if there was "some reasonable assurance that we will have the support of the American people and their elected representatives in Congress."[41] Similar thinking informed the Powell Doctrine during the administration of George H. W. Bush.

Would presidents credited with foreign policy triumphs have fared differently had they acted on their sweeping claims of executive power? Ronald Reagan is the most interesting case because his admirers claim he "won" the Cold War against the Soviet Union, despite being locked in a particularly stormy relationship with Congress. Reagan enjoyed strong bipartisan support in Congress for his large buildup in defense spending, the strategy that ultimately brought about the Soviet Empire's collapse. He also endeavored to attack communist insurgencies around the globe, but was constrained by a Democratic majority in the House and a Republican majority in the Senate. Lawmakers limited his military initiatives to aid, to relatively minor deployments of troops in places

[40] Berman (2001).

[41] GlobalSecurity.org, "The Weinberger Doctrine in the Post–Cold War Era," http://www.global
security.org/military/library/report/1992/MCF.htm (accessed June 1, 2010).

like Granada, and to poorly resourced covert operations in Central America and parts of Africa. The disparity between Reagan's fierce Cold War rhetoric and his relatively modest use of force may have resulted from his limited party coalition in Congress.[42] Yet one cannot help wondering if his standing as a successful foreign policy president would have held up if lawmakers had given him what he wanted with respect to El Salvador and Nicaragua.

In addition to political legitimacy, Congress serves presidents' other needs in addressing the foreign policy agenda. Most administrations come into office with particular strategic goals in mind, but they are quickly overtaken by events. International crises erupt, bureaucratic infighting among the various national security agencies breaks out, and domestic political agendas demand attention. Presidents soon find themselves putting out fires, rather than pursuing broad goals of statecraft. Senior senators with few reelection worries and years of policy expertise can use their committees and professional staff to pick up the slack. Among the many examples of lawmakers who stepped in to plug major policy gaps are Senators Charles Grassley (R-IA) and Barry Goldwater (R-AZ), who led reform of the military procurement process; Senator Sam Nunn (D-GA), who developed innovative approaches to securing nuclear materials after the collapse of the Soviet Union; and Senator John Kerry (D-MA), who made frequent trips to Kabul to smooth the troubled U.S. relationship with Afghan President Hamid Karzai.

Presidents will continue to see Congress as an institution to be bullied or ignored unless the institution develops greater capacity for overseeing foreign affairs than exists today. No doubt the great majority of lawmakers will continue to prioritize domestic policy and favor local constituencies over national interests. And some will find scope for their political ambitions in demagoguery rather than statesmanship. Nevertheless, the president does not need 535 congressional advisors; a handful of Madison's "masters of the public business" should suffice to command White House respect and push U.S. foreign policy toward greater procedural regularity, transparency, and public accountability.

Conclusion

The present state of congressional oversight of national security policy inspires few defenders either on or off Capitol Hill. In the past, reformers have turned to procedural constraints on the executive to redress the imbalance of war powers. Yet this book demonstrates that serious obstacles for achieving presidential accountability lie within the legislative branch. Imperial presidents cannot rule without the collaboration of complicit lawmakers. Reform of Congress's national security watchdogs is necessary for the nation to engage thoughtfully in

---

[42] Howell and Pevehouse (2007).

what Webster termed the "great question" of war and peace. For reforms to succeed, they must address the reasons behind the behavior that appears so counterproductive. The roots of the problem are complex, resulting from major institutional and political developments, as well as deeply engrained patterns within the congressional committee system. Nevertheless, change is possible, and relatively small adaptations at the margins could have a big payoff if they induced a small number of senators to produce collective goods for the institution as a whole.

The record of the national security committees from 1947 to 2008 indicates that they did a better job in the past. In addition, the historical perspective provided by this study shows why the conditions for improving the Senate's watchdog committees are challenging. The Senate does not need revolutionary reforms, but it does require a handful of lawmakers to see the political opportunities in revitalizing the national security committees. In Chapter 7, I put forward a variety of proposals that create incentives for a more responsible partnership between the legislative and executive branches in foreign affairs.

CHAPTER 7

Reforming National Security Oversight in the Senate

SEVERAL WEEKS BEFORE HIS INAUGURATION, President-Elect Barack Obama met with two former secretaries of state to discuss improving means for consultation about foreign policy between the White House and Capitol Hill. James Baker, who served under President George H. W. Bush, and Warren Christopher, who served during the Clinton administration, jointly chaired the National War Powers Commission, which had issued recommendations for reform during the summer of 2008.[1] The meeting raised expectations that a more constructive process of dialogue would replace acrimonious debates between the branches before the United States committed to "any significant military action."[2] Although the bipartisan commission was not the only group pushing ways to rethink decision making about the use of force, its prominent chairmen and prestigious membership gave the report special credibility.[3] The proposal languished after an initial flurry of activity, however, until Senators John McCain (R-AZ) and Tim Kaine (D-VA) revived it in January 2014 by introducing legislation to implement the commission's recommendations. In a statement accompanying the bill, Senator McCain noted, "Unless we in Congress are prepared to cede our constitutional authority over matters of war to the executive, we need a more workable arrangement ... to create a broader and more durable national consensus on foreign policy and national security [and] ... to make internationalist policies more politically sustainable."[4]

---

[1] http://millercenter.org/policy/commissions/warpowers (accessed May 2013).

[2] http://www.nytimes.com/2008/12/12/us/politics/11web-baker.html?_r=0 (accessed January 2014).

[3] See also the War Powers Committee Report (June 2005), proposal by a group of former members of Congress and academics, http://www.constitutionproject.org/wp-content/uploads/2012/10/28.pdf (accessed May 2009); Kay King, "Congress and National Security," Special Report No. 58, Council on Foreign Relations, November 2010, http://www.cfr.org/congress/congress-national-security/p23359 (accessed March 2013). Former Senator Jim Webb has also pushed for a revival of congressional war powers. See Webb, "Congressional Abdication," *National Interest*, March–April 2013, http://nationalinterest.org (accessed March 19, 2013).

[4] http://web1.millercenter.org/commissions/warpowers/2014_0116_CongressionalRecord-KaineMcCain.pdf (accessed April 2014).

Congress attempted to reestablish a role for itself after Vietnam with the War Powers Resolution of 1973. Over four decades, this effort at reform failed repeatedly as presidents denied its constitutionality and lawmakers proved unable to enforce its provisions. The disappointing history of the resolution not only illustrates the difficulty of legislating cooperation between the two branches but also raises doubts about whether a different set of rules can accomplish the goal of generating "durable" consensus about U.S. actions abroad. Indeed, the case studies and empirical findings throughout this book suggest reasons for skepticism.

The report of the National War Powers Commission focused primarily on the initial decision to mobilize the armed forces. While this decision is vitally important, the greater challenge to the legality of the president's actions and the sustainability of foreign interventions has arisen from lengthy U.S. commitments abroad. Since the end of World War II, the bitterest disagreements about foreign affairs emerged during America's four long wars.[5] Greater consultation before undertaking such missions would not have spared policy makers and citizens the Hobson's choice of "stay the course" or "cut and run" posed by Korea, Vietnam, Iraq, and Afghanistan. International conflicts developed their own dynamics, changing over time in unexpected ways that diplomats and generals could not have foreseen at the start. Moreover, public support for the president typically diminished as the strategic objectives of an operation proved elusive or more costly than policy makers predicted. What the nation needed more than interbranch consultation at the beginning of its most divisive overseas engagements was greater review of the mission's implementation and public discussion about alternatives once forces were engaged.

Several obstacles, as we have seen throughout this book, stand in the way of building a more constructive relationship between the legislative and executive branches in foreign affairs. The challenge for Congress is inadequate capacity to generate credible information in a timely manner and to sustain a serious review of the president's proposals for more than a day. The first barrier to effective partnering with the president lies in the devaluation of committee specialization and expertise, particularly in the more prestigious and visible Senate. The second difficulty arises from the goals of members on the national security committees that bias the frequency and content of the inquiries they launch. The third stumbling block results from the political calculations that inhibit a frank, public appraisal of a mission once casualties begin to rise and the public becomes alarmed. Although critics fault the president for withholding vital security materials from Congress, the Senate Armed Services and Foreign Relations Committees have demonstrated serious weaknesses in generating information.

This chapter provides a critique of existing reform proposals and outlines an agenda for improving the oversight capacity of the Senate's national security

---

[5] Griffin (2013).

committees. My recommendations look beyond consultation about the initiation of conflicts to generate a more robust review of the implementation of administration policies over time. I focus on the underlying incentives that drive committee inquiries into the performance of the Departments of Defense and State with an eye to the self-correcting mechanisms at the heart of the American Constitution that balance relations between the branches. Consequently, my aim is not to change the entire Congress, but rather to suggest ways of motivating a relatively small number of senators to promote the interests of the institution and to educate the public while fulfilling their personal ambitions. By focusing on improved capabilities for the Senate Armed Services and Foreign Relations Committees, my proposals avoid the necessity of passing legislation and winning the president's signature. Well-functioning committees that promote the rule of law in foreign affairs through regular, predictable, and public deliberation make a revised war powers act unnecessary; in the absence of such regular order, new rules for consultation seem likely to fail.

WAR AND INSTITUTIONAL REFORM

America's past wars typically sparked congressional oversight of the president's conduct of hostilities and then generated reforms to correct mistakes after a conflict had ended. Lawmakers not only evaluated how the executive branch used its discretion to engage the enemy but also provided a public accounting of the mission's cost in lives and tax dollars. The lengthy wars in Afghanistan and Iraq, however, did not follow the usual pattern in American politics. Legislators conducted comparatively few formal public hearings regarding military operations and showed relatively little interest in evaluating the decisions of the executive branch once combat troops had withdrawn from Iraq and had begun coming home from Afghanistan.[6]

Critics have found fault with Congress for generations, but the pressures of war exposed institutional weaknesses that generated reform efforts throughout the twentieth century. After World War I, for example, Congress altered its budget process and ended its experiment with governance through the party caucuses. With the end of World War II, Congress again examined its internal operations and passed the 1946 Legislative Reorganization Act to improve its capacity for oversight of the president by strengthening its committees. By 1947, members also had adopted legislation to heighten the president's ability to integrate defense, intelligence, and diplomacy by unifying the military services

---

[6] In the winter of 2014, the Senate Intelligence Committee wrapped up a lengthy investigation of the CIA's use of rendition and torture during the years of the Bush administration. The report generated a major crisis over access of committee staff to CIA documents, which was unresolved at the time of this writing, and its major conclusions consequently have not been made public.

under civilian command at the Pentagon and establishing the National Security Council. The cessation of hostilities in Korea in 1953 prompted an unsuccessful Republican attempt to constrain the president's discretion to initiate military conflict through the Bricker Amendment and led to wide-ranging hearings on foreign policy.[7] Following Vietnam, reformers attempted to rein in presidential war making with the passage of the 1973 War Powers Resolution and promoted greater accountability to Congress by creating new intelligence committees and adopting restrictions on covert action and executive agreements.

The reforms of the 1970s were the last serious attempts in Congress to counter presidential war power. They depended heavily, moreover, upon voluntary compliance by the executive branch, which routinely violated both the spirit and the letter of the new rules. Presidents of both parties denied the constitutionality of the War Powers Resolution, and they suffered few consequences for concealing covert actions from lawmakers. Nevertheless, committees undertook major investigations of presidential conduct throughout the 1970s and well into the 1980s with some notable results and some undeniable failures. Since this period of "resurgence," the congressional appetite for monitoring the president's conduct of foreign affairs has diminished steadily to the low levels we see today.

CURRENT REFORM PROPOSALS

Congress is a frequent target for reform, although legislative institutions are notoriously "sticky" and resistant to change. We should not expect otherwise, since legislators make the rules they live by. Several different approaches have circulated in Washington: major legislation, changes in the legislative culture, and incremental tinkering with chamber rules. The only active proposal as of this writing is the McCain-Kaine bill, which was introduced in the second session of 113th Congress, to translate the War Powers Commission recommendations into law. The proposal has serious limitations that raise doubts about its feasibility and efficacy, however.

The centerpiece of the proposed War Powers Consultation Act is repeal of the 1973 War Powers Resolution in favor of a new mechanism for cooperation between the legislative and executive branches. The 1973 act was not only unconstitutional in the eyes of many of its critics, but also widely understood to be unenforceable. The commission's chairmen, James Baker and Warren Christopher, hoped to replace it with a process that presidents would respect and that would provide a pragmatic solution to the asymmetrical relationship between the two branches in conducting modern warfare. Their goal was to establish "a constructive, workable, politically acceptable legal framework that will best

---

[7] McCormick and Wittkopf (1990).

promote effective, cooperative, and deliberative action by both the President and Congress in matters of war."[8]

The proposed bill established new procedures for the legislature, but contained ambiguous language regarding the executive. The main feature was creation of a Joint Congressional Consultation Committee (JCCC), which included the key party leaders in the Senate and House and the chairs and ranking members of the related committees: Armed Services in the Senate and House, Foreign Relations in the Senate, Foreign Affairs in the House, Intelligence, and Appropriations in both chambers. The language did not specify which officials from the executive branch would serve on the committee. Moreover, the proposed bill did not require much from the president other than to "encourage" communication: through notification of an impending armed conflict; consultation during its duration at least every two months; and provision of a monthly classified written report to the committee regarding any significant armed conflict, other than covert operations. In addition, it contained numerous exemptions to the president's obligation to seek congressional input and lacked penalties for flouting the law.

The proponents of the plan argued that it was better to have a legal framework the president would accept than the current ambiguous situation about the initiation of war. Some scholars have shared this perspective,[9] but others have severely criticized it. Louis Fisher, who disputes the notion that the Constitution is ambiguous about congressional authority and has written persuasively about the misguided provisions of the War Powers Resolution of 1973, argued that this new procedure was even worse in terms of marginalizing the legislative branch in foreign affairs.[10] William Howell opposed it on the practical grounds that it would not work.[11] In his view, the president still would enjoy the upper hand in dealing with a fragmented legislature and face powerful incentives to exploit its loopholes. He further argued that Congress would be no more able to enforce the JCCC Act than was the case for the War Powers Act. Finally, Howell called attention to the fact that partisan politics, rather than procedural requirements, would continue to influence presidents' initiation of the use of force and its duration.

My research suggests a further set of objections to the Baker-Christopher proposal. First, the proposal does not address the fundamental changes to the congressional committee system in the past thirty years. Senators today devalue the time spent on committee work, so the logic of creating yet another committee seems flawed. Second, members will bring the goals and strategic premises of existing committees to their deliberations within the new joint committee. If

---

[8] Text of proposed War Powers Consultation Act, http://millercenter.org/policy/commissions/warpowers (accessed March 2013).

[9] Kassop (2013).

[10] Fisher (2012).

[11] Howell (2013).

senators on Armed Services, for example, fear undermining public support for the Pentagon by asking hard questions in their own hearing rooms, why would we expect them to behave otherwise on the JCCC? Third, the proposal says nothing about subpoena powers, which means that the new committee would have fewer levers over the executive branch than existing committees have. Fourth, the new committee would depend upon the efforts of party leaders and committee chairs already deeply engaged in managing the legislature's business and lack the time for intensive examination of the president's proposals and reports. Fifth, McCain-Kaine concentrates on one very specific type of oversight, the decision by presidents to commit U.S. troops in a "significant" way. Such events, however, represent just one piece of a much greater legislative obligation that involves budgets, police patrols, and fire alarms. Most important, the proposal does little to encourage ongoing oversight once the president initiates hostilities other than asking for reports. As I noted in the previous chapter, review of ongoing conflicts may well be the graver matter for the legitimacy of U.S. foreign policy than initial consultation.

Together, the flaws in the commission's approach raise questions about its viability. The bigger drawback, however, is its failure to address the need for procedural regularity that is a fundamental condition of the rule of law. The president still would determine when consultation took place by proposing policies that activated the committee and exercising discretion about what and when to report. The ad hoc nature of the resulting process, of course, arises from the need to get the president's signature on the legislation. No president will agree in advance to meaningful constraints on executive discretion or serious mechanisms of enforcement. In short, the proposed law confers an enormous public relations benefit on a war-minded president, fails to impose any meaningful criteria for gauging and enforcing White House compliance, and ignores the fundamental problems with oversight that this book identifies.

Other prestigious groups have weighed in about the need for change, including a group of former House members, scholars, and policy experts affiliated with an organization called the Constitution Project. In addition, the Brookings Institution and the Council on Foreign Relations offered critiques and recommendations.[12] All of these groups concurred that Congress has not lived up to its constitutional responsibilities and that a dysfunctional legislature posed a threat to both national security and democratic accountability. Their various publications sought to alter expectations among elites in Washington about what lawmakers ought to do. They also stressed how polarized politics undermined the comity, expertise, and professionalism necessary for effective legislative participation in foreign and defense policy.

---

[12] King, "Congress and National Security." See various short reports on Congress and national security at the Constitution Project, War Powers Committee, http://millercenter.org/policy/com missions/warpowers/ (accessed January 2014).

The most detailed report, titled "Congress and National Security" and issued in November 2010 by the Council on Foreign Relations (CFR), analyzed how broad changes in electoral and partisan politics contributed to the gridlock and abysmal public approval ratings of Congress. According to the report's author, Kay King, Congress cannot be a meaningful participant in foreign policy unless it reforms the way it does business: by revamping outdated rules, improving its budget processes, offering "timely" advice and consent to treaties and nominations, consulting regularly with the executive branch, and finding resources to improve its expertise.[13] The CFR report recommends a return to regular order in budget authorization; expansion of reporting requirements, such as the Pentagon's Quadrennial Review; increased funding for the Government Accountability Office, Congressional Research Service, and Congressional Budget Office; and increased educational efforts for members and their constituents. King's arguments, thus, are similar to points other observers of Congress have made about widespread weaknesses in the institution.[14]

The report further contains recommendations to bring the committees responsible for defense and foreign policy of both chambers together for regular consultation. Interestingly, in light of the findings in Chapter 3, the report recommends that members reduce the number of subcommittee and committee assignments to "better focus their attention and develop greater depth of expertise."[15] The council's objectives are worthy, but they require the wholesale undoing of thirty years of institutional change. While the public waits for this to happen, however, ongoing threats to democratic accountability in foreign policy remain.

Political scientist Christopher Deering offered a more limited menu consistent with his expectation that sweeping changes to the status quo were unlikely. Under one of his scenarios, Congress would make small changes to existing rules or add specific requirements to individual statutes.[16] Such piecemeal approaches to reform have been commonplace in Congress,[17] and Deering has given examples of possible strategies: grant permanent tenure on the House and Senate Intelligence Committees; remove the Super A designation from the Senate Foreign Relations Committee to make it more attractive to prospective members; and pass narrowly targeted legislation, similar to the North Korean Human Rights Act. Deering was pessimistic, however, that such small adjustments could restore the institutional balance of power in Washington. "Unable to legislate, unwilling to abdicate," he concluded, "Congress likely will tinker, leaving the conduct of foreign affairs and war largely to the discretion of the president."[18]

[13] King, "Congress and National Security," 31.
[14] Mann and Ornstein (2006; 2012).
[15] King, "Congress and National Security," 38.
[16] Deering (2005, 375).
[17] Schickler (2001).
[18] Deering (2005, 376). See also Fisher (2013, chap. 9, 201–32).

RENEWING FOREIGN POLICY OVERSIGHT

Is it possible to tinker with the Senate's national security committees to make them better stewards of U.S. defense and foreign policy? The results of this study suggest one promising avenue: enhance regular order in the oversight activities of the Senate Armed Services and Foreign Relations Committees. The first target is to elevate the frequency, predictability, and visibility of interactions between committee members and administration officials. The second objective is to rethink the use of executive sessions as venues for exchange between the two branches. The third is to reinvigorate incentives for ambitious lawmakers on Armed Services and Foreign Relations to engage in entrepreneurial oversight.

The challenge of redirecting the energies of the Senate's national security watchdogs is considerable, but my proposals offer several practical virtues. They need induce behavioral change among only a relatively small number of legislators rather than the entire Congress, they require approval of the Senate's majority party caucus rather than majorities in both chambers, and they do not have to have the signature of the president.

If members of the Senate want to strengthen the watchdog capabilities of the national security committees, the Constitution grants them the power to make their own rules. Reforming the committee system is notoriously difficult, because members gravitate toward those that serve their political interest and resist efforts to alter their turf.[19] Furthermore, a legislative body like the Senate, with its emphasis on individual autonomy and its provisions for minority veto, is particularly resistant to reform proposals. Nevertheless, different interests came together in search of mutual gain in the past at times of institutional stress. They frequently operated through the party caucuses and tended to produce a "disjointed" process of reform rather than a coherent set of proposals.[20] The key to revitalizing national security oversight thus is to empower individuals to further the collective well-being of the institution as they pursue their own goals.[21]

Reinventing the Senate's National Security Committees

Improving the performance of the Senate's national security committees depends first upon addressing the reasons behind their reduced workload. In the

[19] King (1997); Adler (2002).

[20] Schickler (2001).

[21] Schickler (2007) has made a persuasive argument that entrepreneurial lawmakers provide valuable collective goods for Congress as a whole as a byproduct of other goal-seeking activity. He and Kriner (2012) have elaborated this perspective in their current research on investigations. Dodd and Schott (1979) and Sundquist (1981) link periods of institutional revival among members to their realization that individual power depends upon congressional power.

absence of frequent hearings, members lose opportunities to query administration officials and inadvertently invite stonewalling by the executive branch. What new incentives could offset the effects of the downward trends in total committee hearing activity so evident in Figures 1.1 and 1.3 and in the statistical results of Chapter 3? The old inducements relied on a norm of apprenticeship and a hierarchy of influence. The former is obsolete and the latter tactic of designating Armed Services and Foreign Relations as Super A Committees no longer works,[22] even though the rule is routinely violated in the chamber. What I have in mind is to stimulate the ambitions of a small number of senators to counter the dominance of the president in international affairs.

We know from the statistical analyses in Chapter 3 that several different trends influenced changes in the frequency of committee hearings for both the Senate Armed Services and Foreign Relations Committees. Both committees reduced the total of all types of hearings, for example, as members took on a greater number of assignments. Moreover, the end of the Cold War Consensus coincided with a shift away from control of the Senate by a small number of senior committee chairs. Finally, the total number of hearing days rose when the number of days in session and mentions in the *New York Times* approached their maximum values. Interestingly, party polarization, which has been blamed for many of the ills affecting the contemporary Congress, was not a significant factor in the decline in committee workloads. These statistical patterns suggest some likely targets for altering behavior and also indicate that the two committees will diverge in responding to changes.

Increasing the length of legislative sessions and dramatically decreasing the mean number of committee assignments held by senators are promising avenues for raising hearing activity. Both of these options require chamber-wide alterations in well-entrenched patterns of behavior, however, and do not warrant serious attention on feasibility grounds.

Enhancing media visibility, however, has solid payoffs in terms of predicted activity levels for both committees. At first glance, reversing the declining trend in media coverage seems beyond the capacity of the Senate's national security committees. The press does not find Congress newsworthy and prefers to devote its diminished coverage of the federal government to the president. Even when reporters pay attention to the legislative branch, they have difficulty framing a coherent narrative in such a decentralized and fragmented institution. Upon reflection, the committees could attract more attention from journalists by designing hearings that directly engage the media's news values of authoritative sources, conflict, black-and-white issues, and human drama. Many of the most noteworthy Senate hearings have had these characteristics.

The national security committees could generate greater media coverage by making more effective use of their ability to call administration witnesses to

[22] Deering (2005).

Capitol Hill. What I have in mind is analogous to the Question Period in the British Parliament in which the prime minister and cabinet officials appear regularly before the chamber to respond to members' inquiries. Under current law, Armed Services and Foreign Relations have the prerogative to examine the executive branch and the authority through their subpoena power to enforce it. What the committees have never done, however, is routinize these appearances.[23]

Three characteristics of the House of Commons sessions would make the national security hearings more salient to the press, and all would move the oversight process in the direction of enhancing regular order. The first requirement would be to build routine sessions with top administrators, whether weekly or biweekly, into the Senate committee calendar. The consistent provision of information at a predictable time and place by people with power to make decisions is the foundation of the Washington beat system.[24] By announcing a schedule of hearings at the beginning of each month, department heads, lawmakers, and journalists would know that salient events and decisions would receive timely public attention from authoritative sources. This approach to policy making increased the likelihood that reporters showed up at the White House and was an important factor in the development of the federal bureaucracy.[25] In addition, the prospect of repeat performances at specific intervals would make it more difficult for administration officials to stonewall the committees with evasive answers.

A second feature of the British system with the potential to raise the profile of national security oversight in the Senate would require administration officials to answer senators' inquiries without reading from prepared testimony or fobbing tough questions off on subordinates. Any one who has watched the debates in the House of Commons quickly develops an appreciation for the spontaneity, wit, and hard-hitting exchanges between ministers and MPs. As intensely human dramas, such hearings satisfy the media's enthusiasm for spectacle and create the possibility that a presidential spokesperson might make news by saying something unexpected or acknowledging the need for additional consideration or possible revision of a policy.

A final possibility for enhancing media visibility is to provide a defined amount of time for committee members of the opposition party to query Cabinet officials. Giving opponents a platform to air differences with the executive branch would generate the possibility of conflict, which is another key element of the media's values regarding newsworthy events. The combination of a predictable,

---

[23] Galloway (1946, 212–21) favored a proposal put forward by Senators Kefauver and Fulbright to establish a regular question time each day when members could interrogate administration officials through a resolution of inquiry or through the standing committees of the House and Senate. David Mayhew pointed me to Galloway's classic.

[24] Cook (1998).

[25] Carpenter (2001).

easily accessed venue with authoritative sources making news would compensate for many of the difficulties the press has experienced in covering Congress. Over time, the national security question periods could partially redress the imbalance in attention to the two branches that has accelerated since the 1980s.

The simple, but profound change of routinizing communication between the Senate's national security committees and the executive branch has several benefits for enhancing the rule of law in international affairs. A predictable schedule would enable members of Foreign Relations and Armed Services to take a more deliberative approach to oversight rather than merely react to events. The presence of reporters on a regular basis would provide incentives for senators to show up, while the prospect of sparring with agency officials would enable members to build reputations as policy experts and test their mettle as future candidates for president. The minority party would have the opportunity to shape discussion about policy options through presenting its views. Most important, the heightened visibility could generate greater interest among senators in serving on Armed Services and Foreign Relations, thus restoring some of their lost prestige. Political scientist Samuel Kernell famously argued that presidents developed the strategy of "going public" to compensate for the institutional weaknesses of their office.[26] Nothing prevents the Senate national security committees from doing the same.

The public would benefit in several ways from heightened visibility of the Senate's national security committees by gaining access to sustained discourse among foreign policy elites. Committee members would still have discretion over how they addressed particular issues, but the regularity of public appearances by the secretaries of defense and state might make it more difficult to engage in the kind of strategic behavior we saw in Chapter 4 regarding total oversight days and Chapter 5 regarding police patrols and fire alarms. Perhaps Armed Services would be more attuned to the president's use of force *prior* to the deployment of troops or address rising casualties publicly *before* the costs of war approached high levels. Most important, Armed Services' seeming inclination to protect Republican presidents might be more difficult to implement. And perhaps Foreign Relations would become more responsible in its treatment of the budget for international affairs and more inclined to focus less on state of the world inquiries in order to pay more attention to the president's use of force. Greater visibility might encourage the committee to do more to generate information that the public cares about and can use to evaluate national security threats.

The emergence of a rival "beat" on Capitol Hill for national security has the additional advantage of encouraging the president to provide more information about his policies. Today, presidents decide when they will hold press conferences or take informal questions at public events, and they fill their schedules

---

[26] Kernell (1997).

with scripted events that protect them from having to defend their policies. With senators holding forth in the hearing rooms of the Armed Services and Foreign Relations Committees, presidents would be less able to manage the news cycle.

On balance, the reforms to generate greater public visibility and regularity of national security oversight would likely produce different effects on the two committees. Foreign Relations was most adversely affected by institutional changes in the Senate, particularly the big decline in media coverage and the loss of internal status. It has the most to gain from the creation of a new "beat" for foreign policy within the Senate's committee rooms. Nevertheless, it is poorly positioned with its current membership to implement proposals for a regular question period. Intervention from the party caucuses would be necessary, therefore, to induce senators with stature inside the chamber to transfer to the committee and to persuade promising newcomers to remain and invest in its success.

Armed Services, in contrast, operated comfortably out of the public eye over the sixty-two years of the study and could prove reluctant to call attention to operations within the Defense Department. The committee had a recurring pattern of deemphasizing oversight during Republican administrations and moving hearings behind closed doors to deal with controversial issues, such as the use of force or rising casualties, in order to protect the committee's internal consensus. Nevertheless, Armed Services engaged in a considerable amount of oversight over the years of the study to ensure that the Defense Department implemented the committee's priorities. It also showed an inclination to use oversight during periods of budget tightening and during high levels of public concern about national security in order to build support for Pentagon programs and military personnel. Improving the performance of Armed Services, therefore, is less about quantity than about content. The committee would need greater diversity among its members to mitigate its ongoing bias toward the delivery of economic benefits to organized constituencies. Only active intervention from the party caucuses is likely to make the membership less homogeneous and better able to raise issues with the Pentagon.

Reinvigorated national security committees would benefit greatly from improved mechanisms within Congress for greater coordination and expertise. A common thread in the reform proposals noted above is dealing with the fragmentation among the various House and Senate committees with jurisdiction over defense and foreign policy. Executive branch officials rightly complain about appearing before multiple committees in both chambers to present the same testimony, a pattern so evident in the investigation of the Walter Reed scandal. An additional concern is the need for greater expertise in addressing the complexities of defense and foreign policy. In the 1950s and 1960s, the Senate Armed Services and Foreign Relations Committees frequently conducted joint hearings, and both enjoyed reputations at various times for excellent staff.

Nevertheless, more is needed to boost the capabilities of both committees in ways that would make them less dependent upon the skills, predilections, and party loyalties of their individual chairs.

Models for a legislative support agency to focus on national security policy already exist. Congress has the Joint Committee on Taxation and the Congressional Budget Office (CBO), both of them highly professional organizations with stellar reputations for nonpartisan expertise. It is instructive, I think, that Congress has paid attention to its need for independent, expert advice with respect to its power of the purse, while neglecting institutional support for its war powers. My preferred model is the CBO, which prepares analyses and professional advice for both chambers and for multiple committees. The agency's reports are widely available to lawmakers who serve on other committees and frequently are quoted in the press. The CBO has issued economic forecasts that historically have been more accurate than those of its counterpart in the White House, the Office of Management and Budget (OMB). In addition, CBO analysts have proved more resistant than OMB staff to political pressures to cook the numbers. Multiple masters with widely divergent ideological views turn out to be better guarantors of disinterested expertise than a single-minded executive.

Rethinking the Role of Secrecy

All democracies wrestle with conflicting needs for secrecy and accountability in the conduct of war and diplomacy. With respect to oversight, secrecy promotes the public interest when the legislative and executive branches can deliberate candidly. Yet, it also makes lawmakers complicit in hiding the truth from citizens. Both Armed Services and Foreign Relations need to rethink their use of secrecy, albeit in different ways.

The responsibilities of the national security committees of necessity require secrecy. Two patterns suggest that the committees need to step up their meetings behind closed doors. First is the decline in executive sessions as a result of members' increased number of committee assignments. Second is the absence of trust during periods of divided government, which seems to reduce the frequency of informal interaction between the committees and the administration. Both committees devoted a disproportionate amount of their closed-door meetings to oversight during the period of study. Moreover, Armed Services substituted fire alarm hearings for police patrols when it felt obliged to deal with the use of major force or rising casualties. Without an increase in the centrality of committee work in the Senate and longer legislative sessions, therefore, it is hard to devise remedies that would enable Armed Services and Foreign Relations to improve their use of executive sessions.

Some readers may find my support for more secret committee meetings to be counterproductive. After all, the loss of accountability resulting from secret hearings motivated liberal reformers in the 1970s to advocate fewer executive sessions.[27] Moreover, this study indicates that some percentage of the secret meetings, particularly in the Armed Forces hearing rooms, strategically favored Republican presidents rather than promoted the public good.

Despite these concerns, implementing a British-style question period and creating a CBO-type agency could promote a more constructive use of secrecy on both committees. By regularizing public give-and-take between committee members and administration officials, lawmakers could more carefully set priorities for the closed-door sessions that require interbranch consultation. By developing a source of independent expertise, senators, especially those in the minority party, would be better equipped to participate in hearings out of public view. Closed sessions, moreover, would be particularly valuable for creating opportunities for joint meetings that included multiple committees from the Senate and House with jurisdiction over aspects of international affairs. Over time, a regularized pattern of private exchange involving multiple parties has the potential for the two branches to develop the trust that is currently lacking in their deliberations.

Rewarding Individual Policy Entrepreneurs

Legislatures, by their very nature, confront serious obstacles of coordination that handicap members in dealing with the president.[28] Oversight of foreign policy is a collective good for Congress as an institution and for the public at large whose benefits are widely dispersed and burdens narrowly focused. Consequently, the amount of monitoring of the executive will always be suboptimal.[29] In the past the institution offered members inducements for generating valuable information,[30] and over time, many individuals have assumed the costs of

---

[27] Kravitz (1990). Reformers argued that closed meetings protected deal making among committees, agencies, and interest groups in "iron triangles," which were contrary to the public interest. With reference to national security, they believed that the defense establishment escaped scrutiny of wasteful spending and contended that the Johnson and Nixon administrations had been able to mislead the public about the Vietnam War because so much congressional oversight occurred behind closed doors.

[28] Moe (1985); Moe and Howell (1999). Congress, as a body of two chambers and 535 individuals, must overcome substantial transaction costs to confront the executive branch. Most members will be free riders unless institutions organize them into a coherent defense of legislative prerogatives or individuals assume the responsibility for bearing the costs of providing the collective good of institutional power. The president, in contrast, is a single actor whose personal and institutional interests coincide in promoting the power of the executive. This is an uneven fight, and lawmakers will seldom prevail without extraordinary efforts to overcome barriers to collective action that impede their ability to act as one.

[29] Schickler (2006).

[30] Fenno (1973); Krehbiel (1991).

overseeing the president's conduct of foreign policy, with considerable impact.[31] For reform of the oversight process to work, therefore, the national security committees must inspire ambition for engaging in oversight in at least some of their members.

It is important to recognize how aspirations for the presidency encouraged oversight effort among individual members over the period of this study. For many years, service on Foreign Relations, and to a lesser extent Armed Services, was perceived as an important credential for presidential candidates, and Democrats continue to adhere to this view. Among those who ran for president between 2000 and 2012, for example, many had previously served on one of the two committees, including Vice President Al Gore (previously D-TN) and Senators John Kerry (D-MA), Paul Wellstone (D-MN), Hillary Clinton (D-NY), Joe Lieberman (D-CT), Joe Biden (D-DE), Christopher Dodd (D-CT), and Barack Obama (D-IL). The ranks of senior Democratic senators have thinned with the departure of Senators Biden, Dodd, and Kerry, and few have stepped forward to serve as counterweights or partners to the Obama administration.

The GOP, in contrast, has been more likely to draw candidates from its governors. Consequently, the list of senators who ran for president with experience on either Armed Services or Foreign Relations is much shorter: Senators John McCain (R-AZ) and Orrin Hatch (R-UT) served on Armed Services, while Richard Lugar (R-IN) had a long tenure on Foreign Relations. As noted in Chapter 3, rising Senate stars in the GOP have shunned the Foreign Relations Committee since the mid-1990s,[32] and with the defeat of Senator Lugar in the 2012 primary, no incumbent Republicans on Foreign Relations have the stature of a Vandenberg or Lodge to challenge the president.

The timing is good for both parties to develop new approaches to international affairs. The Republican brand on foreign policy needs refurbishing after the war in Iraq,[33] and the Democratic alternatives lack coherence. Indeed, both parties seem uncertain about how best to deal with the dramatic changes wrought by globalization of the world economy and the emergence of consequential new actors in the international system. Postwar periods historically have been times for the political parties to reinvent themselves, and senators on the national security committees frequently have been involved in past reorientations of American policy. The way is open for Senate entrepreneurs to begin the national conversation.

If the reforms noted above increase the prestige and visibility of the national security committees, we might see more efforts among members to develop an

---

[31] See, for example, Mayhew (2000); Schickler (2006); Carter and Scott (2009).

[32] Former Senator Fred Thompson (R-TN) served very briefly on Foreign Relations. His short bid for the Republican nomination occurred after he left the Senate.

[33] See, for example, Daniel W. Drezner, "Rebooting Republican Foreign Policy," *Foreign Affairs*, January/February 2013, http://www.cfr.org/us-strategy-and-politics/rebooting-republican-foreign-policy/p29717 (accessed March 2013).

aura of statesmanship. Two nonstatutory changes could help things along. The first would be for party leaders to reaffirm the role of the chairs and ranking minority members of the national security committees as spokespersons. The majority and minority leaders, so enmeshed in the day-to-day affairs and individual quirks of their members, have little time to develop expertise and nuance with respect to foreign and defense policy.

Alternatively, the Senate parties could create a position in their respective leadership ranks equivalent to the chair of each caucus's Policy Committee. At present, the leadership structure is geared largely to domestic affairs; a new position would assign responsibility to a respected senator for crafting a party position on major foreign and defense policy issues and conveying it to the press and public. Working in concert with the leaders of the national security committees, the designated senator in each caucus could help develop hearing agendas to offer a counterweight to the personal, political goals of the committee members. In this way, the mission of the parties would expand beyond bill passage to include coordination of national security oversight.

Conclusion

The present state of national security oversight inspires few defenders either on or off Capitol Hill. Lawmakers made major efforts in 1946 and again in the 1970s to improve the ability of congressional committees to monitor the performance of the executive. Another round of reform is long overdue, but not enough members appreciate what has been lost and why it matters.

Lawmakers retain many prerogatives for exerting influence in foreign affairs,[34] and they typically have followed periods of exceptional delegation of power to the president with resurgent activity.[35] At various moments in American foreign policy, lawmakers have taken an active role, at times thwarting the president and at other times offering political cover and support.[36] According to one noted scholar, members have recognized that participation in foreign policy making has been essential for the legislature "to hold its own" in the national government.[37]

[34] See Jones (2005) for how the system of separated powers in the United States constrains the presidency.

[35] Dodd and Schott (1979); Sundquist (1981).

[36] Sundquist (1981); Destler (1985); Ripley and Lindsay (1993); Lindsay (1992–93; 1994); Meernik (1993; 1995); Hinckley (1994); Auerswald and Cowhey (1997); Henderson (1998; 2002); Wolfensberger (2005); Johnson (2006); Schickler (2007); Carter and Scott (2009); Zelizer (2010).

[37] Mayhew (2000, 123). Mayhew draws parallels with the British experience in the seventeenth century, as an increasingly assertive Parliament engaged with the king over foreign affairs. Katznelson and Lapinski (2006) further stress the importance of legislative constraints over the monarch, arguing that the British Empire would have foundered had Parliament not reined in the king at various key points.

As the most visible and consequential overseers of U.S. foreign policy, the Senate Armed Services and Foreign Relations Committees could play a major role in the revival of Congress as a responsible partner to the president. Accustomed for several decades to furthering the personal and partisan agendas of the members, the two committees have been fitful in their adherence to regular order. They have been biased in their dealings with administrations of different parties and overly sensitive to budgetary politics and routine administration at the expense of more consequential matters. They have emphasized matters of concern to relatively narrow constituencies rather than generate information of widespread public interest. Of the two, Armed Services has been the more responsible watchdog in terms of reacting to the president's use of force and scheduling additional hearings during times of rising casualties. Yet, it has often been slow to react to rising casualties, overly protective of the Pentagon, and satisfied with hearings of relatively short duration. Foreign Relations has lost sight of its past history as a major player in U.S. foreign policy, settled for second-class status in the Senate and contented itself with broad inquiries into the "state of the world" instead of sustained attention to difficult issues.

More hearings alone will not restore the rule of law to U.S. foreign policy. Repeated House committee inquiries during the 113th Congress, for example, about the 2012 murder in Benghazi, Libya, of four Americans, including the ambassador, contributed little to presidential accountability or to public understanding. Nevertheless, regular and visible interaction between executive officials and a few senatorial "masters" of the public business would help to restore institutional balance in the making of war and peace. With a better process for generating information about U.S. actions in world affairs, the public might better hold its guardians accountable.

Coding Congressional Committee Hearings

CONGRESSIONAL HEARINGS are a rich source of information for scholars and are becoming more useful for empirical research because of the availability of electronically searchable databases. The Policy Agendas Project at the University of Washington has provided an invaluable resource to scholars in coding hearings by policy type.[1] In addition, recent researchers on congressional investigations have used keyword searches to identify relevant hearings.[2] For a variety of reasons, neither the Agendas Project nor the keyword method was suitable for my purposes. First, the former does not have a separate code for oversight, while the latter method is prone to error, since committees do not consistently use the words such as "review," "oversee," or "oversight." Second, neither approach differentiates among types of oversight content nor takes account of executive sessions. Below I describe the methods and content codes that I used for the system of fine-grained coding of hearings. I have provided more detail than is perhaps necessary so that scholars who choose a similar research strategy do not have to reinvent the wheel.

CODING PUBLIC HEARINGS

Congressional committees confer significance on hearings by deciding to publish them, and I follow their lead by focusing on the published record. The Congressional Information Service (CIS) provides abstracts of all published hearings that include the hearing title, the dates, the relevant bill numbers, committees and subcommittees, the witness list, and a summary of the content. The CIS abstracts also contain information regarding unpublished hearings and some executive sessions, which I address later.

---

[1] The data were originally collected by Frank R. Baumgartner and Bryan D. Jones, with the support of National Science Foundation grants SBR 9320922 and 0111611, and were distributed through the Department of Government at the University of Texas at Austin.

[2] Parker and Dull (2009; 2012); Kriner and Shen (2007); Kriner and Schickler (2014).

The content codes for each type of hearing include (1) nominations for presidential appointees and military promotions, (2) treaty ratification, (3) budgets dealing with reauthorization of programs for the next fiscal year, (4) statutes creating new programs or regulations or substantially modifying existing programs, and (5) oversight.

The oversight category includes hearings of the following types: (1) general overview of situations in the international arena, major regions or specific countries, such as challenges confronting a new administration in the coming year or perspectives on developments in China; (2) agenda setting to push the executive branch to act on a particular international problem, such as human trafficking; (3) program implementation, such as military training and other personnel matters, weapons systems, or aid programs; (4) progress on treaty negotiations; (5) implementation of approved treaties; (6) scandal or incompetence; (7) resolutions urging nonmilitary action on the president, which I subsequently collapsed with the code for agenda setting; and (8) conflicts in which American forces are engaged in hostilities or are deployed in an area that experiences a crisis, such as the demilitarized zone in Korea. I also included in this latter category crises in which vital American strategic interests created the possibility that the United States would become involved in the use of military operations. For example, the Egyptian seizure of the Suez Canal in the 1950s and the reflagging of Kuwait ships in the 1990s were coded as crises; the genocide in Darfur, despite its horrific nature, was not. I included resolutions to authorize the president's use of force or urge the deployment of troops in this category, as well.

Until the mid-1970s, the two committees dealt with covert operations, a task they now share with the Senate Intelligence Committee. I did not include hearings for the Intelligence Committee in the study because data were lacking for the first half of the time series and because Senate members are term-limited. One needs to bear in mind, however, that the hearing agenda changed for committees midway in the time series.

Two different Dartmouth undergraduates coded the CIS abstract information for each hearing. I then matched their separate spreadsheets with an Excel program that identified discrepancies. I resolved all of these differences, often referring to the hearing record, and I then rechecked each observation to clarify any linkage to an international crisis or U.S. military operation against lists of military engagements in Howell and Pevehouse (2007) and Kriner (2010) and descriptions in the *New York Times*. I chose to combine active military operations and diplomatic crises that *could have led* to hostilities because I found it difficult to draw consistent boundaries around military conflicts and because many of the emergencies that ended up with a diplomatic solution sometimes spilled over into violence.

I accessed the hearings from the online CIS abstracts rather than the printed volumes. I subsequently learned that the Policy Agendas Project relies on the printed record, but could not obtain a clear sense of how large the differences were. Based on my own digging, I discovered that sources of error in the published record arose from the unpublished hearings prior to 1970, the censoring of sensitive hearing testimony, and the historical time series issued by Foreign Relations, which included testimony and documents in executive session for key events. For example, multiple historical series were issued over time for the same event to include additional days of testimony, so care was crucial to avoid double counting, as I explain below. Finally, I went back to the hearing abstracts from 2004 through 2010 to include any that were published after the first round of coding.

Prior to 1970, committee record keeping was quite idiosyncratic. The Legislative Reorganization Act of 1970 standardized committee procedures, established a commitment to greater transparency, and provided additional staff to carry out these directives. The CIS staff went through the records for all committees from the pre-1970 period to determine what was missing from the public record and to make important unpublished hearings available. The problem in reconstructing the record of committee activity prior to 1970 was deciding which public hearings had not been published, which nonpublic hearings were so minor that publication was not warranted, and which were too sensitive in the eyes of the committee to put in the public domain.[3] Apparently, the Senate Armed Services and Foreign Relations Committees had better records for the pre-1970 period than did most committees.[4] The CIS staff were able to compile the unpublished hearings in "Red Books," which I sampled systematically by examining every fifth hearing in the volumes for the 1960s. This search turned up a few hearings for the Senate Foreign Relations Committee that dealt with approval for new programs, but nothing substantial for Armed Services. I concluded, therefore, that I was on safe ground in relying on the CIS abstracts of public hearings, at least for my two committees.[5] The major problem for both committees, therefore, appears to be censored data for hearings that the committees chose to conceal from the public. To deal with the potential for undercounts of oversight activity, I did extensive sleuthing, described in the next section.

---

[3] Interview with August Imholz, 2006.

[4] Interview with August Imholz, 2006.

[5] Something odd appears in the Policy Agendas Project data set, which shows unpublished hearings dropping to zero for Armed Services in 1965, for Foreign Relations in 1972, and for all committees in 1973. The CIS continues to list unpublished hearings to the present. I spot-checked the list for my committees and concluded that like the Red Books, they contain content that is minor and routine. The category of unpublished hearings also produced abstracts for executive sessions, however, for which the content was not available, but which provided invaluable summary information of topics, dates, and witnesses noted below.

Coding Executive Session Hearings

Executive sessions, in which committees convene behind closed doors, occurred frequently for the Armed Services and Foreign Relations Committees. Hearings in closed sessions often dealt with matters of high politics involving sensitive treaty negotiations, military operations, or emerging crises. But some executive sessions took place for reasons that did not appear related to policy issues. The challenge, then, was to develop a data set of hearings that were comparable to the public sessions in terms of their importance, policy content, and engagement with the executive branch. I used several strategies to accomplish these goals by consulting the CIS hearing abstracts, the Historical Series of hearings of key foreign policy decisions published by the Senate Foreign Relations Committees, and the committee calendars for Armed Services and Foreign Relations in the *Daily Digest*. Each of these sources had drawbacks, but together they provided a comprehensive view of the oversight activity of Armed Services and Foreign Relations hearings in closed session from 1947 to 2008.

The CIS published abstracts for hearings conducted during executive session and released years or decades later. Some were compilations for a particular year that included multiple topics, while others included multiple hearings over several years for a particular topic. These turned out to be fraught with error in terms of counting the number of hearing days. For example, a single abstract might list twelve to fifteen different dates (and in a few instances fifty or sixty) for hearings by the Foreign Relations or Armed Services Committee. Closer examination revealed, moreover, that the entries covered multiple topics, some involving oversight, others examining budget authorizations, and still others dealing with treaty negotiations.[6] I found it necessary, therefore, to inspect each abstract carefully and adjust the coding accordingly.

Over the years, the Senate Foreign Relations Committee also published extensive volumes of hearings of historical documents and executive sessions, many of which were joint sessions with the Senate Armed Services Committee. These volumes, which coveed such events as the Truman Doctrine, the Korean and Vietnam Wars, and various conflicts between Israel and its Arab neighbors, are a gold mine of information, but also pose difficulties. First, a volume in the Historical Series often included both public and executive session hearings, such as the creation of NATO. Second, an individual volume, for example the one on the Marshall Plan or the Cuban Missile Crisis, contained important hearings that also appeared in other volumes. Third, Foreign Relations issued different versions of the same volume multiple times, with the first compilation about the Truman Doctrine appearing in the mid-1950s and subsequent ver-

---

[6] The Policy Agendas Project hearing data appear to have this problem because each abstract is coded as a single observation. This is not an issue for the studies by Jones and Baumgartner (2005) because they typically look at annual figures and broad policy domains.

sions appearing multiple times in later years as new information was included. Fourth, nothing comparable to the Historical Series volumes has appeared since the mid-1980s. Thus, the combination of the CIS abstracts and the Historical Series raised the dual possibility of overcounting some public or executive session hearings and missing others altogether.

Therefore, I turned to description of Senate committee activity in the *Daily Digest*, which contains the calendar of activities each day for each committee. This is the approach that Joel Aberbach used for his study of oversight.[7] The calendar specifies which meetings are "closed," "partially closed," or in "executive session," and it provides titles that identify the content and gives lists of the witnesses appearing before the committee.[8] With respect to counting the number of days for each hearing, most calendar entries dealt with a specific topic for only a day or two. When a topic resulted in multiple hearing days, I grouped them together by quarter.

The *Digest*, too, generated problems with respect to determining the content, salience, and interaction of the executive branch. The criteria I used for eliminating a meeting from the list of closed, partially closed, or executive session hearings include the following: (1) committee housekeeping and procedures; (2) routine approvals, such as authorization of a U.S. delegation to an international convention; and (3) legislative markups, unless executive branch officials were present. Nominations were problematic because they involved confidential discussion among senators about the fitness of a nominee that might or might not be relevant to oversight of the executive branch. I did not include these sessions unless witnesses other than the nominee appeared before the committee. In the end, so few hearings met this criterion that I dropped them from the analysis.

The coding for the content of executive sessions was usually straightforward because the hearing titles were clear and the list of witnesses reinforced my judgment regarding the nature of the hearing. A hearing with the title "Taiwan" in 1954 or 1955 that brought the secretary of defense, the chair of the Joint Chiefs, and the chief of naval operations to Capitol Hill obviously involved military conflict, in this case over the islands of Quemoy and Matsu. Other entries were less recognizable and required judgment calls on my part. Frequently, I was able to match up the date and witnesses with a hearing in the Foreign Relations Historical Series or in a subsequently published compilation of executive

[7] Aberbach (1990; 2002). Note that Aberbach looked at the first six months of each session, which would lead to serious undercounting in the realm of foreign and defense policy because of the incidence of crises in the second half of the year that stimulate Senate inquiries.

[8] LexisNexis has digitized the journals of the House and Senate, which are searchable by keywords, such as "executive session" (Interview with August Imholz, 2006), but the Dartmouth College subscription to LexisNexis Congressional did not provide access to this service. Consequently, I examined all calendar entries, and when I could not obtain committee calendars online, I used the printed *Digest* in the Senate historian's office.

sessions. At other times, however, the title was simply "Briefing" and the text included a list of witnesses. These appeared to be oversight hearings, but the type of oversight was unclear. If the hearing involved one or more of the major national security officials, especially if several appeared together, I coded the hearing content as "crisis." Again, I consulted the Historical Series to double-check and usually was able to confirm my judgment call. In addition, I also consulted Howell and Pevehouse's and Kriner's lists of events involving U.S. military forces to see if the dates overlapped, as well as the *New York Times* for the relevant dates. For a handful of cases, thirteen in total and all from Armed Services in the 1950 and 1960s, I was unable to confirm the content, so I included these "briefing" sessions in the category of total oversight, but dropped them from the analysis of specific types of oversight, even though I suspect they pertained to crises of some sort.

The last issue was dealing with executive sessions that did not appear on the committee calendars. To fill in this gap, I went back to the Historical Series and the committees' compilations of unpublished executive sessions. I was pleased to see that most of the hearings from the calendar were also showing up in these other places, but I did find some omissions that I added to the data set.

The Senate's rules permit committees to maintain the secrecy of executive session hearings for twenty-five years, however, which means that the record from 1983 may have gaps. On the one hand, the *Daily Digest* entries for the more recent Congresses were specific about the topic and the administration officials scheduled to testify, and I experienced few difficulties in coding the hearing content. On the other hand, I did find hearings published after the date of the session but before the mandatory time limit. I have no means of cross-checking for omissions, however, as I was able to do for the Congresses prior to the mid-1980s. In sum, I have exhausted all of the possibilities for ensuring the accuracy of the executive session data, but cannot guarantee that I captured every relevant hearing that took place in the Senate Armed Services and Foreign Relations Committees behind closed doors.

Description of Dependent and Independent Variables

DESCRIPTIVE STATISTICS FOR DEPENDENT VARIABLES

	Armed Services				
Dependent Variables	Mean	Median	Standard Deviation	Range	N
Total Hearing Days (year)	96.39	94	32.84	46–173	62
Days per Hearing	2.58	1	3.32	1–34	2,329
Public Sessions					
Total Public Hearing Days (year)	66.87	65	21.94	20–119	62
Total Public Hearings Days (quarterly)	16.72	12	15.48	0–64	248
Days per Hearing	2.76	1	2.97	1–24	1,517
Oversight Days (year)	20.23	17	14.71	3–89	62
Oversight Days (quarterly)	5.06	3	6.57	0–44	248
Budget Days (year)	29.90	26	16.60	1–66	62
Budget Days (quarterly)	7.48	1	12.31	0–52	248
Patrol Days (year)	13.32	10	13.33	0–85	62
Patrol Days (quarterly)	3.33	1	5.31	0–43	248
Alarm Days (year)	7.15	6	9.03	0–62	62
Alarm Days (quarterly)	1.79	0	4.00	0–43	248
Executive Sessions					
Total Exec Hearing Days (year)	29.52	26	17.29	0–68	62
Total Exec Hearing Days (quarterly)	7.38	4	9.91	0–54	248
Days per Hearing	2.25	1	3.86	1–34	812
Oversight Days (year)	13.61	12	8.69	0–46	62
Oversight Days (quarterly)	3.40	2	4.28	0–41	248
Budget Days (year)	13.98	11	13.54	0–54	62
Budget Days (quarterly)	3.50	1	8.11	0–52	248
Patrol Days (year)	7.27	6	6.73	0–31	62
Patrol Days (quarterly)	1.82	1	2.98	0–21	248
Alarm Days (year)	5.89	4	6.83	0–44	62
Alarm Days (quarterly)	1.47	0	3.25	0–40	248

Dependent Variables	Mean	Median	Standard Deviation	Range	N
Total Hearings					**2,329**
Total Public Hearings					1,517
Total Exec Hearings					812
Total Hearing Days					**6,019**
Total Public Hearing Days					4,189
Total Exec Hearing Days					1,830

	Foreign Relations				
Dependent Variables	Mean	Median	Standard Deviation	Range	N
Total Hearing Days (year)	84.79	76	33.35	39–173	62
Days per Hearing	1.72	1	1.92	1–26	3,052
Public Sessions					
Total Public Hearing Days (year)	53.56	50	19.49	21–111	62
Total Public Hearings Days (quarterly)	13.39	12	9.84	0–55	248
Days per Hearing	1.91	1	2.09	1–25	1,740
Oversight Days (year)	30.45	30	15.53	1–79	62
Oversight Days (quarterly)	7.61	7	7.02	0–43	248
Budget Days (year)	6.87	7	6.54	0–39	62
Budget Days (quarterly)	1.72	0	3.70	0–23	248
Patrol Days (year)	24.52	24	13.65	0–76	62
Patrol Days (quarterly)	6.13	5	5.67	0–27	248
Alarm Days (year)	6.15	3	7.98	0–44	62
Alarm Days (quarterly)	1.54	0	3.80	0–43	248
Executive Sessions					
Total Exec Hearing Days (year)	31.23	28	21.29	1–81	62
Total Exec Hearing Days (quarterly)	7.81	5	7.67	0–38	248
Days per Hearing	1.48	1	1.64	1–26	1,312
Oversight Days (year)	24.76	22	16.27	1–62	62
Oversight Days (quarterly)	6.20	4	6.00	0–33	248
Budget Days (year)	2.08	0	4.98	0–28	62
Budget Days (quarterly)	0.52	0	2.00	0–17	248
Patrol Days (year)	13.74	11	12.04	0–42	62
Patrol Days (quarterly)	3.44	2	4.25	0–21	248
Alarm Days (year)	10.92	9.5	7.28	0–35	62
Alarm Days (quarterly)	2.73	2	3.33	0–21	248
Total Hearings					**3,052**
Total Public Hearings					1,740
Total Exec Hearings					1,312
Total Hearing Days					**5,257**
Total Public Hearing Days					3,321
Total Exec Hearing Days					1,936

Descriptive Statistics for Independent Variables

Independent Variables	Mean	Median	Standard Deviation	Range	N
Mean Committee Assign (Congress)	2.681	2.5	0.504	2.1–4.1	31
Length Session (year)	159.2	160.5	24.41	105–211	62
Polarization-Senate (Congress)	0.631	0.615	0.107	0.428–0.883	31
Polarization-AS (Congress)	0.598	0.637	0.189	0.215–0.953	31
Polarization-FR (Congress)	0.636	0.639	0.168	0.334–0.951	31
NY Times-Congress (year)	7606	7630	1737.7	4425–11403	62
NY Times-AS (year)	150	122	89.3	27–490	62
NY Times-FR (year)	249	243	132.6	42–569	62
Seniority Ratio-AS (year)	1.064	1.058	0.119	.794–1.394	62
Seniority Ratio-FR (year)	1.222	1.105	0.346	.701–2.097	62
Defense Budget (billions of dollars per year)	178.14	100.87	150.27	9.11–616.07	62
International Budget (billions of dollars per year)	10.63	7.278	7.83	1.59–34.59	62
Presidential Approval (year)	53.70	55.122	12.313	27.56–75.92	62
Presidential Approval (quarterly)	53.70	54.71	13.02	24.33–87.13	248
Important Problem (year)	0.158	0.154	0.135	0–0.471	62
Casualties (quarterly)	392.57	8	1045.9	0–7948	248
Casualties (year)	1570.29	50	3681.03	0–16619	62
Total Hearing Days-AS (year)	96.39	94	32.84	46–173	62
Total Hearing Days-FR (year)	84.79	76	33.35	39–173	62

Methodological Appendix to Chapter 3

Note: Tables C1, C2 and C3 present summaries of the statistical results for the models in Chapter 3.

Table C.1. Poisson Regression Results for All Senate Committee Public Hearing Days, 1947–2008

Independent Variables	All Senate Public Hearings
NY Times Mentions	0.018
	0.033
Senate Polarity	0.032
	0.053
Mean Committee Assign	−0.371***
	0.052
Days in Session	0.059**
	0.029
Cold War Consensus	−0.393***
	0.063
Constant	8.566***
	0.031
N	62
Wald χ^2	244.69***

Independent variables are standardized. Robust standard errors in italics. *$p < .05$. **$p < .01$. ***$p < .001$.

Table C.2. Poisson Regression Results for the Armed Services Committee: Public, Executive, and Total Hearing Days, 1947–2008

Independent Variables	Public Days	Executive Days	Total Days
NY Times Mentions	0.062	0.115	0.078
	0.052	0.080	0.051
Committee Polarity	−0.055	0.375**	0.087
	0.067	0.119	0.065
Mean Committee Assign	−0.162***	−0.386***	−0.233***
	0.038	0.085	0.038
Days in Session	0.060	0.186***	0.098**
	0.037	0.055	0.036
Cold War Consensus	−0.422***	0.048	−0.261**
	0.124	0.196	0.119
Constant	4.952***	3.922***	3.254***
	0.055	0.097	0.054
N	62	62	62
Wald χ^2	24.68***	40.15***	45.95***

Independent variables are standardized. Robust standard errors in italics. $*p < .05$. $**p < .01$. $***p < .001$.

Table C.3. Poisson Regression Results for the Foreign Relations Committee: Public, Executive, and Total Hearing Days, 1947–2008

Independent Variables	Public Days	Executive Days	Total Days
NY Times Mentions	0.256***	0.123**	0.202***
	0.076	0.072	0.060
Committee Polarity	0.042	0.081	0.046
	0.067	0.073	0.057
Mean Committee Assign	−0.091	−0.748***	−0.266***
	0.078	0.096	0.059
Days in Session	−0.007	0.223***	0.088**
	0.037	0.055	0.039
Cold War Consensus	−0.613***	−0.275**	−0.418***
	0.108	0.125	0.095
Constant	4.173***	13.326***	3.155***
	0.055	0.061	0.045
N	62	62	62
Wald χ^2	48.87***	221.63***	134.82***

Independent variables are standardized. Robust standard errors in italics. $*p < .05$. $**p < .01$. $***p < .001$.

The models in Chapter 3 required a number of methodological judgments. This appendix outlines the choices I made, the reasons behind them, and the various checks I used to confirm the robustness of the results.

STATISTICAL MODEL

The dependent variables in this chapter are, first, the total number of public hearing days per year conducted by all Senate committees and then, the public, executive session, and total hearing days of the Senate Armed Services and Foreign Relations Committees. Such count data typically violate the assumptions for ordinary least squares (OLS) regression. Of the alternative models, Poisson regression is the most restrictive, assuming that the mean and variance for the dependent variable are the same. For the total hearing data, the mean and variance were close to equivalence for all Senate Committees and for Armed Services, while the distribution of total Foreign Relations hearing days was slightly skewed in a positive direction. For the two committees' public and executive session observations, the mean and variances were not as close, but still within a reasonable range of each other. Consequently, the use of the Poisson model was appropriate.

I ran the models for the Senate as a whole and for both committees using OLS and negative binomial regression, however. The substantive results were the same in terms of the significance, relative size, and direction of the coefficients. Moreover, the dispersion parameter in the negative binomial regression was relatively small and not always significant statistically. I used the fitstat program with the "force" option in Stata to compare the Poisson results with those from OLS and negative binomial regression. The Poisson method generated a modestly better Bayesian information criterion (BIC) statistic compared to the negative binomial regression model and was markedly better than the OLS model. I also considered versions of the Poisson and negative binomial regression techniques that correct for truncation in the dependent variable. There were no years with zero total public hearing days, although there were quite a few years without executive session days, both proved inferior to the standard Poisson approach according to tests for goodness of fit.

LEVEL OF ANALYSIS

Two of the five independent variables were coded on a yearly basis, including the *New York Times* mentions and the number of days in session. The polarization and mean number of committee assignments variables, however, were available only by each two-year Congress. The seniority ratio variable was calculated by year, but typically was similar for both sessions of Congress. I ran the analysis both by year and by Congress, and the pattern of coefficients was essentially the same with a few minor differences in the p values. I opted for the larger N and reported the results for the analysis by year.

STANDARDIZED VARIABLES

Often in statistical analysis, one or two variables with large variances can dominate the results. To compensate for this problem, I standardized the variables by subtracting each observation from the mean of the variable and dividing by the standard deviation. This procedure enabled me to compare the size of the coefficients in each model directly and to graph the predicted number of hearing days in an easily understandable fashion by using percentiles. It also had the excellent side effect of reducing problems of multicollinearity discussed below.

STANDARD ERRORS

I used robust standard errors, but also ran the models with standard errors clustered by Congress and with bootstrapped standard errors (with one thousand repetitions). The pattern of significant variables did not change with either the cluster or bootstrap procedure.

MULTICOLLINEARITY

The correlations among several of the independent variables, committee polarization, mean number of committee assignments, and Cold War consensus were substantial. The variance inflation factor (VIF) values for these variables were in the 3.5 to 5.5 range, a signal of multicollinearity. The indicators were least serious for the Senate as a whole and most serious for Foreign Relations. The seniority ratio variable was also highly correlated with mean committee assignments and polarization for Armed Services, and especially for Foreign Relations. I ran successive models, dropping each of the correlated variables in turn, and confirmed that the significance of the coefficients changed for these variables depending on which of the others I included.

The most problematic was the dummy variable for Cold War, which was highly correlated with the variables measuring committee polarization, the seniority ratio, and mean committee assignments (.68 to .84, depending on the variable). I had strong theoretical reasons for including all of these variables for the Armed Services and Foreign Relations Committees and worried about misspecification of the models if I dropped any major ones. Fitstat tests confirmed that they were all important, and the substantive effects were nontrivial, so I kept all but the seniority ratio, which I subsequently used to confirm the robustness of the models for Armed Services and Foreign Relations.

For the full Senate hearings, the Cold War dummy, which was correlated with chamber polarization, reduced the predicted number of hearings by 19 percent. One study of polarization demonstrated that party divisions increased in the 1990s because of the disappearance of Cold War pressures.[1] Again, the VIF value ruled against its inclusion, but the fitstat procedure comparing the fit of the various models ruled strongly in its favor.

Standardization of the variables solved the multicollinearity problem for the aggregate Senate committees and for Armed Services, according to the VIF test, and the procedure greatly reduced the problem for Foreign Relations. Nevertheless, the VIF values continued to be less than optimal for Foreign Relations. Each of the correlated variables taps a different theoretical dimension of committee behavior, however, so I retained them.

Time Trends

I presume that the collinear relationships among mean committee assignments, the seniority ratio, and polarization occur because the values of each had a strong trend over time, as shown in the graphs in Chapters 1, 2, and 3. Models for count data lack good options for dealing with time trends, as near as I can tell from consulting with knowledgeable colleagues. I experimented with lagged dependent variables using OLS, as well as lagged independent variables in the Poisson models, without discernible improvement. Fitstat tests did not support using lagged dependent variables with OLS or lagged independent variables with either negative binomial regression or the Poisson model.

Variables

The specification of the variables can influence statistical results. In the analysis, I coded *New York Times* mentions in any part of the newspaper that referenced the whole Congress and its members, or the Armed Services or Foreign Relations Committees and their members. The procedure for creating the variable is in the discussion of Figure 2.2 in Chapter 2. I ran all of the models with *New York Times* mentions for each committee as a percentage of all coverage of Congress. The relative size, sign, and significance were the same as the raw counts for both committees.

One could define the Cold War in various ways. Many scholars argue that the Cold War period from 1947 to 1968 was unusual in U.S. foreign policy and

---

[1] Parent and Bafumi (2012).

produced a distinctive politics that coincidentally overlapped with the era of the "textbook" Congress. This is the stance I adopted, but I also considered a dummy variable that included the years from 1947 to 1989, when the Berlin Wall collapsed and signaled the termination of the Cold War. This variable proved highly unstable in the various models and also had the same problems of high correlation with the other independent variables as the Cold War dummy variable that ran from 1947 to 1968. I also examined the effects of a dummy variable for the years 1995 to 2008, and it proved so highly correlated with other independent variables that Stata could not generate goodness-of-fit statistics.

Often interactions between two independent variables provide important information about the patterns in the data. I examined the interaction of the Cold War consensus variable with polarization and seniority ratio. The coefficient was not significant and did not improve the fit of the models.

Divided government is a highly significant variable in many types of analyses of congressional behavior. I considered divided government to be a short-term influence that explained variation in committees' oversight behavior from year to year and had no expectations that it was a factor in the long-term institutional changes examined in this chapter. I did try it as a control, with and without the Cold War dummy, and also examined its interaction with the other independent variables. It was never significant and did not improve the fit of the models according to the fitstat test.

I had included committee staff size in the initial models as a control variable because Aberbach (1990) had found it to be significant in his analysis of congressional oversight. Its theoretical value was negligible, its VIF value was very high, and its correlation with mean committee assignments was over .8. Fitstat tests using the BIC statistic confirmed that committee staff size did nothing to improve the overall fit of the models, so I dropped it from the analysis.

Methodological Appendix to Chapter 4

Note: Tables D1, D2, D3, D4, and D5 present summaries of the statistical results for the models in Chapter 4.

Table D.1. External Influences on Armed Services Oversight Hearing Days, by Public and Executive Session, 1947–2008

	Public Hearings		Executive Hearings	
Goal-Related Variables				
Divided	0.124	0.132	−0.321**	−0.319**
	0.155	*0.154*	*0.136*	*0.128*
Budget (billions of dollars per year)		0.000		0.001**
		0.001		*0.000*
Major Force (date)		0.304		0.231
		0.183		*0.156*
Control Variables				
NY Times Mentions (year)	0.002***	0.002***	0.001	0.001*
	0.001	*0.001*	0.001	*0.001*
Approval (quarterly lag)	0.003	0.003	0.004	0.006
	0.007	*0.007*	*0.005*	*0.005*
Total Hearing Days (year)	0.006**	0.006**	0.007***	0.010***
	0.007	*0.003*	*0.002*	*0.002*
Constant	1.865***	1.450***	1.688***	0.897*
	0.474	*0.511*	*0.381*	*0.446*
N	62	62	62	62
Wald χ^2	28.56*	34.16***	34.02***	44.49***

Negative binomial regression. Robust standard errors in italics. $*p < .05$. $**p < .01$. $***p < .001$.

Table D.2. External Influences on Foreign Relations Oversight Hearing Days, by Public and Executive Session, 1947–2008

Variables	Public Hearings		Executive Hearings	
Goal-Related Variables				
Divided	0.168	0.365***	−0.271**	−0.349***
	0.110	*0.105*	*0.104*	*0.090*
Budget (billions of dollars)		0.049***		−0.046***
		0.010		*0.010*
Major Force (date)		−0.114		−0.099
		0.128		*0.092*
Control Variables				
NY Times Mentions (year)	−0.002***	−0.001	0.001*	−0.001
	0.001	*0.000*	*0.000*	*0.001*
Approval (quarterly lag)	0.001	0.006	0.004	−0.001
	0.007	*0.005*	*0.005*	*0.005*
Total Hearing Days (year)	0.005***	0.013***	0.016***	0.013***
	0.002	*0.002*	*0.002*	*0.002*
Constant	2.759***	1.409**	1.566***	2.976***
	0.427	*0.515*	*0.363*	*0.481?*
N	62	62	62	62
Wald χ^2	14.79***	74.35***	138.6***	213.54***

Negative binomial regression. Robust standard errors in italics. *$p < .05$. **$p < .01$.
***$p < .001$.

Table D.3. Armed Services Choice of Oversight or Budget Hearing, by Public and Executive Session Hearing, 1947–2008

Variables	Oversight Hearing		Budget Hearing	
	Public	Executive	Public	Executive
Goal-Related Variables				
Divided	−0.049	−0.044	0.193	−0.063
	0.117	*0.165*	*0.134*	*0.176*
Budget (FY, billions of dollars	0.003***	0.000	0.002***	0.001*
	0.000	*0.001*	*0.001*	*0.000*
Major Force (date)	0.366***	0.384*	0.057	−0.565**
	0.126	*0.186*	*0.148*	*0.207*
Control Variables				
NY Times Mention (year)	0.001	0.001	−0.003***	−0.002
	0.001	*0.001*	*0.001*	*0.001*
Approval (quarterly)	0.007	0.004	−0.011*	−0.002
	0.005	*0.007*	*0.005*	*0.007*
Total Hearing Days (year)	−0.007***	−0.003	0.010***	−0.003
	0.002	*0.003*	*0.002*	*0.003*
N	1,517	812	1,517	812
LR χ^2	113.83***	8.98	64.25***	16.40**

Model is conditional logit (clogit) grouped by quarter. Standard errors in parentheses.
*$p < .05$. **$p < .01$. ***$p < .001$.

Table D.4. Foreign Relations Choice of Oversight or Budget Hearing, by Public and Executive Session Hearing, 1947–2008

Variables	Oversight Hearing		Budget Hearing	
	Public	Executive[a]	Public	Executive
Goal-Related Variables				
Divided	0.208	−0.147	−0.001	−0.099
	0.115	*0.174*	*0.198*	*0.313*
Budget (FY, billions	0.067***	0.135***	−0.038	−0.238***
of dollars)	*0.012*	*0.030*	*0.021*	*0.072*
Major Force (date)	0.075	−0.173	0.289	0.118
	0.115	*0.173*	*0.201*	*0.321*
Control Variables				
NY Times Mentions	−0.003***	−0.002*	0.000	0.000
(year)	*0.001*	*0.001*	*0.001*	*0.002*
Approval (quarterly)	0.008	−0.008	−0.015*	0.036**
	0.005	*0.007*	*0.007*	*0.014*
Total Hearing Days	0.004	0.008**	0.004	−0.007
(year)	*0.002*	*0.003*	*0.004*	*0.007*
N	1,740	1,312	1,740	1,312
LR χ²	219.5***	99.48***	20.6***	50.62***

Model is conditional logit (clogit) grouped by quarter. Standard errors in parentheses.
*p < .05. **p < .01. ***p < .001.
[a]For Foreign Relations executive oversight hearings, the model did not converge, so the results are for regular logit with quarterly dummies and Wald χ².

Table D.5. Number of Days per National Security Committee Hearing, by Public and Executive Session Hearing, 1947–2008

Variables	Armed Services		Foreign Relations	
	Public	Executive	Public	Executive
Goal-Related Variables				
Individual Hearing Type				
Oversight Hearing	0.282***	−0.310*	0.179***	−0.267***
	0.054	*0.142*	*0.046*	*0.074*
Budget Hearing	0.928***	0.382**	0.473***	0.217
	0.055	*0.149*	*0.069*	*0.119*
Divided	0.067	−0.051	0.093*	−0.051
	0.040	*0.063*	*0.042*	*0.063*
Budget (billions of	−0.005***	−0.001***	−0.016***	−0.001***
dollars)	*0.000*	*0.000*	*0.004*	*0.000*
Major Force (date)	0.113**	0.157*	0.031	0.157*
	0.044	*0.070*	*0.460*	*0.070*
Control Variables				
NY *Times* Mentions	0.001***	0.000	0.001***	0.000
(year)	*0.000*	*0.000*	*0.000*	*0.000*
Approval (quarterly)	0.002	0.001	−0.006***	0.001
	0.002	*0.003*	*0.002*	*0.003*
Total Hearing Days	0.003***	0.004***	0.001	0.004***
(year)	*0.001*	*0.001*	*0.001*	*0.001*
Constant	0.413**	0.745**	1.899***	2.397***
	0.158	*0.281*	*0.222*	*0.256*
N	1,517	812	1,740	1,312
Wald χ^2	377.67***	146.97***	266.47***	78.88***

Model is negative binomial regression with quarterly random effects. Standard errors in parentheses. $*p < .05$. $**p < .01$. $***p < .001$.

Statistical Model

There are three types of dependent variables in this chapter, and they have different characteristics: (1) the total number of all types of oversight hearing days per year; (2) two dichotomous variables, which take the value of one in each case if an individual hearing was about either an oversight topic or a budget topic, and zero otherwise; (3) the duration of an individual hearing measured as the number of days per type of hearing.

For the yearly analysis of total oversight hearing days, the distribution of the dependent variable was highly skewed, especially for the Foreign Relations Committee, and violated basic assumptions of ordinary least squares and Poisson regression. I opted for negative binomial regression, although I ran comparisons and confirmed with the Long and Freese countfit software that I had made the correct choice. Because there are no years with negative or zero hearing days in the data set, I also ran tests using versions that correct for truncation and tested them with countfit. A tobit model for the number of hearing days per year produced very satisfying coefficients in terms of my theoretical expectations, but generated predicted values of negative hearings days. In effect, the model demonstrated that some combinations of variables deterred the committees to varying degrees from holding oversight hearings. I thought the resulting graphs were confusing, so I stayed with the negative binomial regression model despite the fact that the N of sixty-two is relatively small.

For the analysis of two of the dependent variables, hearing type and days per hearing, time constraints on the committee calendars, especially for Armed Services, indicated the need to take account of panel effects in the data that resulted from unobservable factors. I first ran the models with separate dummy variables for the first, second, and third quarters and then compared them to the versions with random quarterly effects. In some cases the coefficients were nearly identical in sign and direction, but in others there was sufficient variation in the size of the coefficients, particularly for divided government, to warrant concern. I adopted the conditional logit model (clogit) grouped by quarter for the models of hearing type, and I employed the negative binomial regression model (xtnbreg) with quarterly random effects for the model predicting days per hearing. I chose a random effects model because the committees exercised discretion over when they held hearings and how many hearings would take place in each quarter. In other words, the calendar effects could vary over time and were not correlated with the predictor variables.

This decision to account for quarterly effects created several complications in the analysis of the dichotomous dependent variables regarding hearing type. First, one of the clogit models predicting whether the Foreign Relations Committee opted for an executive oversight hearing would not converge, a problem that seemed to be attributable to the high frequency of executive session hearings devoted solely to oversight, as shown in Chapter 1.

Second, my intention to use a multinomial logit model with three categories, oversight, budget, and other, was frustrated by the fact that a model for a trichotomous dependent variable comparable to clogit (or xtlogit) does not exist in Stata. The alternative involved multilevel modeling, which not only was beyond my comfort level and but also produced results that were difficult to explain. Consequently, I ran separate models for the likelihood that a hearing would be about oversight and the likelihood that it would be about budgets. I checked the resulting pattern of coefficients against a standard multinomial logit model using quarterly controls. The predicted values were not exact, but in most cases they were so close that the graphs of the predicted values appeared quite accurate. The negative binomial regression models with random quarterly effects predicting the number of days per hearing proved straightforward.

Third, assessing the substantive impact of individual hearings in fixed effects models required the use of Stata's predict command with the pu0 option for the clogit analysis and the nu0 option for the negative binomial regression analysis. To simplify the graphs, I identified points at the 10th, 25th, 50th, 75th and 90th percentile, which masks the curvilinear relationship between the dependent and independent variables.

LEVEL OF ANALYSIS

For the analysis of the annual oversight hearing counts, more than half of the key variables were measured by year. These included divided government (with 2001 counted as divided), budget authorizations for defense and international programs, *New York Times* mentions, and total hearing days. The variable for major force was coded by date, which means that the variable takes the value of one at the start of a deployment and continues until its end date. I collapsed this variable by year and quarter, with the result that it ranged from 0 to .25 to .5 to .75 to 1. I also converted the quarterly measure of presidential approval to the mean for the year. For the analyses of individual hearing type and days per hearing, I disaggregated the independent variables by date or quarter where possible.

STANDARD ERRORS

For the analysis of yearly oversight hearings, I used robust standard errors, but also examined the results from clustering them by Congress. I also compared the results with the bootstrapping procedure (using one thousand iterations). The differences in significance of the coefficients were trivial. With the models using random effects, Stata's xtnbreg procedure supposedly allows for computing robust standard errors and clustering, but the manual advises not to specify an option if one plans to use the predict command.

MULTICOLLINEARITY

I ran the usual tests and found the VIF values for the independent variables to be very good to excellent.

TIME TRENDS

Historical data often result in the violation of the assumption of constant variance, which influences confidence intervals and tests of significance, although the estimated coefficients will be unbiased and consistent. Time was a potential issue for the dependent and independent variables. I did not uncover evidence of autocorrelation for the dependent variables for either Armed Services or Foreign Relations. I tested various lagged versions of each of the independent variables with nbreg and compared their contribution to the overall fit of the model using fitstat. The results indicated that I did not need a lagged version of the dependent variable, but I did adopt a lag for presidential approval in the yearly analysis of Armed Services and Foreign Relations oversight hearing days.

PLOTS OF OUTLIERS

For each model, I plotted the predicted values of public or executive oversight hearing days against the actual observations. I checked each model without the outliers and obtained essentially the same pattern in the coefficients.

VARIABLES AND ROBUSTNESS CHECKS

I considered several different ways of measuring the key independent variables and tested them with fitstat by using negative binomial regression and quarterly dummies. I looked at scatter plots of the dependent variable with each type of potential independent variable, as well. For divided government, I substituted the size of the president's party coalition in the Senate. For budget expenditures, I tested lagged values, first differences, and quadratic relationships. For the use of force, I examined the number of times the president initiated force in each quarter, and I looked at the timing of initiation without considering its duration. I also considered the ideological distance between each committee's median DW-Nominate score and that of the president.[1] I evaluated the interaction of the key independent variables with divided government, none of which yielded interesting results.

---

[1] McGrath (2013) obtained significant results using this type of measure. Compiled for each Congress, the scores depend upon two years of roll calls and may be too highly aggregated for examining individual hearings. In addition, ideological divisions based on floor voting do not translate directly in conflicts among committee members for a committee like Armed Services. Finally, foreign policy has not been divided cleanly along liberal and conservative lines for most of the period of this study either for Congress or the president.

Methodological Appendix to Chapter 5

Note: Tables E1, E2, E3, E4, E5, and E6 present summaries of the statistical results for the models in Chapter 5.

Table E.1. Effect of Casualties and Public Opinion on Armed Services Quarterly Police Patrol Oversight, by Public and Executive Session Hearing Days, 1947–2008

	Public Patrol Hearing Days		Executive Patrol Hearing Days	
Party Reputation Variables				
Divided-Dem. Pres.	0.080	0.009	−0.399	−0.548
	0.268	*0.300*	*0.355*	*0.387*
Unified-Rep. Pres.	−0.010	−0.150	0.557**	0.509**
	0.226	*0.231*	*0.232*	*0.232*
Divided-Rep. Pres.	−0.274	−0.164	0.040	0.190
	0.344	*0.364*	*0.404*	*0.426*
Important Problem		1.461**		0.177
(year)		*0.642*		*0.700*
Casualties (ln)		−0.087**		−0.043
(quarterly lag)		*0.032*		*0.035*
Control Variables				
Budget (billions of	0.001	0.001	0.001	0.001
dollars per year)	*0.001*	*0.001*	*0.001*	*0.001*
Approval (quarterly)	0.013*	0.008	0.008	0.004
	0.006	*0.006*	*0.006*	*0.007*
Total Hearing Days	0.007**	0.008**	0.012***	0.011***
(year)	*0.003*	*0.003*	*0.002*	*0.003*
Constant	−2.021***	−1.713**	−2.238***	−1.807**
	0.515	*0.604*	*0.523*	*0.637*
N	248	248	248	248
Wald χ^2	11.00	21.56**	44.51***	47.87***

Negative binomial regression with random effects (quarter). Standard errors in italics.
*$p < .05$. **$p < .01$. ***$p < .001$.

Table E.2. Effect of Casualties and Public Opinion on Foreign Relations Quarterly
Police Patrol Oversight, by Public and Executive Session Hearing Days, 1947–2008

	Public Patrol Hearing Days		Executive Patrol Hearing Days	
Party Reputation Variables				
Divided-Dem. Pres.	0.920***	0.701***	−1.020***	−1.084***
	0.188	0.202	0.305	0.315
Unified-Rep. Pres.	0.509***	0.522***	0.157	0.148
	0.170	0.169	0.169	0.169
Divided-Rep. Pres.	−0.711***	−0.522**	0.635	0.696*
	0.223	0.228	0.347	0.355
Important Problem		−0.977		−0.290
(year)		0.541		0.481
Casualties (ln)		−0.022		−0.006
(quarterly lag)		0.025		0.023
Control Variables				
Budget (billions of	0.056***	0.053***	−0.031**	−0.033**
dollars per year)	0.008	0.009	0.011	0.012
Approval (quarterly)	0.012**	0.010*	0.004	0.004
	0.004	0.002	0.005	0.005
Total Hearing Days	0.012***	0.011***	0.014***	0.013***
(year)	0.002	0.002	0.002	0.002
Constant	−2.433***	−1.926***	−0.495	−0.367
	0.423	0.450	0.460	0.488
N	248	248	248	248
Wald χ^2	81.69***	90.56***	140.29***	141.06***

Negative binomial regression with random effects (quarter). Standard errors in italics.
*$p < .05$. **$p < .01$. ***$p < .001$.

Table E.3. Effect of Casualties and Public Opinion on Armed Services Quarterly Fire Alarm Oversight, by Public and Executive Session Hearing Days, 1947–2008

	Public Alarm Hearing Days		Executive Alarm Hearing Days	
Party Reputation Variables				
Divided-Dem. Pres.	−0.386	0.012	−0.404	0.086
	0.344	*0.397*	*0.316*	*0.363*
Unified-Rep. Pres.	−0.840**	−0.724**	−0.472	−0.400
	0.312	*0.318*	*0.271*	*0.279*
Divided-Rep. Pres.	0.610	0.229	0.282	−0.183
	0.441	*0.481*	*0.387*	*0.426*
Important Problem		−1.436		−0.758
(year)		*0.902*		*0.820*
Casualties (ln)		0.149***		0.152***
(quarterly lag)		*0.050*		*0.043*
Control Variables				
Budget (billions of	0.003***	0.003***	0.003***	0.003***
dollars per year)	*0.001*	*0.001*	*0.001*	*0.001*
Approval (quarterly)	−0.006	0.002	−0.005	0.004
	0.008	*0.008*	*0.008*	*0.008*
Total Hearing Days	0.002	0.005	0.001	0.004
(year)	*0.004*	*0.004*	*0.003*	*0.003*
Constant	−1.257*	−2.229**	−0.691	−1.968**
	0.631	*0.789*	*0.608*	*0.758*
N	248	248	248	248
Wald χ^2	21.84***	28.65***	32.2***	44.04***

Negative binomial regression with random effects (quarter). Standard errors in italics. $^*p < .05.$ $^{**}p < .01.$ $^{***}p < .001.$

Table E.4. Effect of Casualties and Public Opinion on Foreign Relations Quarterly Fire Alarm Oversight, by Public and Executive Session Hearing Days, 1947–2008

	Public Alarm Hearing Days		Executive Alarm Hearing Days	
Party Reputation Variables				
Divided-Dem. Pres.	−1.004	−0.700	0.048	0.095
	0.547	*0.574*	*0.232*	*0.251*
Unified-Rep. Pres.	0.178	0.243	−0.126	−0.130
	0.314	*0.321*	*0.203*	*0.205*
Divided-Rep. Pres.	1.293*	0.979	−0.018	−0.062
	0.032	*0.630*	*0.304*	*0.318*
Important Problem		0.404		0.325
(year)		*0.877*		*0.537*
Casualties (ln)		0.067		−0.002
(quarterly lag)		*0.044*		*0.028*
Control Variables				
Budget (billions of	0.075***	0.072***	0.003	0.004
dollars per year)	*0.017*	*0.017*	*0.011*	*0.011*
Approval (quarterly)	−0.003	0.000	−0.004	−0.005
	0.008	*0.008*	*0.005*	*0.006*
Total Hearing Days	0.015***	0.014***	0.009***	0.010
(year)	*0.003*	*0.004*	*0.002*	*0.002*
Constant	−3.323***	−3.752***	−0.358	−0.453***
	0.762	*0.829*	*0.477*	*0.515*
N	248	248	248	248
Wald χ^2	49.17***	54.33***	28.10***	28.24***

Negative binomial regression with random effects (quarter). Standard errors in parentheses. *$p < .05$. **$p < .01$. ***$p < .001$.

Table E.5. Effect of Casualties and Public Opinion on Armed Services Quarterly Crisis Oversight, by Public and Executive Session Hearing Days, 1947–2008

	Public Crisis Hearing Days		Executive Crisis Hearing Days	
Party Reputation Variables				
Divided-Dem. Pres.	−0.728	−0.533	−0.595	0.010
	0.470	*0.527*	*0.339*	*0.394*
Unified-Rep. Pres.	−1.518***	−1.386***	−0.698**	−0.658*
	0.441	*0.449*	*0.292*	*0.300*
Divided-Rep. Pres.	0.922	0.906	0.439	0.039
	0.598	*0.604*	*0.424*	*0.458*
Important Problem		−1.413		−0.606
(year)		*1.299*		*0.856*
Casualties (ln)		0.104		0.170***
(quarterly lag)		*0.072*		*0.047*
Stennis		−2.714**		−0.635*
		1.035		*0.324*
Control Variables				
Budget (billions of	0.006***	0.005***	0.003***	0.003***
dollars per year)	*0.001*	*0.001*	*0.001*	*0.001*
Approval (quarterly)	0.001	−0.004	−0.001	0.006
	0.012	*0.012*	*0.008*	*0.009*
Total Hearing Days	0.002	0.067	0.000	0.006
(year)	*0.006*	*0.005*	*0.004*	*0.004*
Constant	−2.721**	−2.629**	−0.987	−2.265*
	0.988	*1.137*	*0.658*	*0.809*
N	248	248	248	248
Wald χ^2	50.42***	51.55***	30.73	45.52***

Negative binomial regression with random effects (quarter). Standard errors in italics.
*$p < .05$. **$p < .01$. ***$p < .001$.

Table E.6. Effect of Casualties and Public Opinion on Foreign Relations Quarterly Crisis Oversight, by Public and Executive Session Hearing Days, 1947–2008

	Public Crisis Hearing Days		Executive Crisis Hearing Days	
Party Reputation Variables				
Divided-Dem. Pres.	−0.817	−0.099	0.059	0.142
	0.660	*0.710*	*0.238*	*0.258*
Unified-Rep. Pres.	0.183	0.312	−0.078	−0.092
	0.436	*0.449*	*0.212*	*0.215*
Divided-Rep. Pres.	1.108	0.424	−0.202	−0.277
	0.727	*0.771*	*0.313*	*0.327*
Important Problem		0.692		0.686
(year)		*1.218*		*0.578*
Casualties (ln) (quarterly		0.170**		−0.008
lag)		*0.064*		*0.030*
Control Variables				
Budget (billions of	0.105***	0.090***	0.008	0.011
dollars per year)	*0.022*	*0.022*	*0.012*	*0.012*
Approval (quarterly)	0.004	0.012	0.003	0.003
	0.010	*0.011*	*0.006*	*0.006*
Total Hearing Days	0.009	0.008	0.007**	0.007**
(year)	*0.005*	*0.006*	*0.003*	*0.003*
Constant	−4.432***	−5.272***	−0.671	−0.839
	1.011	*1.114*	*0.517*	*0.555*
N	248	248	248	248
Wald χ^2	53.29***	69.24***	10.73	12.25

Negative binomial regression with random effects (quarter). Standard errors in italics.
*$p < .05$. **$p < .01$. ***$p < .001$.

Method of Analysis

I used negative binomial regression with random quarterly effects to assess the effects of party reputation on the frequency of police patrols and fire alarms, for the same reasons as in Chapter 4. Given the high frequency of quarters lacking either patrol or fire alarm hearings, I tested models that adjusted for large numbers of zeroes, using zero inflated negative binomial regression (ZINB). This technique employs a regular negative binomial regression model for the main equation and a separate logit estimate for the inflation parameter (which may or may not be a variable in the full model). The idea behind the second estimate is that the zeroes are the result of some inherent characteristic of the decision maker rather than choice. Examples include the prediction of fish catches in a park based on the number of visitors who visited but had no fishing gear and the prediction of live births among the female population that included women over fifty Both committees, however, had the option to meet during quarters that had missing values, and they scheduled sessions, some of which were quite lengthy, at all times of year. Armed Services and Foreign Relations thus were not in an analogous situation to campers without fishing gear or women past childbearing age. Although there was no theoretical reason to use ZINB, I ran the models with calendar quarter as the inflation parameter. The inflation-adjusted models did not produce major differences in the results and performed poorly on the executive session hearing data for both committees.

I checked the fit of the models in two ways. I was not able to find protocols for testing model fit with xtnbreg comparable to the Stata's suest procedure. As a rough approximation, I ran the analyses with straight negative binomial regression and quarterly dummies and then used the suest and test commands to determine if the models were significantly different from each other. The results indicated that I could reject the null hypothesis of no difference in seven of the eight cases. The exception was for the comparison of Armed Services' public and executive fire alarm hearings.

Second, I graphed the actual days per quarter for each hearing type with the predicted number of hearings. For Armed Services, the fit was exceptionally good for both public and executive session hearings. For Foreign Relations, the fit also was extremely good, except for public police patrol hearings.

Level of Analysis

The observations are by the number of days per quarter for each type of hearing. Several independent variables are measured at the quarterly level, including casualties, total hearing days, and presidential approval. The others, most important problem, budget, and the dummy variable regarding the president's party, are annual measures.

Dependent Variable

The dependent variable for the second part of the analysis is the frequency of days for each type of hearing content per quarter. The major question was whether my classification of police patrols and fire alarms was the appropriate one. The biggest source of potential error was with the hearings involving treaties, which was primarily an issue for Foreign Relations. I experimented with various groupings involving treaty progress, treaty implementation, and treaty ratification. Because the number of treaty-related hearings per quarter was small, there was little evidence that it mattered where I grouped them.

Standard Errors

Stata's xtnbreg procedure supposedly allows for computing robust standard errors and clustering, but the manual advises not to specify an option if one plans to use the predict command. I ran the models using the standard nbreg procedure with quarterly dummies with the robust option and clustering on Congress for the standard errors and found no reason to think that the statistical significance of the key variables was affected.

Multicollinearity

The tests for multicollinearity revealed no problems. The VIF values were between 1.18 and 1.66. Dummy variables for individual committee chairs did generate problems, so I did not use more than one or two in a model.

Time Trends

Some scholars consider the diagnostic tools for count models to be undeveloped. I did not uncover evidence of autocorrelation for either committee after experimenting with lagged and differenced versions of the dependent variables. I also tried using Congress as a time indicator, which was not significant and did not improve the fit of any of the models.

Plots

Plots of the predicted and actual values of public and executive oversight hearing days indicated outliers for both committees for observations in 1951. In addition, Foreign Relations had unusually low frequencies of hearing days in 1948, when the chair, Arthur Vandenberg (R-MI) was seriously ill, and in 1980 when Senator Frank Church (D-ID) was chair and engaged in a bruising reelection battle. I ran each model without these outliers and found no differences in the overall results.

To generate the predicted values of public and executive session hearings, I used Stata's predict command with the option, nu0, that treats the quarterly effects as zero.

Variables

As with Chapters 3 and 4, I spent considerable time determining which variables provided the better fit. For example, I coded dummy variables for divided government, with Democratic and Republican presidents, and Republican presidents under unified government. In addition, I examined various lagged forms of the independent variables, as well as first differences and quadratic versions. Following conventional practice in the literature, I transformed the casualty variable with the natural log before lagging it by quarter. I tested the efficacy of the different modifications with scatter plots of each type with the dependent variable. In addition to interactions between the continuous independent variables and the dummy variables for divided government or Republican president, I also looked at the interaction between casualties and public opinion (Gallup's important problem). None of these experiments yielded interesting results.

Both committees have had chairs who were major historical figures or had more or less inclination for oversight. I created dummy variables for each one and ran models testing the impact of individual chairs on the frequency of different types of hearing content. If the coefficient for an individual chair attained statistical significance, I retained the variable for further analysis; more than one or two led to problems of convergence in the models. After a lot of trial and error, I identified John Stennis (D-MI) and Barry Goldwater (R-AZ) as potentially significant actors for Armed Services and Arthur Vandenberg (R-MI), John Connally (D-TX), John Sparkman (D-AL), and Jesse Helms (R-NC) for Foreign Relations. Only Sparkman showed a consistently strong effect, although his tenure as chair was short.

References

Aberbach, Joel D. *Keeping a Watchful Eye: The Politics of Congressional Oversight*. Washington, DC: Brookings Institution, 1990.

——. "What's Happened to the Watchful Eye?" *Congress & the Presidency* 29, no. 1 (2002): 3–23.

Acheson, Dean. *Present at the Creation: My Years in the State Department*. New York: Norton, 1969.

Ackerman, Bruce A. *The Decline and Fall of the American Republic*. Cambridge, MA: Harvard University Press, 2010.

Adler, E. Scott. *Why Congressional Reforms Fail*. Chicago: University of Chicago Press, 2002.

Adler, E. Scott, and John S. Lapinski. "Demand-Side Theory and Congressional Committee Composition: A Constituency Characteristics Approach." *American Journal of Political Science* 41, no. 3 (1997): 895–918.

——, eds. *The Macropolitics of Congress*. Princeton: Princeton University Press, 2006.

Aldrich, John H. "A Model of a Legislature with Two Parties and a Committee System." In *Positive Theories of Congressional Institutions*, edited by Kenneth A. Shepsle and Barry R. Weingast, 173–99. Ann Arbor: University of Michigan, 1995a.

——. *Why Parties? The Origin and Transformation of Political Parties in America*. Ann Arbor: University of Michigan, 1995b.

Aldrich, John H., Christopher Gelpi, Peter Feaver, Jason Reifler, and Kristin Thompson Sharp. "Foreign Policy and the Electoral Connection." *American Annals of Political Science* 9 (2006): 477–502.

Aldrich, John H., and David W. Rohde. "The Logic of Conditional Party Government: Revisiting the Electoral Connection." In *Congress Reconsidered*, 7th ed., edited by Lawrence C. Dodd and Bruce I. Oppenheimer, 269–92. Washington, DC: CQ Press, 2001.

——. "Congressional Committees in a Partisan Era." In *Congress Reconsidered*, 9th ed., edited by Lawrence C. Dodd and Bruce I. Oppenheimer, 249–70. Washington, DC: CQ Press, 2005.

Aldrich, John H., John Sullivan, and Eugene Borgida. "Foreign Policy and Voting in Presidential Elections: Do Candidates Waltz before a Blind Audience?" *American Political Science Review* 83, no. 1 (1989): 123–41.

Ansolabehere, Stephen, James M. Snyder, Jr., and Charles Stewart III. "The Effects of Party and Preferences on Congressional Roll-Call Voting." *Legislative Studies Quarterly* 36 (2001): 533–72.

Arnold, R. Douglas. *Congress, the Press, and Political Accountability*. Princeton: Russell Sage Foundation, Princeton University Press, 2004.

Auerswald, David P., and Colton C. Campbell, eds. *Congress and the Politics of National Security*. New York: Cambridge University Press, 2012.

Auerswald, David, and Peter Cowhey. "Ballotbox Diplomacy: The War Powers Resolution and the Use of Force." *International Studies Quarterly* 85, no. 2 (1997): 508–28.

Auerswald, David, and Forrest Maltzman. "Policymaking through Advice and Consent: Treaty Consideration by the United States Senate." *Journal of Politics* 65, no. 4 (2003): 1097–110.

Balla, Steven, and Christopher Deering. "Police Patrols and Fire Alarms: An Empirical Examination of the Legislative Preference for Oversight." *Congress & the Presidency* 40, no. 1 (2013): 27–40.

Balla, Steven J., and John R. Wright. "Interest Groups, Advisory Committees, and Congressional Control of the Bureaucracy." *American Journal of Political Science* 45, no 4 (2001): 799–812.

Bartels, Larry M. "Constituency Opinion and Congressional Policy-Making: The Reagan Defense Build Up." *American Political Science Review* 85, no. 2 (1991): 457–74.

Baum, Matthew A. "Sex, Lies, and War: How Soft News Brings Foreign Policy to the Inattentive Public." *American Political Science Review* 96, no. 1 (2002): 91–109.

———. *Soft News Goes to War: Public Opinion and American Foreign Policy in the New Media Age*. Princeton: Princeton University Press, 2003.

Baum, Matthew A., and Tim J. Groeling. *War Stories: The Causes and Consequences of Public Views of War*. Princeton: Princeton University Press, 2010.

Baum, Matthew A., and Philip B. K. Potter. "The Relationships between Mass Media, Public Opinion, and Foreign Policy: Toward a Theoretical Synthesis." *Annual Review of Politics* 11 (2008): 39–65.

Bendor, Jonathan, Amihai Glazer, and Thomas Hammond. "Theories of Delegation." *Annual Review of Political Science* 4, no. 1 (2001): 235–69.

Bennett, W. Lance. "An Introduction to Journalism Norms and Representation of Politics." *Political Communication* 13, no. 4 (1996): 373–84.

———. "Toward a Theory of Press-State Relations in the United States." *Journal of Communication* 40, no. 2 (1990): 103–27.

Bennett, W. Lance, Regina G. Lawrence, and Steven Livingston. *When the Press Fails: Political Power and the News Media from Iraq to Katrina*. Chicago: University of Chicago Press, 2007.

Bennett, W. Lance, and David L. Paletz, eds. *Taken by Storm: The Media, Public Opinion, and U.S. Foreign Policy in the Gulf War*. Chicago: University of Chicago Press, 1994.

Berinsky, Adam J. "Assuming the Costs of War: Events, Elites, and American Public Support for Military Conflict." *Journal of Politics* 69, no. 4 (2007): 975–97.

———. *In Time of War: Understanding American Public Opinion from World War II to Iraq*. Chicago: University of Chicago Press, 2009.

Berman, Larry. *No Peace, No Honor: Nixon, Kissinger and Betrayal in Vietnam*. New York: Free Press, 2001.

Binder, Sarah. "Legislative Productivity and Gridlock." In *The Oxford Handbook of the American Congress*, edited by Eric Schickler and Frances E. Lee, 641–59. Oxford: Oxford University Press, 2011.

———. *Stalemate: Causes and Consequences of Legislative Gridlock*. Washington, DC: Brookings Institution, 2003.

Boettcher, William A., III, and Michael D. Cobb. "Echoes of Vietnam? Casualty Framing and Public Perceptions of Success and Failure in Iraq." *Journal of Conflict Resolution* 50, no. 6 (2006): 831–54.

Bolton, John R. "Wrong Turn in Somalia." *Foreign Affairs* 73, no. 1 (1994): 56–66.

Brody, Richard A. "Crisis, War, and Public Opinion." In *Taken by Storm: The Media, Public Opinion, and U.S. Foreign Policy in the Gulf War*, edited by W. Lance Bennett and David L. Paletz, 210–30. Chicago: University of Chicago Press, 1994.

Brown, Alan W. "U.S. Armed Forces Abroad: Selected Congressional Roll Call Votes since 1982." Report RL31693, Congressional Research Service, Library of Congress, 2003.

Bueno de Mesquita, Bruce, and David Lalman. *War and Reason: Domestic and International Imperatives*. New Haven: Yale University Press, 1992.

Bueno de Mesquita, Bruce, Alastair Smith, Randolph M. Siverson, and James D. Morrow. *The Logic of Survival*. Cambridge, MA: MIT Press, 2003.

Burgin, Eileen. "Representatives' Decisions on Participation in Foreign Policy Issues." *Legislative Studies Quarterly* 16, no. 4 (1991): 521–46.

Burk, James. "Public Support for Peacekeeping in Lebanon and Somalia: Assessing the Casualties Hypothesis." *Political Science Quarterly* 114, no. 1 (1999): 53–78.

Cameron, Charles M., and Peter B. Rosendorff. "A Signaling Theory of Congressional Oversight." *Games and Economic Behavior* 5, no. 1 (1993): 44–70.

Canes-Wrone, Brandice. *Who Leads Whom? Presidents, Policy, and the Public*. Chicago: University of Chicago Press, 2006.

Canes-Wrone, Brandice, William G. Howell, and David Lewis. "Toward a Broader Understanding of Presidential Power: A Reevaluation of the Two Presidencies Thesis." *Journal of Politics* 70, no. 1 (2008): 1–16.

Canon, David T., and Charles Stewart III. "Parties and Hierarchies in Senate Committees, 1789–1946." In *U.S. Senate Exceptionalism*, edited by Bruce I. Oppenheimer, 157–81. Columbus: Ohio State University Press, 2002.

Carpenter, Daniel P. *The Forging of Bureaucratic Autonomy: Reputations, Networks, and Policy Innovation in Executive Agencies, 1862–1928*. Princeton: Princeton University Press, 2001.

Carson, Austin. "Blame Dynamics and Audience Cost Theory." Paper presented at the Research in International Politics Workshop, Ohio State University, March 4, 2011. http://scholar.google.com/scholar?q=Austin+Carson+%22Blame+Dynamics%22&btnG=&hl=en&as_sdt=0%2C5. Accessed July 2012.

Carter, Ralph G., and James M. Scott. *Choosing to Lead: Understanding Congressional Foreign Policy Entrepreneurs*. Durham, NC: Duke University Press, 2009.

Cheney, Dick. "Congressional Overreaching in Foreign Policy." In *Foreign Policy and the Constitution*, edited by Robert A. Goldwin and Robert A. Licht, 101–21. Washington, DC: American Enterprise Institute, 1990.

Clark, David H. "Agreeing to Disagree: Domestic Institutional Congruence and U.S. Dispute Behavior." *Political Research Quarterly* 53 (2000): 375–401.

Clark, David H., and Timothy Nordstrom. "Democratic Variants and Democratic Variance: How Domestic Constraints Shape Interstate Conflict." *Journal of Politics* 67, no. 1 (2005): 250–70.

Cohen, Jeffrey E. "The Impact of the Modern Presidency on Presidential Success in the U.S. Congress." *Legislative Studies Quarterly* 7 (1982): 515–32.

Cook, Timothy E. *Governing with the News*. Chicago: University of Chicago Press, 1998.

Cox, Gary W., and Mathew D. McCubbins. *Setting the Agenda: Responsible Party Government in the U.S. House of Representatives*. New York: Cambridge University Press, 2005.

———. *Legislative Leviathan: Party Government in the House*. 2nd ed. New York: Cambridge University Press, 2007.

Crabb, Cecil V., and Pat M. Holt. *Invitation to Struggle: Congress, the President and Foreign Policy*. 4th ed. Washington, DC: CQ Press, 1992.

Crocker, Chester A. "The Lessons of Somalia: Not Everything Went Wrong." *Foreign Affairs* 74, no. 3 (1995): 2–8.

Crovitz, L. Gordon, and Jeremy A. Rabkin, eds. *The Fettered Presidency: Legal Constraints on the Executive Branch*. Washington, DC: American Enterprise Institute, 1989.

Daalder, Ivo H., and James M. Lindsay, eds. *America Unbound: The Bush Revolution in American Foreign Policy*. Washington, DC: Brookings Institution, 2003.

Deering, Christopher J. "Principle or Party? Foreign and National Security Policymaking in the Senate." In *The Contentious Senate: Partisanship, Ideology and the Myth of Cool Judgment*, edited by Colton C. Campbell and Nicol C. Rae, 21–42. Lanham, MD: Rowman & Littlefield, 2001.

———. "Foreign Affairs and War." In *The Legislative Branch and American Democracy: Institutions and Performance*, edited by Paul J. Quirk and Sarah Binder, 349–81. New York: Oxford University Press, 2005.

Deering, Christopher J., and Steven S. Smith. *Committees in Congress*. Boston: Little, Brown, 1984.

———. *Committees in Congress*. 3rd ed. Boston: Little, Brown, 1997.

Den Hartog, Chris, and Nathan W. Monroe. *Agenda Setting in the U.S. Senate: Costly Consideration and Majority Party Advantage*. Cambridge: Cambridge University Press, 2011.

Destler, I. M. "Executive-Congressional Conflicts in Foreign Policy: Explaining It, Coping with It." In *Congress Reconsidered*, 3rd ed., edited by Lawrence C. Dodd and Bruce I. Oppenheimer, 343–63. Washington, DC: CQ Press, 1985.

Diermeier, Daniel, and Timothy J. Fedderson. "Information and Congressional Hearings." *American Journal of Political Science* 44, no. 1 (2000): 51–65.

Dodd, Lawrence C., and Richard L. Schott. *Congress and the Administrative State*. New York: John Wiley, 1979.

Doyle, Michael. "Three Pillars of the Liberal Peace." *American Political Science Review* 99, no. 3 (2005): 463–66.

Edwards, George C., III. *On Deaf Ears: The Limits of the Bully Pulpit*. New Haven: Yale University Press, 2003.

Edwards, George C., III, and B. Dan Wood. "Who Influences Whom? The President, Congress and the Media." *American Political Science Review* 93, no. 2 (1999): 327–44.

Eichenberg, Richard C. "Victory Has Many Friends: U.S. Public Opinion and the Use of Military Force, 1981–2005." *International Security* 30, no. 1 (2005): 140–77.

Eichenberg, Richard C., Richard J. Stoll, and Matthew Lebo. "War President: The Approval Ratings of George W. Bush." *Journal of Conflict Resolution* 50, no. 6 (2006): 783–808.

Epstein, David, and Sharyn O'Halloran. *Delegating Powers: A Transaction Cost Politics Approach to Policy Making under Separate Powers*. New York: Cambridge University Press, 1999.

Evans, C. Lawrence. *Leadership in Committee: A Comparative Analysis of Leadership Behavior in the U.S. Senate*. Ann Arbor: University of Michigan Press, 1991.

————. "Congressional Committees." In *The Oxford Handbook of the American Congress*, edited by Eric Schickler and Frances E. Lee, 396–425. Oxford: Oxford University Press, 2011.

Evans, Diana. "Congressional Oversight and the Diversity of Members' Goals." *Political Science Quarterly* 109, no. 4 (1994): 649–87.

Farnsworth, David N., and James W. McKenney. *U.S.-Panama Relations, 1903–1978: A Study in Linkage Politics*. Boulder, CO: Westview, 1983.

Farnsworth, Stephen J., and S. Robert Lichter. *The Mediated Presidency: Television News and Presidential Governance*. Lanham, MD: Rowman & Littlefield, 2006.

Fatovic, Clement. "Constitutionalism and Presidential Prerogative: Jeffersonian and Hamiltonian Perspectives." *American Journal of Politics Science* 48, no. 3 (2004): 429–44.

Fearon, James D. "Domestic Political Audiences and the Escalation of International Disputes." *American Political Science Review* 88, no. 3 (1994): 577–92.

Feaver, Peter D., and Christopher Gelpi. *Choosing Your Battles*. Princeton: Princeton University Press, 2004.

Fenno, Richard F., Jr. *Congressmen in Committees*. Boston: Little, Brown, 1973.

————. *Home Style: House Members in Their Districts*. Boston: Little, Brown, 1978.

Fisher, Louis. *Presidential War Power*. Lawrence: University Press of Kansas, 1995.

————. *Congressional Abdication on War and Spending*. College Station: Texas A&M University Press, 2000.

————. "Congressional Investigations: Subpoenas and Contempt Power." Congressional Research Service Report RL 31836, April 2, 2003.

————. "Deciding on War against Iraq: Institutional Failures." In *The Meaning of American Democracy*, edited by Robert Y. Shapiro, 115–36. New York: Academy of Political Science, 2005.

————. *In the Name of National Security: Unchecked Presidential Power and the Reynolds Case*. Lawrence: University Press of Kansas, 2006.

————. *The Constitution and 9/11: Recurring Threats to America's Freedoms*. Lawrence: University Press of Kansas, 2008.

————. "The Baker-Christopher War Powers Commission." *Presidential Studies Quarterly* 39 (2009): 128–40.

————. "The Baker-Christopher War Powers Commission." Current Legal Topics, Law Library of Congress, August 3, 2012. http://loc.gov/law/help/usconlaw/pdf/baker.christopher.pdf. Accessed March 2013.

————. *Presidential War Power*. 3rd ed. Lawrence: University Press of Kansas, 2013.

Fisher, Louis, and David Gray Adler. "The War Powers Resolution: Time to Say Goodbye." *Political Science Quarterly* 113 (1998): 1–20.

Fite, Gilbert C. *Richard B. Russell, Jr., Senator from Georgia*. Chapel Hill: University of North Carolina Press, 1991.

Fowler, Linda L. "Congressional War Powers." In *The Oxford Handbook of the American Congress*, edited by Eric Schickler and Frances E. Lee, 812–33. Oxford: Oxford University Press, 2011.

Fowler, Linda L., and R. Brian Law. "Make Way for the Party: The Rise and Fall of the Senate National Security Committees, 1947–2006." In *Why Not Parties? Party Effects in the United States Senate*, edited by Nathan W. Monroe, Jason M. Roberts, and David W. Rohde, 121–41. Chicago: University of Chicago Press, 2008a.

———. "Seen but Not Heard: Committee Visibility and Institutional Change in the Senate National Security Committees, 1947–2006." *Legislative Studies Quarterly* 33, no. 3 (2008b): 357–86.

Fry, Joseph A. *Debating Vietnam: Fulbright, Stennis and Their Senate Hearings*. Lanham, MD: Rowman & Littlefield, 2006.

Gailmard, Sean, and Jeffery A. Jenkins. "Negative Agenda Control in the Senate and House: Fingerprints of Majority Party Power." *Journal of Politics* 69, no. 3 (2007): 689–700.

Galloway, George B. *Congress at the Crossroads*. New York: Thomas Y. Crowell, 1946.

Gartner, Scott Sigmund. "The Multiple Effects of Casualties on Public Support for War: An Experimental Approach." *American Political Science Review* 102, no. 1 (2008): 95–106.

Gartner, Scott Sigmund, and Gary M. Segura. "War, Casualties and Public Opinion." *Journal of Conflict Resolution* 42, no. 3 (1998): 278–300.

———. "All Politics Are Still Local: The Iraq War and the 2006 Midterm Elections." *PS: Political Science & Politics* 41, no. 1 (2008): 95–100.

Gartner, Scott Sigmund, Gary M. Segura, and Michael Wilkening. "All Politics Are Local: Local Losses and Individual Attitudes toward the Vietnam War." *Journal of Conflict Resolution* 41, no. 5 (1997): 669–94.

Gelpi, Christopher, Peter D. Feaver, and Jason Reifler. "Success Matters: Casualty Sensitivity and the War in Iraq." *International Security* 30, no. 3 (2005): 7–46.

———. "Iraq the Vote: Retrospective and Prospective Foreign Policy Judgments on Candidate Choice and Casualty Tolerance." *Political Behavior* 29, no. 2 (2007): 151–74.

Goodwin, Doris Kearns. *Lyndon Johnson and the American Dream*. New York: St. Martin's, 1976.

Gowa, Joanne. "Politics at the Water's Edge: Parties, Voters and the Use of Force Abroad." *International Organization* 52, no. 2 (1998): 307–24.

Graber, Doris A. *Mass Media and American Politics*. Washington, DC: CQ Press, 1989.

Griffin, Stephen M. *Long Wars and the Constitution*. Cambridge, MA: Harvard University Press, 2013.

Groeling, Tim, and Matthew A. Baum. "Crossing the Water's Edge: Elite Rhetoric, Media Coverage, and the Rally-Round-the-Flag Phenomenon." *Journal of Politics* 70, no. 4 (2008): 1065–85.

Grose, Christian R., and Bruce I. Oppenheimer. "The Iraq War, Partisanship, and Candidate Attributes: Variation in Partisan Swing in the 2006 U.S. House Elections." *Legislative Studies Quarterly* 32, no. 4 (2007): 531–57.

Groseclose, Tim, and David C. King. "Committee Theories Reconsidered." In *Congress Reconsidered*, 7th ed., edited by Lawrence C. Dodd and Bruce I. Oppenheimer, 269–92. Washington, DC: CQ Press, 2001.

Groseclose, Tim, and Charles Stewart III. "The Value of Committee Seats in the House, 1947–91." *American Journal of Political Science* 42, no. 2 (1998): 453–74.

Grynaviski, Jeffrey D. "A Bayesian Learning Model with Applications to Party Identification." *Journal of Theoretical Politics* 18, no. 3 (2006): 323–46.

Hall, Richard L. *Participation in Congress*. New Haven: Yale University Press, 1996.

Hall, Richard L., and Kristina Miler. "What Happens after the Alarm? Interest Group Subsidies to Legislative Overseers." *Journal of Politics* 70, no. 4 (2008): 990–1005.

Hamilton, Alexander, John Jay, and James Madison. *The Federalist: A Commentary on the Constitution of the United States.* New York: Modern Library, 1962.

Healy, Gene. *The Cult of the Presidency.* Washington, DC: Cato Institute, 2008.

Henderson, Ryan C. "War Powers, Bosnia and the 104th Congress." *Political Science Quarterly* 113, no. 2 (1998): 241–58.

———. *The Clinton Wars: The Constitution, Congress, and War Powers.* Nashville: Vanderbilt University Press, 2002.

Hersman, Rebecca K. C. *Friends and Foes: How Congress and the President Really Make Foreign Policy.* Washington, DC: Brookings Institution Press, 2000.

Hess, Stephen. "The Decline and Fall of Congressional News." In *Congress, the Press, and the Public,* edited by Thomas E. Mann and Norman J. Ornstein, 141–56. Washington, DC: American Enterprise Institute and Brookings Institution, 1994.

Hill, Seth J., Michael C. Herron, and Jeffrey B. Lewis. "Economic Crisis, Iraq, and Race: A Study of the 2008 Presidential Election." *Election Law Journal* 9, no. 1 (2010): 41–62.

Hinckley, Barbara. *Less Than Meets the Eye: Foreign Policy and the Myth of the Assertive Congress.* Chicago: University of Chicago Press, 1994.

Holsti, Ole R. *Public Opinion and American Foreign Policy.* 2nd ed. Ann Arbor: University of Michigan Press, 2004.

Howell, William G. *Power without Persuasion: The Politics of Direct Presidential Action.* Princeton: Princeton University Press, 2003.

———. "Resolved, Congress Should Pass the War Powers Consultation Act: Con." In *Debating Reform: Conflicting Perspectives on How to Fix the American Political Systems,* 2nd ed., edited by Richard J. Ellis and Michael Nelson. Washington, DC: CQ Press, 2013.

Howell, William G., Saul P. Jackman, and John C. Rogowski. *The Wartime President: Executive Influence and the Nationalizing Politics of Threat.* Chicago: University of Chicago Press, 2013.

Howell, William G., and Jon C. Pevehouse. "Presidents, Congress, and the Use of Force." *International Organization* 59 (2005): 209–32.

———. *While Dangers Gather: Congressional Checks on Presidential War Powers.* Princeton: Princeton University Press, 2007.

Huntington, Samuel P. "Congressional Responses to the Twentieth Century." In *Congress and America's Future,* edited by David B. Truman, 6–38. Englewood Cliffs, NJ: Prentice Hall, 1973.

Huth, Paul K., and Todd L. Allee. *The Democratic Peace and Territorial Conflict in the Twentieth Century.* New York: Cambridge University Press, 2002.

Irons, Peter H. *War Powers: How the Imperial Presidency Hijacked the Constitution.* New York: Metropolitan Books, 2005.

Jacobs, Lawrence R., and Benjamin I. Page. "Who Influences U.S. Foreign Policy?" *American Political Science Review* 99, no. 1 (2005): 107–24.

Jacobson, Gary C. *A Divider, Not a Uniter: George W. Bush and the American People: The 2006 Election and Beyond.* New York: Pearson, 2006.

James, Scott C. "The Evolution of the Presidency: Between the Promise and the Fear." In *The Executive Branch,* edited by Joel D. Aberbach and Mark A. Peterson, 3–41. New York: Oxford University Press, 2005.

Jentleson, Bruce W. "The Pretty Prudent Public: Post Post-Vietnam American Opinion on the Use of Military Force." *International Studies Quarterly* 36, no. 1 (1992): 49–73.

Jentleson, Bruce W., and Rebecca L. Britton. "Still Pretty Prudent: Post-Cold War American Public Opinion on the Use of Military Force." *Journal of Conflict Resolution* 42, no. 4 (1998): 395–417.

Johnson, Robert David. *Congress and the Cold War*. Cambridge: Cambridge University Press, 2006.

Jones, Bryan D., and Frank J. Baumgartner. *The Politics of Attention: How Government Prioritizes Problems*. Chicago: University of Chicago Press, 2005.

Jones, Charles O. *The Presidency in a Separated System*. Washington, DC: Brookings Institution, 2005.

Karol, David, and Edward Miguel. "The Electoral Costs of War: Iraq Casualties and the 2004 U.S. Presidential Election." *Journal of Politics* 69, no. 3 (2007): 633–48.

Kassop, Nancy. "The War Power and Its Limits." *Presidential Studies Quarterly* 33, no. 3 (2003): 509–29.

———. "Resolved, Congress Should Pass the War Powers Consultation Act: Pro." In *Debating Reform: Conflicting Perspectives on How to Fix the American Political Systems*, 2nd ed., edited by Richard J. Ellis and Michael Nelson. Washington, DC: CQ Press, 2013.

Katznelson, Ira, and John S. Lapinski. "At the Crossroads: Congress and American Political Development." *Perspectives on Politics* 4 (2006): 243–60.

Kernell, Samuel. *Going Public: New Strategies of Presidential Leadership*. Washington, DC: CQ Press, 1997.

Kiewiet, D. Roderick, and Mathew D. McCubbins. *The Logic of Delegation: Congressional Parties and the Appropriations Process*. Chicago: University of Chicago Press, 1991.

King, David C. *Turf Wars: How Congressional Committees Claim Jurisdiction*. Chicago: University of Chicago Press, 1997.

Kingdon, John W. *Agendas, Alternatives, and Public Policies*. 2nd ed. New York: HarperCollins, 1995.

Kinsella, David. "No Rest for the Democratic Peace." *American Political Science Review* 99, no. 3 (2005): 453–57.

Kleinerman, Benjamin A. "Can the Prince Really Be Tamed? Executive Prerogative, Popular Apathy, and the Constitutional Frame in Locke's *Second Treatise*." *American Political Science Review* 101, no. 2 (2007): 209–22.

Koh, Harold Hongju. *The National Security Constitution: Sharing Power after the Iran-Contra Affair*. New Haven: Yale University Press, 1990.

Kravitz, Walter. "The Advent of the Modern Congress: The Legislative Reorganization Act of 1970." *Legislative Studies Quarterly* 15, no. 3 (1990): 375–99.

Krehbiel, Keith. *Information and Legislative Organization*. Ann Arbor: University of Michigan Press, 1991.

———. "Where's the Party?" *Journal of Politics* 23, no. 2 (1993): 235–66.

———. *Pivotal Politics: A Theory of U.S. Lawmaking*. Chicago: University of Chicago Press, 1998.

Kriner, Douglas L. "Can Enhanced Oversight Repair 'the Broken Branch'?" *Boston University Law Review* 89, no. 2 (2009): 765–93.

———. *After the Rubicon: Congress, Presidents, and the Politics of Waging War*. Chicago: University of Chicago, 2010.

Kriner, Douglas L., and Eric Schickler. "Investigating the President: The Dynamics of Congressional Committee Probes, 1898–2006." Manuscript, 2012.

———. "Investigating the President: Committee Probes and Presidential Approval, 1953–2006." *Journal of Politics* 76, no. 2 (2014): 521–34.

Kriner, Douglas L., and Liam Schwartz. "Divided Government and Congressional Investigations." *Legislative Studies Quarterly* 33 (2008): 295–321.

Kriner, Douglas, and Francis X. Shen. "Iraq Casualties and the 2006 Senate Elections." *Legislative Studies Quarterly* 32, no. 4 (2007): 507–30.

———. "Responding to War on Capitol Hill: Battlefield Casualties, Congressional Response, and Public Support for the War in Iraq." *American Journal of Political Science* 58, no. 1 (2014): 157–74.

Kull, Steven, Clay Ramsey, and Evan Lewis. "Misperceptions, the Media, and the Iraq War." *Political Science Quarterly* 118, no. 4 (2003–4): 569–98.

Kull, Stephen, and I. M. Destler. *Misreading the Public: The Myth of a New Isolationsism*. Washington, DC: Brookings Institution, 1999.

Lawrence, Eric D., Forrest Maltzman, and Steven S. Smith. "Who Wins? Party Effects in Legislative Voting?" *Legislative Studies Quarterly* 31, no. 1 (2006): 33–70.

Lee, Frances E. "Dividers, Not Uniters: Presidential Leadership and Senate Partisanship, 1981–2004." *Journal of Politics* 70, no. 4 (2008): 914–28.

———. *Beyond Ideology: Politics, Principles, and Partisanship in the U.S. Senate*. Chicago: University of Chicago Press, 2009.

Lichter, Robert S., and Daniel R. Amundson. "Less News Is Worse News: Television News Coverage of Congress, 1972–92." In *Congress, the Press, and the Public*, edited by Thomas E. Mann and Norman J. Ornstein, 131–40. Washington, DC: American Enterprise Institute and Brookings Institution, 1994.

Lindsay, James M. "Congress and Foreign Policy: Why the Hill Matters." *Political Science Quarterly* 107, no. 4 (1992–93): 607–28.

———. *Congress and the Politics of U.S. Foreign Policy*. Baltimore: Johns Hopkins University Press, 1994.

Lippmann, Walter. *Public Opinion*. New York: Harcourt, Brace, 1922.

Luttwak, Edward N. "Where Are the Great Powers?" *Foreign Affairs* 73 (1994): 23–28.

Maass, Arthur. *Congress and the Common Good*. New York: Basic Books, 1983.

MacKenzie, John P. *Absolute Power: How the Unitary Executive Theory Is Undermining the Constitution*. New York: Century Foundation, 2009.

Madison, James. *Notes on Debates in the Federal Convention of 1787*. New York: Norton, 1987.

Maltzman, Forrest. *Competing Principals: Committees, Parties and the Organization of Congress*. Ann Arbor: University of Michigan Press, 1997.

Manley, John F. *The Politics of Finance: The House Committee on Ways and Means*. Boston: Little, Brown, 1970.

Mann, Thomas E., and Norman J. Ornstein. *The Broken Branch: How Congress Is Failing America and How to Get It Back on Track*. New York: Oxford University Press, 2006.

———. *It's Even Worse Than It Looks: How the American Constitutional System Collided with the New Politics of Extremism*. New York: Basic Books, 2012.

Marshall, Bryan W. "Presidential Success in the Realm of Foreign Affairs: Institutional Reform and the Role of House Committees." *Social Sciences Quarterly* 84, no. 3 (2003): 685–703.

Martin, Lisa L. *Democratic Commitments: Legislatures and International Cooperation*. Princeton: Princeton University Press, 2000.

Mayer, Jane. *The Dark Side: The Inside Story of How the War on Terror Turned into a War on American Ideals*. New York: Doubleday, 2008.

Mayhew, David R. *Congress: The Electoral Connection*. New Haven: Yale University Press, 1974.

———. *Divided We Govern: Party Control, Lawmaking, and Investigations, 1946–1990*. New Haven: Yale University Press, 1991.

———. *America's Congress*. New Haven: Yale University Press, 2000.

———. "Wars and American Politics." *Perspectives* 3, no. 3 (2005): 473–93.

———. *Divided We Govern: Party Control, Lawmaking, and Investigations, 1946–2002*. 2nd ed. New Haven: Yale University Press, 2006.

McCarty, Nolan, Keith T. Poole, and Howard Rosenthal. *Polarized America: The Dance of Ideology and Unequal Riches*. Cambridge, MA: MIT Press, 2008.

McCormick, James M. "Decision Making in the Foreign Affairs and Foreign Relations Committees." In *Congress Resurgent: Foreign and Defense Policy on Capitol Hill*, edited by Randall B. Ripley and James M. Lindsay, 115–53. Ann Arbor: University of Michigan Press, 1993.

McCormick, James M., and Michael Black. "Ideology and Senate Voting on the Panama Canal Treaties." *Legislative Studies Quarterly* 8, no. 1 (1983): 45–63.

McCormick, James M., and Eugene R. Wittkopf. "Bipartisanship, Partisanship, and Ideology in Congressional-Executive Foreign Policy Relations, 1947–1988." *Journal of Politics* 52, no. 4 (1990): 1077–1100.

McCubbins, Mathew D., and Thomas Schwartz. "Congressional Oversight Overlooked: Police Patrols versus Fire Alarms." *American Journal of Political Science* 28 (1984): 165–79.

McCulloch, David. *Truman*. New York: Simon & Schuster, 1992.

McGrath, Robert J. "Congressional Oversight Hearings and Policy Control." *Legislative Studies Quarterly* 38, no. 3 (2013): 349–76.

Meernik, James. "Presidential Support in Congress: Conflict and Consensus on Foreign and Defense Policy." *Journal of Politics* 55, no. 3 (1993): 569–87.

———. "Congress, the President, and the Commitment of the U.S. Military." *Legislative Studies Quarterly* 20 (1995): 377–92.

Milkis, Sidney M. "Executive Power and Political Parties: The Dilemmas of Scale in American Democracy." In *The Executive Branch*, edited by Joel D. Aberbach and Mark A. Peterson, 379–418. New York: Oxford University Press, 2005.

Milner, Helen V. *Interests, Institutions, and Information: Domestic Politics and International Relations*. Princeton: Princeton University Press, 1997.

Moe, Terry M. "The Politicized Presidency." In *New Directions in American Politics*, edited by John E. Chubb and Paul E. Peterson, 235–71. Washington, DC: Brookings Institution, 1985.

Moe, Terry M., and William G. Howell. "Unilateral Action and Presidential Power: A Theory." *Presidential Studies Quarterly* 29, no. 4 (1999): 850–72.

Monroe, Nathan W., Jason M. Roberts, and David W. Rohde, eds. *Why Not Parties? Party Effects in the United States Senate*. Chicago: University of Chicago Press, 2008.

Moore, Will H., and David J. Lanoe. "Domestic Politics and U.S. Foreign Policy: A Study of Cold War Conflict Behavior." *Journal of Politics* 65, no. 2 (2003): 376–96.

Mucciaroni, Gary, and Paul J. Quirk. *Deliberative Choices: Debating Policy in Congress*. Chicago: University of Chicago Press, 2006.

Mueller, John E. *War, Presidents, and Public Opinion*. New York: John Wiley, 1973.

———. *Policy and Opinion in the Gulf War*. Chicago: University of Chicago Press, 1994.

———. "The Iraq Syndrome." *Foreign Affairs* 84, no. 6 (2005): 44–54.

Munger, Michael C. "Allocation of Desirable Committee Assignments: Extended Queues Versus Committee Expansion." *American Journal of Political Science* 32, no. 2 (1988): 317–44.

Nyhan, Brendan. "Scandal Potential: How Political Context and News Congestion Affect the President's Vulnerability to Media Scandal." *British Journal of Political Science*, FirstView (2014): 1–32. http://journals.cambridge.org/action/displayAbstract?from Page=online&aid=9161701&fileId=S0007123413000458.

Ogul, Morris S. *Congress Oversees the Bureaucracy: Studies in Legislative Supervision*. Pittsburgh: University of Pittsburgh Press, 1976.

Ogul, Morris S., and Bert A. Rockman. "Overseeing Oversight: New Departures and Old Problems." *Legislative Studies Quarterly* 15, no. 1 (1990): 5–24.

Oleszek, Mark J., and Walter J. Oleszek. "Institutional Challenges Confronting Congress after 9/11: Partisan Polarization and Effective Oversight." In *Congress and the Politics of National Security*, edited by David P. Auerswald and Colton C. Campbell, 45–70. New York: Cambridge University Press, 2012.

Olson, William. "The U.S. Congress: An Independent Force in World Politics." *International Affairs* 67 (1991): 547–63.

Ornstein, Norman J., and Thomas E. Mann. "When Congress Checks Out." *Foreign Affairs* (2006): http://www.foreignaffairs.com/articles/62091/norman-j-ornstein-and -thomas-e-mann/when-congress-checks-out. Accessed January 2007.

———. "The Hill Is Alive with the Sound of Hearings." *Foreign Affairs* (2009): http:// www.foreignaffairs.com/articles/64245/norman-j-ornstein-and-thomas-e-mann/ the-hill-is-alive-with-the-sound-of-hearings. Accessed January 2010.

Ostrom, Charles, and Brian Job. "The President and the Political Use of Force." *American Political Science Review* 80, no. 2 (1986): 541–66.

Packer, George. *The Assassins' Gate: America in Iraq*. New York: Farrar, Straus and Giroux, 2005.

Page, Benjamin I., and Marshall M. Bouton. *The Foreign Policy Disconnect: What Americans Want from Our Leaders but Don't Get*. Chicago: University of Chicago Press, 2006.

Page, Benjamin I., and Robert Y. Shapiro. *The Rational Public: Fifty Years of Trends in Americans' Policy Preferences*. Chicago: University of Chicago Press, 1992.

Parent, Joseph, and Joseph Bafumi. "International Polarity and America's Polarization." *International Politics* 49, no. 1 (2012): 1–35.

Parker, David C. W., and Matthew Dull. "Divided We Quarrel: The Politics of Congressional Investigations, 1947–2004." *Legislative Studies Quarterly* 34, no. 3 (2009): 319–45.

———. "Rooting Out Waste, Fraud, and Abuse: The Politics of House Committee Investigations, 1947 to 2004." *Political Research Quarterly* 6, no. 4 (2012): 1–15.

Peake, Jeffrey. "Coalition Building and Overcoming Gridlock in Foreign Policy, 1947–1998." *Presidential Studies Quarterly* 32, no. 1 (2002): 67–83.

Peterson, Paul. "The President's Dominance in Foreign Policy Making." *Political Science Quarterly* 109 (1994): 215–34.

Petrocik, John R. "Issue Ownership in Presidential Elections, with a 1980 Case Study." *American Journal of Political Science* 40, no. 3 (1996): 825–50.

Petrocik, John R., William L. Benoit, and Glenn J. Hansen. "Issue Ownership and Presidential Campaigning, 1952–2000." *Political Science Quarterly* 118, no. 4 (2003–4): 599–626.

Pitkin, Hannah F. *The Concept of Representation*. Berkeley: University of California Press, 1967.

Poole, Keith T., and Howard Rosenthal. *Congress: A Political-Economic History of Roll Call Voting*. New York: Oxford University Press, 1997.

Prins, Brandon C., and Bryan W. Marshall. "Congressional Support of the President: A Comparison of Foreign, Defense, and Domestic Policy Decision Making during and after the Cold War." *Presidential Studies Quarterly* 31, no. 4 (2001): 660–78.

Quirk, Paul. "Deliberation and Decision Making." In *The Legislative Branch and American Democracy: Institutions and Performance*, edited by Paul J. Quirk and Sarah Binder, 314–48. New York: Oxford University Press, 2005.

Reiter, Dan, and Allan C. Stam. *Democracies at War*. Princeton: Princeton University Press, 2002.

Ripley, Randall B., and Grace A. Franklin. *Congress, the Bureaucracy, and Public Policy*. 5th ed. Pacific Grove, CA: Brooks/Cole, 1990.

Ripley, Randall B., and James M. Lindsay, eds. *Congress Resurgent: Foreign and Defense Policy on Capitol Hill*. Ann Arbor: University of Michigan Press, 1993.

Rohde, David W. *Parties and Leaders in the Postreform House*. Chicago: University of Chicago Press, 1991.

———. "Partisanship, Leadership, and Congressional Assertiveness in Foreign and Defense Policy." In *The New Politics of American Foreign Policy*, edited by David A. Deese, 76–101. New York: St. Martin's, 1994.

———. "Parties and Committees in the House: Members' Motivations, Issues, and Institutional Arrangements." In *Positive Theories of Congressional Institutions*, edited by Kenneth A. Shepsle and Barry R. Weingast, 119–37. Ann Arbor: University of Michigan Press, 1995.

———. "Committees and Policy Formulation." In *The Legislative Branch*, edited by Paul J. Quirk and Sarah Binder, 201–24. New York: Oxford University Press, 2005.

Rozell, Mark J. "Press Coverage of Congress, 1946–1992." In *Congress, the Press, and the Public*, edited by Thomas E. Mann and Norman J. Ornstein, 59–130. Washington, DC: American Enterprise Institute and Brookings Institution, 1994.

Rudalevige, Andrew. *The New Imperial Presidency: Renewing Presidential Power after Watergate*. Ann Arbor: University of Michigan Press, 2006.

Rundquist, Barry, and Thomas M. Carsey. *Congress and Defense Spending: The Distributive Politics of Military Procurement*. Norman: University of Oklahoma Press, 2002.

Schickler, Eric. *Disjointed Pluralism: Institutional Innovation and the Development of the U.S. Congress*. Princeton: Princeton University Press, 2001.

———. "Entrepreneurial Defenses of Congressional Power." In *Formative Acts: American Politics in the Making*, edited by Stephen Skowronek and Matthew Glassman, 293–314. Philadelphia: University of Pennsylvania Press, 2007.

Schiller, Wendy. *Partners and Rivals: Representation in U.S. Senate Delegations*. Princeton: Princeton University Press, 2000.

Schlesinger, Arthur. *The Imperial Presidency*. Boston: Houghton Mifflin, 1973.

Schultz, Kenneth A. "Domestic Opposition and Signaling in International Crises." *American Political Science Review* 92, no. 4 (1998): 829–44.

———. *Democracy and Coercive Diplomacy*. Cambridge: Cambridge University Press, 2001.

———. "Tying Hands and Washing Hands: The U.S. Congress and Multilateral Humanitarian Intervention." In *Locating the Proper Authorities: The Interaction of Domestic and International Institutions*, edited by Daniel W. Drezner, 105–44. Ann Arbor: University of Michigan Press, 2003.

Scott, James M., and Ralph G. Carter. "Acting on the Hill: Congressional Assertiveness in U.S. Foreign Policy." *Congress & the Presidency* 29, no. 2 (2002): 151–69.

Sheingate, Adam D. "Structure and Opportunity: Committee Jurisdiction and Issue Attention in Congress." *American Journal of Political Science* 50, no. 4 (2006): 844–59.

Shepsle, Kenneth A. *The Giant Jigsaw Puzzle: Democratic Committee Assignments in the Modern House*. Chicago: University of Chicago Press, 1978.

Shepsle, Kenneth A., and Barry R. Weingast. "The Institutional Foundations of Committee Power." *American Political Science Review* 81 (1987): 85–104.

Shipan, Charles R. "Regulatory Regimes, Agency Actions, and the Conditional Nature of Congressional Influence." *American Political Science Review* 98, no. 3 (2004): 467–80.

Silverstein, Gordon. *Imbalance of Powers: Constitutional Interpretation and the Making of American Foreign Policy*. New York: Oxford University Press, 1997.

Sinclair, Barbara. *The Transformation of the U.S. Senate*. Baltimore: Johns Hopkins University Press, 1989.

———. "The New World of U.S. Senators." In *Congress Reconsidered*, 9th ed., edited by Lawrence C. Dodd and Bruce I. Oppenheimer, 1–22. Washington, DC: CQ Press, 2005.

———. *Party Wars: Polarization and the Politics of National Policy Making*. Norman: University of Oklahoma Press, 2006.

———. "The New World of U.S. Senators." In *Congress Reconsidered*, 10th ed., edited by Lawrence C. Dodd and Bruce I. Oppenheimer, 1–26. Washington, DC: CQ Press, 2012a.

———. *Unorthodox Lawmaking: New Legislative Processes in the U.S. Congress*. 4th ed. Washington, DC: CQ Press, 2012.

Skowronek, Stephen. *The Politics Presidents Make: Leadership from John Adams to George H. W. Bush*. Cambridge, MA: Harvard University Press, 1993.

———. *Presidential Leadership in Political Time*. Lawrence: University Press of Kansas, 2011.

Slantchev, Branislav L. "Politicians, the Media, and Domestic Audience Costs." *International Studies Quarterly* 50 (2006): 445–77.

Smith, Steven S. "Parties and Leadership in the Senate." In *The Legislative Branch*, edited by Paul J. Quirk and Sarah A. Binder, 255–78. New York: Oxford University Press, 2005.

———. *Party Influence in Congress*. New York: Cambridge University Press, 2007.

Stam, Allan C. *Win, Lose or Draw: Domestic Politics and the Crucible of War*. Ann Arbor: University of Michigan Press, 1996.

Stewart, Charles, III. "The Value of Committee Assignments in Congress since 1994." Paper presented at the annual meeting of the Midwest Political Science Association, Chicago, April 12–15, 2012.

Stewart, Charles, III, and Tim Groseclose. "The Value of Committee Seats in the United States Senate, 1947–91." *American Journal of Political Science* 43 (1999): 963–73.

Sundquist, James. *The Decline and Resurgence of Congress*. Washington, DC: Brookings Institution, 1981.

Suskind, Ron. *The Price of Loyalty: George W. Bush, the White House, and the Education of Paul O'Neill*. New York: Simon & Schuster, 2004.

Swers, Michele. "Building a Reputation on National Security: The Impact of Stereotypes Related to Gender and Military Experience." *Legislative Studies Quarterly* 32, no. 4 (2007): 559–95.

Theriault, Sean M. *Party Polarization in Congress*. New York: Cambridge University Press, 2008.

Thompkins, C. David. *Senator Arthur H. Vandenberg: The Evolution of a Modern Republican, 1884–1945*. East Lansing: Michigan State University Press, 1970.

Thorpe, Rebecca U. *The American Warfare State: The Domestic Politics of Military Spending*. Chicago: University of Chicago Press, 2014.

Tocqueville, Alexis de. *Democracy in America*. Vol. 1. New York: Vintage, 1945.

Tomz, Michael. "Domestic Audience Costs in International Relations: An Experimental Approach." *International Organization* 61, no. 4 (2006): 824–40.

Tomz, Michael, Jason Wittenberg, and Gary King. *CLARIFY: Software for Interpreting and Presenting Statistical Results*. Version 2.1. Cambridge, MA: Harvard University, January 2003. http://king.harvard.edu/clarify.

Trager, Robert, and Lynn Vavreck. "The Political Costs of Crisis Bargaining: Presidential Rhetoric and the Role of Party." *American Journal of Political Science* 55, no. 3 (2011): 526–45.

Vanderbush, Walt, and Patrick J. Haney. "Clinton, Congress and Cuba Policy between Two Codifications: The Changing Executive-Legislative Relationship in Foreign Policy Making." *Congress & the Presidency* 29, no. 2 (2002): 171–94.

Voeten, Erik, and Paul R. Brewer. "Public Opinion, the War in Iraq and Presidential Accountability." *Journal of Conflict Resolution* 50, no. 6 (2006): 809–30.

Volden, Craig. "A Formal Model of the Politics of Delegation in a Separation of Powers System." *American Journal of Political Science* 46, no. 1 (2002): 111–33.

Waldron, Jeremy. "Separation of Powers in Thought and Practice?" *Boston College Law Review* 54 (2013): 433–68. http://bclawreview.org/files/2013/03/01_waldron.pdf. Accessed December 2013.

Wawro, Gregory J., and Ira Katznelson. "Designing Historical Social Scientific Inquiry: How Parameter Heterogeneity Can Bridge the Methodological Divide between Quantitative and Qualitative Approaches." *American Journal of Political Science* 58, no. 2 (2014): 526–46.

Weingast, Barry R., and W. J. Marshall. "The Industrial Organization of Congress; or, Why Legislatures, Like Firms, Are Not Organized for Markets." *Journal of Political Economy* 96 (1988): 132–63.

Weingast, Barry R., and Mark J. Moran. "Bureaucratic Discretion or Congressional Control? Regulatory Policymaking by the Federal Trade Commission." *Journal of Political Economy* 9, no. 5 (1983): 765–800.

Whittington, Keith E., and Daniel P. Carpenter. "Executive Power in American Institutional Development." *Perspectives on Politics* 1, no. 3 (2003): 495–513.

Wildavsky, Aaron. "The Two Presidencies." *Trans-Action* 4 (1966): 7–14.

Wilson, Woodrow. *Congressional Government: A Study in American Politics*. Boston: Houghton Mifflin, 1885.

Wittkopf, Eugene R., and James M. McCormick. "Congress, the President, and the End of the Cold War: Has Anything Changed?" *Journal of Conflict Resolution* 42, no. 4 (1998): 440–66.

Wolfensberger, Donald R. "Congress and Policymaking in an Age of Terrorism." In *Congress Reconsidered*, 9th ed., edited by Lawrence C. Dodd and Bruce I. Oppenheimer, 343–62. Washington, DC: CQ Press, 2005.

Wood, B. Dan. "Congress and the Executive Branch: Delegation and Presidential Dominance. In *The Oxford Handbook of the American Congress*, edited by Eric Schickler and Frances E. Lee, 789–811. Oxford: Oxford University Press, 2011.

Woodward, Bob. *Bush at War*. New York: Simon & Schuster, 2002.

———. *Plan of Attack*. New York: Simon & Schuster, 2004.

———. *State of Denial*. New York: Simon & Schuster, 2006.

Woon, Jonathan, and Jeremy C. Pope. "Made in Congress? Testing the Electoral Implications of Party Ideological Brand Names." *Journal of Politics* 70, no. 3 (2008): 823–36.

Yoo, John. *The Powers of War and Peace: The Constitution and Foreign Affairs after 9/11*. Chicago: University of Chicago Press, 2005.

Zaller, John R. "Elite Leadership of Mass Opinion: New Evidence from the Gulf War." In *Taken by Storm: The Media, Public Opinion, and U.S. Foreign Policy in the Gulf War*, edited by W. Lance Bennett and David L. Paletz, 186–209. Chicago: University of Chicago Press, 1994.

———. *The Nature and Origins of Mass Opinion*. New York: Cambridge University Press, 1992.

Zaller, John, and Dennis Chiu. "Government's Little Helper: U.S. Press Coverage of Foreign Policy Crises, 1945–1991." *Political Communication* 13, no. 4 (1996): 385–405.

Zegart, Amy B. "The Domestic Politics of Irrational Intelligence Oversight." *Political Science Quarterly* 126, no. 1 (2011): 1–25.

Zeisberg, Mariah. *War Powers: The Politics of Constitutional Authority*. Princeton: Princeton University Press, 2013.

Zelizer, Julian E. *Arsenal of Democracy: The Politics of National Security—From World War II to the War on Terrorism*. New York: Basic Books, 2010.

Index

Note: Page numbers followed by *f* indicate a figure; those with *t* indicate a table.